D0429026

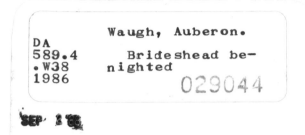

DA
589.4
.W38
1986

Waugh, Auberon.

  Brideshead be-
nighted

029044

SEP 1 '88

Lake Tahoe Community College
Learning Resources Center
So. Lake Tahoe, CA   95702

BRIDESHEAD
BENIGHTED

BRIDESHEAD BENIGHTED

Auberon Waugh

Little, Brown and Company
Boston   Toronto

LAKE TAHOE COMMUNITY COLLEGE
LEARNING RESOURCES CENTER

029044

COPYRIGHT © 1986 BY Auberon Waugh

ALL RIGHTS RESERVED. NO PART OF THIS BOOK MAY BE REPRODUCED
IN ANY FORM OR BY ANY ELECTRONIC OR MECHANICAL MEANS,
INCLUDING INFORMATION STORAGE AND RETRIEVAL SYSTEMS,
WITHOUT PREMISSION IN WRITING FROM THE PUBLISHER, EXCEPT
BY A REVIEWER WHO MAY QUOTE BRIEF PASSAGES IN A REVIEW.

FIRST AMERICAN EDITION

Library of Congress Catalog Card No. 86–81010

All of these articles were first published
in *The Spectator*. This book was first
published in Great Britain with the title,
Another Voice.

*Published simultaneously in Canada
by Little, Brown & Company (Canada) Limited*

PRINTED IN GREAT BRITAIN

CONTENTS

PART III

Ideological War

For Alexander Chancellor
Staunch friend and sometimes fearless leader

ANOTHER VOICE

Introduction and Guide by Auberon Waugh

Journalists who reprint their newspaper or magazine articles and decide to dignify them with the description of "essays" are sometimes mocked by their colleagues – especially by those who have never been exposed to the temptation of pretending that their daily or weekly commentaries on the passing scene merit serious consideration in the *belles lettres* department of English literature. The scoffers are absolutely right, of course. The essence of journalism is that it should stimulate its readers for a moment, possibly open their minds to some alternative perception of events, and then be thrown away, with all its clever conundrums, its prophecies and comminations, in the great wastepaper basket of history. Timeless journalism is bad journalism. Although there are some pieces in this collection which treat of general subjects, many more address themselves to the affairs of the moment and, as such, will be more or less incomprehensible in ten years' time. A few may be hard enough to follow even now for those with a poor memory or little interest in current affairs.

I offer the book simply as a diversion. It is taken from ten years of weekly articles in the *Spectator*, the articles being chosen on the basis of their supposed merit. The choice was made by other hands than mine. I cannot claim that it was modesty which prevented me from reading through the 500-odd articles involved, nor even the gentlemanly English quality of laziness. The reason was that I could not spare the time from other, more remunerative occupations. I made a few recommendations for articles which I vaguely remembered as having thought good at the time, and some of these have been adopted.

Reading through the final selection, I sometimes find myself proud of what I have written, at other times acutely embarrassed by it. The problem is that remarks which seemed funny and relevant under the Labour Governments of Harold Wilson and James Callaghan, when the proletarian movement was in the ascendant, trade unionists threatened to take over the commanding heights and education was avowedly designed as a levelling force, can seem merely boorish ten years later under Mrs Thatcher, when trade unions are on the run and education is under attack from an entirely different direction. A further awkwardness is created by monetary inflation. Sums which seemed disgracefully large in the 1970s, especially if paid to a 'worker', now appear derisory.

I decided that each article should be accompanied by the date on which it first appeared, in large type, to allow readers to make the necessary adjustments. However my publisher, Mr Mark Booth, of Waterstone, to whose enthusiasm the book owes its existence, took the contrary view. Such reminders, he said, might detract from what he was kind enough to call the 'timeless brilliance' of the book. He would prefer the dates in an appendix. Pondering about this objection, I decided that what he probably meant was that if displayed prominently, they would remind readers that the 'essays' are in fact warmed-up magazine articles with the result that fewer people would be tempted to buy the book. I deferred to his greater commercial acumen, then he deferred to my sense of journalistic propriety. As a result, the dates appear in small type at the end of each article, but readers might be well advised to look at them first if they wish to understand what is happening rather than just marvel at the timeless brilliance. Although each chapter is generally organized in chronological order, the chapters themselves are not, with the result that you find an article on the subject of libel – *Express Malice* – In Chapter 8, devoted to the Press, while the piece which gave rise to that article will be found in Chapter 17 under the heading *Our Sacred Duty*. This may seem odd, but careful readers will spot a system in it all, and I dare say it will help to sell a few more copies of the book.

Before summarising the contents of the book I should perhaps describe the background in which the articles first appeared for the benefit of those who are not regular readers of the *Spectator* – as, I fear, few people are outside England and few enough inside. The *Spectator* is a literary and political weekly which has been appearing since 1824. Despite some rough passages, it has generally been considered the brightest and best of the English weeklies, although it was regularly challenged in that position at one time by the slightly more left-wing *New Statesman*. Because it never adopted socialism as its creed, it used sometimes to be described in the 1960s and 1970s as 'right-wing' – despite having solemnly advised its miniscule readership to vote Labour in the 1959 general election when it was edited and owned by Sir Ian Gilmour, later a Conservative Cabinet Minster. With the shifting centre of British politics, few would call it 'right-wing' now, but the greater truth about the *Spectator* is that it has always been an independent rag-bag of more or less eccentric outlooks, bound together only by a concern for decent writing and the intelligent Englishman's refusal to be browbeaten into anything commonplace.

I first started writing a regular column in the *Spectator* in 1967 when the then Editor, Mr Nigel Lawson, hired me as his political correspondent. Lawson later entered politics and at the moment of writing is Chancellor of the Exchequer in Mrs Thatcher's Cabinet – the second editor of the *Spectator* in a row to achieve that office, after the late Iain

Macleod. He was a good journalist and is a great loss to journalism, but his choice of politcal correspondent must seem as a curious one for someone who also had political ambitions. My only qualification at that time, apart from a certain fluency with words, was a mild dislike of politics and politicians which became less mild in the three years or so I spent working for him.

Eventually I was goaded to play a mild prank at the expense of another contributor while subbing the Table of Contents on night duty at the *Spectator's* printers, and Lawson sacked me on the spot. I sued him for breach of contract and won handsome damages, but before the case could come to court he had himself been dismissed as Editor; the contributor, Mr George Gale, had been appointed in his place, and I had been reappointed to write a weekly column on books – by Mr Gale. When the case was eventually heard at St Marylebone Crown Court, Lawson, as a sacked editor, had to defend himself for sacking me, who had since been re-employed, for insulting the man who had since re-employed me.

It was a sad end to a happy relationship, but my absence from the *Spectator* on that occasion was scarcely more than six months. A longer absence was to follow when, after three years or so of reviewing books, I moved on to write a regular column for the *New Statesman* and review books for the *Evening Standard*. The *Spectator* was going through one of its bad patches at that time but after two years it was bought by an old school friend, Mr Henry Keswick, who appointed another old and valued friend, Mr Alexander Chancellor, as editor, and I was happy to go back, in January 1976, to write the column called 'Another Voice' which has been appearing ever since.

It was an uninterrupted continuation of another I had been writing for two and a half years under the title 'First Person' in *New Statesman* which, under the editorship of Anthony Howard, was enjoying its last spell as the civilized, intelligent, literate and humane periodical which had been challenging the *Spectator* for sixty years. Since then it has unfortunately disappeared from sight into the Technical Colleges and Colleges of Further Education where it seems to be enjoyed by the new, only fairly literate but infinitely gullible generation of dispossessed left-wingers. Its disappearance has left *Spectator* alone in the field they once shared. The closeness of the two magazines at that time may be measured by the fact that when I joined *New Statesman* I found that its political correspondent was my predecessor as political correspondent on *Spectator*, Alan Watkins, who also happened to be Howard's brother-in-law. Those who choose to study the published edition of my *New Statesman* pieces – I am sorry to say they came out as 'Fifty Essays' under the title *In the Lion's Den* (Michael Joseph 1976) – may judge for themselves how effortless was the transition from an allegedly left-wing to an allegedly

11

right-wing magazine. Others who have made the same journey, like Mr Paul Johnson, the former editor of *New Statesman* who now writes a regular column in *Spectator*, may not prove the point so well, but wandering, as I have done, from the *Telegraph* to the *Mirror* to *Spectator* to the *Statesman*, then back again to the *Spectator* and *Telegraph*, I am convinced that intelligent educated and literate Englishmen are neither left-wing or right-wing, but are bored by politics and regard all politicians with scorn. That is my political creed, so far as I have one.

So now for the contents of this book which has been ingeniously put together by Mr Peter Kennealy, of Florence. This Guide is intended almost entirely for the benefit of reviewers as a help and encouragement to them in their task. My own experience of reviewing tells me that second only to collections of short stories, these collections of articles (or essays) are almost impossible to review. Even if a reviewer reads everything in the book, he cannot possibly construct a readable article from so many different subjects. The trick is to read the Introduction where the author should reveal his intentions, if not his entire political creed and philosophy of life. Perfectly good reviews can usually be written from the Introduction alone, although it is safer to read at least one article from the collection and refer to it. A grander alternative is to choose two or three articles and tear them to pieces, or praise them extravagantly as the mood takes one. The problem is to find the right article for one's purpose without wasting too much effort on the rest of the book. Other readers may be happy to browse or use the table of contents, but reviewers need help, since chapter and section headings only rarely reveal the line being taken by the author, and can sometimes be misleading. So here goes.

Mr Kennealy has divided his choice of articles under five subject headings, each concerned with a broad aspect of contemporary life. The section most likely to provide copy for reviewers is the first, on Class War. The chapter on Royalty is mostly of whimsical interest, designed to captivate and charm rather than to cause alarm. Princess Anne, as portrayed in the first article, has long since been superseded by the image of someone half way between Mother Teresa and Grace Kelly, but I hope I am not alone in mourning the disappearance of Princess Sourpuss (p. 23). The piece describing the Duke of Edinburgh on housing (p. 25) was written in an attempt to discourage him from taking any further interest in such matters. There is no reason to suppose it has worked. Nigel Dempster's attack on the Princess of Wales, which prompted *Princess Fairytale* (p. 27) was only the first of many attempts to challenge the nation's attitude towards this lovely young woman, as I rather hoped it would be. Although I adore her, too, I found the unremitting adulation tedious.

Brits Old and New, (Chapter 2) as identified on television and in the Sunday Times Colour Supplement, are a constant source of wonder. First, there is a tribute to an old Brit, Mr (now Sir) William Rees-Mogg, on his retirement from *The Times* (p. 30). Norman and Judy, taken from a peculiarly ridiculous article which appeared in *The Times* after Sir William's retirement, seemed excellent specimens of the New variety (p. 33). Two other examples, one called YITS (after the Year of Information Technology) and WAPS (Workers at Play) are discussed in the next article (p. 35) which dwells on the horrors which result from encouraging these New Brits to travel abroad. Finally, there is a look at the battle raging between New and Old Brits within the Security Service, otherwise known as MI5 (p. 38).

However, it is the third Chapter (p. 41) on the Working Classes which will be easiest to write about. *Workers' Power* argues that since all manifestations of trade union influence serve to increase the poverty and discomfort of workers, the middle classes might regard it with greater favour than formerly. *Social Security* (p. 43) urges as many 'workers' as possible to follow the example of Mr Albert Thorogood, who abstained from all work for 25 years. *Two Nations* (p. 45) discusses the philsophical gulf between Liverpool and the rest of England. Although the image of Liverpool has since shifted, with the Militant take over of Liverpool Corporation and the Toxteth riots – not to mention the murder of 36 Italian football fans by Liverpool supporters in Brussels – it seems to me that the philosophical gulf is still the key factor.

Wetness of the Middle Classes (p. 47) advances what I believe to be the one major difference between Britain and the rest of the Western World, which explains more than anything else our comparative decline. *Horrors of Prosperity* (p. 49) praises the trade unions as a great bulwark against the enrichment of the proletariat which efficient capitalism might threaten – bringing with it the unspeakable horrors of a society dominated by proletarian tastes and appetites. Subsequent events might seem to question the validity of this argument, since the defeat of the unions by Mrs Thatcher's government does not seem to have been accompanied by any great increase in proletarian spending power; but then the threat of an efficient industrial system in Britain is still mercifully remote.

Society's Fault (p. 51) is a rather disagreeable attack on what was then the fashionable attitude on crime and punishment, but the chapter ends on a pleasant note with *Model Briton* (p. 54) which advances the claim of a champion darts player to be considered a national hero as well as Mr Albert Thorogood.

The second part, devoted to the Generation War, may seem to be inspired by a somewhat sour view of the contemporary scene. It could be read as a middle-aged man's cry of pain at the current postures of young and old alike, or a cry of terror at the prospect of Mrs Shirley Williams's teenagers and the unspeakable horror of what come after them in the kiddies' division. People might reasonably complain that this is a partial and prejudiced view. They know many old people who are really quite agreeable and active, unaffected by self-pity or resentment; they even know some young persons and kiddies who are polite, handsome, intelligent and kind. So do I. In fact, to tell the truth, I know no one like any of the people described. They are what we read about and glimpse occasionally in trains or out of the window of a cab as we pass. They are our contemporary idea of what the old and young are like, an idea actively promoted by the compassion industry in the media and in the social services.

Shirley Williams's Achievement (p. 57) describes the generation which has resulted from that forthright lady's attempts to reform the education system. Pierre Trudeau's problems are made the subject of a little homily in *Marrying a Younger Woman* (p. 60) and shortcomings in the police force are explained by reference to age-groups in *Unwanted, Angry Policemen* (p. 62). *Father Christmas Day* (p. 65) explores the relevance of Christmas to the Blue Peter generation of kiddies. *Hatred of Children* (p. 67) relates this strange characteristic of the English to their violent reaction against paedophiles. *Potty Training on the NHS* (p. 69) reveals a little-known refinement of the nanny state. *In Praise of Punks* (p. 70) acclaims some original and true spokesmen for their generation which was offered to readers of the *Sunday Times* by one middle-class mother, in the hope, presumably of providing a model for them all.

So much for the chapter on Youth. Chapter 5, on the Old, complains about the practice of dumping old people on the trains, to travel backwards and forwards endlessly until such time as they enter their dotage, when they can safely be put into an old people's home. That appears in *Against Cheaper Tickets* (p. 76). *Uses of the Elderly* (p. 79) proposes ways in which old people might make themselves useful, and therefore better loved.

Part Three, covering what is described as the ideological war, contains most of the pieces which non-political readers will find boring. In the chapter devoted to politics - although by no means all of the articles are exclusively political - *Britain's World Role* (p. 83) explains how my own study of Britain's behaviour during the Nigerian Civil War of 1967-1970 convinced me that Britain is no longer fit for a world role, even if she had the energy or resources for one. Next we examine the plight of a nation which clearly thinks it has a world role - *The Workers' State Without Vodka* (p. 86). *A Political Sex Fantasy* (p. 88) will be understood only by those who shared this particular fantasy during the Wilson years of 1964-1976.

14

The Power Urge (p. 90) explains the entire political phenomenon as I understand it. *British Infertility* (p. 92) warns these planners and political leaders that their policies and attitudes are going to leave them with nobody to plan or lead. *Death of Lucie Gates* (p. 95) examines public reactions to the death of a baby as the result of negligence by its New Brit unmarried mother, and suggests that intensified surveillance by the social services is not a reasonable thing to demand. Our present affluent state is the subject in *Illusions of Poverty* (p. 98). The next piece, *Extending the welfare* (p. 100) takes a rather bitter look at public reactions to another tragedy and sarcastically suggests that parents may soon be able to claim extra State money for not murdering their children, or murdering them, as the case may be. The chapter on policies ends with another gloomy piece, *The Nilson millennium* suggesting that the homosexual mass-murderer, Dennis Nilsen, might represent, in exaggerated form, a larger part of the nation's problems than it is fashionable to believe.

A surprising amount of what I wrote in the last ten years was on the subject of education but inevitably much of it is repetitive. After a brief glance at the Princess of Wales's educational qualifications, *The Lesson of Royalty* (p. 104), the two main themes are summed up in *A Horror of Élites* (p. 106) which examines the proposition that the true purpose of education is to impose equality, at whatever level, and *Disadvantaged Children* (p. 108), which explores the concept that anti-social behaviour springs from social disadvantage.

A chapter on the Press starts with an examination of the sermon preached by Cardinal Hume (p. 110) in the *News of the World* on Easter Sunday, placing it in the context of all the naughty knickers stories which accompanied it. The next piece, *Copper's Nark* (p. 112) examines the Press's self-appointed role as guardian of the public morals. The law of libel is touched upon in the next two pieces. *Express Malice* (p. 114) replies to an article which appeared in the *Express's* William Hickey column, itself lifted from a previous article by me in the *Spectator*. This previous article appears on p. 219 as '*Our sacred duty*'. In *Laughing stock of the World* (p. 117) I draw attention to various anomalies in the libel law, but in the next piece, *The Real Censors* (p. 118) I examine the extent of my real commitment to the idea of a free press. *The Morality of Private Eye* (p. 120) takes the issue a stage further in enquiring into the ethics of gossip, scandalmongering and personal abuse, deciding that for the most part they are perfectly all right. Perhaps I should explain, having not previously done so, that for sixteen years, from 1970 to 1986, I wrote a regular column in *Private Eye*, first on politics, later (1972-1986) a satirical Diary. This may be read in a companion volume to *Another Voice: A Turbulent Decade: Diaries of Auberon Waugh 1976-1985* (Deutsch 1985). Finally, in this chapter, the account of an attempt by Sir James

15

Goldsmith, the businessman, to bring a High Court injunction to prevent my ever mentioning him in print, despite my never having done so previously (*Goldsmith's Injunction*, pp. 122 and 124).

The chapter on religion is plainly addressed to the small minority of intelligent people still interested in the subject. Everybody else should skip it. My first article, *The Folly of God* (p. 125) takes its theme from a sermon preached in the Languedoc on a text from St Paul, drawing attention to the two sides or aspects of the undivided God – the darker side and the lighter side. *Lust within Marriage* (p. 127) provides an ingenious but somewhat far-fetched apologia for Pope John Paul's strange statement that husbands who look at their wives lustfully are committing adultery in their hearts. The keynote article in this religious section, and the one which expresses my personal religious creed, to the extent that I have one, is the piece entitled *Self-abasement* (p. 130). This argues that the Christian religion, by perverting the New Testament notion of humility into a message of self-abasement and self-immolation within the 'Community', is actively assisting the triumph of evil, here identified with the power urge in man. Not many people will be interested in this thesis, I dare say, and even fewer impressed by it, but I would like as many as might be interested to read it. *Religion on Channel 4* (p. 132) examines some of the absurdities of a post-Christian age which still clings to many of the most awkward and improbable propositions of Christian ethics, while *The Problem of Women* (p. 135) which deals with the ordination of women is included, I imagine, mainly for the benefit of feminist readers, so that they can reassure themselves of the author's misogyny (or sexism, or both) and discountenance anything he has to say on any other subject. Cardinal Hume is examined without much affection in *A Thoroughly English Cardinal* (p. 138), Sir John Betjeman's death lamented in *Is Trifle Sufficient?* (p. 139).

Part 4, devoted to Liberal Issues, starts with *Some Racist jokes* (p. 145) which are just that. Greater concern about the race problem is shown in the next piece, *Towards a British Apartheid* (p. 148) but this good impression may be lost by *A Quota System for Schools and Prisons* (p. 000) which examines the race relations industry. Finally, in the chapter on race, the National Front and the Race Relations Board are compared in *Che Guevara in the West Midlands* (p. 153) and found remarkably similar. A notorious racist is presented as an essentially comic figure, and welcomed as such in the rich pageant of our national story.

The chapter on four-legged friends opens with a discussion of fox-hunting, fishing and bull-fighting and ends with a tirade against the familiar target of the compassion industry, with special reference to the thalidomide scandal (*The Pleasures of Compassion*, p. 156). *Death by Ferrets* (p. 158) argues against a further bureaucratic intrusion into private

16

freedom after demands for licensing ferret owners. Some ferrets had escaped to devour a child in a London suburb. *The Case of the Suffering Goldfish* (p. 160) draws attention to yet another injustice inflicted on man by animal lovers, who had prosecuted a goldfish owner for failing to kill his goldfish when it was suffering. Finally, in the animal section, there is a cry of pain against the new law which forbids householders who find their homes invaded by bats to drive them out, touch or disturb them in any way (p. 161).

Two pieces in Chapter 12 try to analyse the extraordinary prominence given in Britain to the welfare services' care of the disabled. *Special Lavatories* (p. 164) discusses the ostentatious signs put up all over London airport, while expressing reservations about the new militancy evinced by one disabled writer in his demand for better facilities at the National Theatre, while *The Country of the Disabled* (p. 167) greets Lord Snowdon's investiture as its President with misgivings (later proved unjustified).

On smoking and drinking (Chapter 13) a piece entitled *The Temperance Fanatics* (p. 168) is self-explanatory. It does not take up cudgels on behalf of the 'drunk' driver who is unfortunate enough to be caught with a few points of alcohol over the limit, so much as express dismay at the attitude of newspapers in condemning these unfortunate people as moral lepers. It also questions the motives of fanatical anti-drink campaigners and examines the excesses they have already perpetuated in the United States. *Smaller Genitals* (p. 171), which title refers to a claim put forward by a Temperance supporter about the baneful effects of alcohol, looks at further arguments advanced by these people, and reveals how much deliberate distortion of the truth is involved, for instance, in the claim that the tobacco and alcohol consumption costs government money, rather than subsidizing non-drinkers and non-smokers from cradle to grave. The Duke of Gloucester advanced exactly the same arguments against tobacco in his maiden speech in the House of Lords; his errors are politely pointed out to him in *ASH* (p. 173).

Chapter 14 is about sex which still, I suppose, counts as a Liberal Issue. The first piece (*Inventing New Sexual Offences*, p. 176) complains about a Bill before Parliament creating the new offence of trying to pick up a girl from a car, while rejoicing that the Bill seems to have been defeated. The second (*Shameful State of British Prostitution*, p. 178) mourns that the wretched Bill has been saved and proceeds to a loud complaint about British prostitutes – their laziness, greed, ugliness, dirt, and lack of interest in their work.

Various evidence of decling masculinity in British males and growing masculinity in British females is adduced in *Changing Sexes* (p. 181) while in *Naked Infants* (p. 184) misgivings are expressed about a new law

17

making it a criminal offence for parents to photograph their children with no clothes on, under penalty of a fine of £10,000 and/or three years imprisonment. The next piece, on p. 185, draws attention to something which is practically never mentioned in public – not only have sexual offences been decreasing in Britain for many years (despite claims of an 'epidemic of rape' by lesbian activists and their supporters, and despite the creation of several new sexual offences) but so has all sexual activity been declining. Finally, there is a plea for compassion towards Lord Wigg (p. 188) a disgusting old man and former Labour Cabinet Minister who had managed to wriggle his way out of a police prosecution for accosting women in the streets of London. The basis of my plea is that any of us might end up in his condition.

A short chapter on drugs is all that remains of voluminous writings on this subject – judged unsuitable for inclusion, I imagine, not so much for reasons of repetition as contradiction. At one time it seemed an obvious crime against human freedom to forbid cannabis, and I urged it would have beneficial social effects in discouraging the workers from producing more hideous and useless artefacts with which to clutter up the world's surface. At another it seemed that while the unspaced-out Soviet Union threatened our security, it would be a mistake for us all to descend into a happy trance of inactivity. The first piece (p. 191) merely points out that we have nothing whatever to learn about the control of drugs from the United States and complains about the huge increase in police powers demanded by a party of MPs who have returned from a visit to the United States. *The Real Case against Heroin* (p. 193) finds that the libertarian case for legalising this dangerous poison does not stand up. Ending the Liberal Issues section, some alarmed noises about a proposal that the police should be allowed to conduct intimate body searches at will – *Nymph in Thy Orifices* (p. 196), and a few arguments are advanced against restoration of the death penalty – not least that the prospect of hanging gives so much pleasure to the working classes, who have done nothing to deserve such a treat. *The Low Taste for Hanging* appears on page 199.

The book ends on a note of unrelieved gloom which some, I hope, will find cheering. The articles which appear under the general heading: the Sad State of Britain, rather speak for themselves: *Surly, Incompetent, Dishonest* (p. 203); *The Laziest People on Earth* (p. 204); *Roll on the Wealth Tax!* (p. 206). This last, rather uncharacteristic exclamation, seems to be explained by the assumption that a wealth tax would speed the Glorious Counter-Revolution for which Britain has been waiting so long. I suppose this seemed a worthwhile thing to say at the time.

The depths of gloom are touched in the piece called *Nothing to be done* (p. 209) which deals with the country's economic prospects, but some sort of hope may be discerned in the next three pieces. *Morocco as the Model* (p. 212) looks at one possible way ahead, while *A Possible Cure for Paralysis* (p. 214) suggests allowing the Socialist Workers Party and National Front to fight it out between them to decide which should control the country, in the hope that the fray would somehow galvanize everyone else. A longish and fairly serious penultimate piece contrasts the French of adjusting themselves to the brutality and hideousness of the modern world to our own, and tentatively suggests that there might be something to learn from them. That is *The French Solution* (p. 216).

Last of all I print the sad letter I received from an unknown lady, written the day before she committed suicide – prompted in part, as it would appear, by gloom engendered by reading my articles in *Spectator*. I hope this book does not have the same effect on many people. That is not its purpose.

PART ONE

CLASS WAR

1

ROYALTY

The Queen and the French President

Perhaps it was no more than an attack of persecution mania brought on by knowledge of my country's abject state, but I can't help wondering whether anybody else who watched the Queen receiving President Giscard d'Estaing outside Buckingham Palace last week noticed something perfunctory in the Frenchman's manner towards our sovereign? She was obviously putting herself out for him in a big way, chatting with great animation in what I am sure was excellent French. Giscard – or so it seemed to me – went through the motions of nodding once or twice while openly looking around to see if there was anybody more interesting to talk to.

At any rate, I was deeply shocked – not so much by the exhibition of bad manners, although that was interesting too, as by the lack of curiosity it revealed. Like many Francophiles of my generation and class, I had always tended to look upon Giscard as something approaching a Messiah. It is true that the French have a much better Constitution than we have – one day I shall bore everyone stiff when I unveil my thesis on how the British Constitution has shaped and fossilised those working-class attitudes which now lead ineluctably to our national ruin – but he nevertheless seemed to have achieved the impossible by emerging from within a recognisably democratic framework, as a leader of intelligence, cultivation, high principles and good sense.

Like many of my generation, I feel I have shed most of those illusions which sustained Englishmen in the past – on the superiority of British workmanship, the splendour of the British working man, the abiding virtue of most British institutions, the wit, wisdom and basic human decency of Lord Hailsham, the basic human decency of the Parliamentary Labour Party etc etc. But one illusion I have always entertained was that foreigners in general – and Frenchmen in particular – are bitterly jealous of our monarchy. Obviously, this jealousy was not to be found among all foreigners, or even among all Frenchmen. There would always be left-wingers, technocrats, people suffering from some form of brain damage and other unfortunates who would loudly proclaim their repudiation of anything so irrational, old-fashioned and sentimental but even among these delinquent and semi-human noises one could usually detect a note of suppressed envy.

Or so I thought. And where Giscard himself was concerned – a shooting man, who knew only too well that the best shotguns and cartridges are made in London, the only grouse fly in Scotland, gentlemen don't shoot quails or even wild pigs and dress themselves in Savile Row, not at some foreign tailor with a permanent wave in the Faubourg St Honoré – Giscard, surely, would fall to his knees in front of our Queen, crossing himself through his tears and uttering strange Gallic cries of delight. After all, the monarchy is now just about the only thing we have to offer in the modern world: our modern architecture is as ugly as everyone else's, our machines are even less reliable than theirs. Only the Queen and the Church of England are left, and nobody has ever shown the slightest interest in the Church of England.

Which is why it came as an ugly shock to see this Frenchman turn his back on the one remaining prop to our national self-esteem. Of course, I was already aware that my idol had at any rate a few clay toes on his nifty little feet. His own party goes out of its way to call itself Independent Republican; one of his first actions on arrival at the Elysée was to decree that officials there should no longer recognise the picturesque 'titles' which give so much harmless pleasure to so many otherwise ordinary Frenchmen and Frenchwomen; his greater political struggle at the present time is to introduce a totally fatuous, totally unwanted capital gains tax which even the French Communist Party is opposing.

Yet undoubtedly he has made a great impact on the British public. A survey conducted among the crowds waiting to cheer him at Victoria Station, found that many of them thought that Valéry Giscard d'Estaing was a female pop singer – surely the ultimate accolade from these pleasant, simple folk. Only the ghastly suspicion remains that, despite the fact we all put on our Sunday best, wore our most ingratiating smiles, trotted up and down in fancy dress, blew trumpets at him, showed him our House of Lords, despite the fact we even sent our happy and glorious Queen to talk French with him, Giscard d'Estaing was not impressed.

Nobody can blame the Queen. I had never seen anyone talk so much French in such a short space of time. If she had been feeling a little more generous, I suppose she might have given him a pair of Purdeys rather than an overweight black labrador bitch which won't understand French and will probably catch rabies before very long. But we must all pull in our belts nowadays, must we not?

But if these wretched foreigners are not going to be impressed, I see no reason to inflict them on the Queen. The Royal Family is something altogether too precious and too essential to our national self-esteem to be exposed to supercilious foreign politicians who, like all politicians, are here today and gone tomorrow. Some people may even feel that the Queen has made rather a fool of herself being seen talking so eagerly in a foreign tongue to someone who plainly didn't want to listen. Perhaps we should let the Queen retire from the centre of the stage for a while and concentrate our attention on Princess Anne, Dame Anne Phillips, who is surely a model for the more insular Royal Family of the future.

3.7.76

*   *   *

Princess Sourpuss

Of all the various forms of press censorship, an unspoken agreement between newspaper editors to exercise voluntary self-censorship strikes me as the most sinister. One such suspicion occurred to me at Easter of last year, when they showed a documentary film about the private life of Princess Anne and Captain Mark Phillips on television. In The Princess Anne Mrs Mark Phillips (or Dame Anne Phillips, as I maintain she should be called after receiving the GCVO for bravery in resisting kidnap by a madman called Ian Ball a short time after her marriage) it seemed to me that a new star had been born. I expected the television critics to be raving about her.

Instead of which, they all tastefully looked the other way. I did not see a single mention in any newspaper of this supremely comic performance. I was in hospital at the time, and it had the patients falling out of their beds. My family, quite independently, watched it in Somerset, and felt so moved they had to telephone me about it. Everybody I met who had seen it felt the same. Yet not a word appeared in the newspapers the next day.

The qualities of gracelessness and charmlessness portrayed in that memorable film were of an epic order in themselves, but when coupled with a readiness to be exposed on television they approached the sublime. To be as awful as that, and prepared to show it off without the slightest awareness of what you were showing suddenly became distinctly lovable. Princess Anne was the original pantomime dame, and if she could reconcile herself to the role she would win an instant place in her people's hearts as well as adding hugely to the general gaiety of the nation. But the newspapers, as I say, ignored her.

From that moment, I followed her career more carefully, even making her the object of a private cult. Her friends, we were told, included Mr Jackie Stewart (the racing driver) and Mr Anthony Andrews, the actor who delighted us all by showing us his bottom in *Brideshead Revisited*. She won golden opinions at the time of the snows by driving a sack of coal (or possibly potatoes or nuts) to an old age pensioner in her neighbourhood. Earlier this year, she opened an abattoir in the North of England and stayed to watch some animals being slaughtered. More recently she visited the Royal Veterinary College in London and stayed to watch some operations being carried out on a cat and a dog. This Dame as I say, has star quality.

Then suddenly last week, the truth dawned. Those lucky enough to see her on television in New Mexico being told that the Princess of Wales had given birth to a son – I saw it three times, and for the first time in my life wished I had a video machine to capture the magic moment – will never forget it:

'Your Royal Highness, any word about Princess Diana?'

'I don't know. You tell me.'

'Your reaction to her having a son?'

'I didn't know she had one.'

'This morning.'

'Oh, good.'

The Palace later explained that she was not sure the reporter was telling her the truth. Earlier, she had heard the rumour of a royal birth which turned out to be false. But this does not explain her answers to other questions on the tour, or, indeed, her answers on this occasion:

'How are you enjoying your visit to New Mexico?'

'Keep your questions to yourself.'

As an answer, this must rank with the classic reply of the prison warder in *Two-Way Stretch*: 'Silence! when you're talking to *me*.'

It was a bravura performance from start to finish. Asked how it felt to be an aunt for the first time, she riposted: 'That's my business, thank you,' which prompted an old lady present to ask (according to the *Daily Mirror*): 'Who would want her for an aunt?'

Well, I would for one. She belongs to a grand old tradition of English aunts, stretching from Wodehouse through Saki and Wilde to Jane Eyre's Aunt Reed and no doubt further back than that. Every child should have at least one aunt like that, and it is one of the sorrows of my life that I never did. The Americans had a word for her, to contrast her with the Prince of Wales – 'his sister's a sourpuss but he's a real sweetie' – and it was this word which the *Mirror* seized on for a memorable leading article, *PRINCESS SOURPUSS*:

'*If Princess Diana is the best advert for Britain, Princess Anne is the worst.*

24

'It is bad enough when she is miserable and rude in this country.

'When she behaves like that abroad, as she has in America, she lets Britain down.

'She doesn't appear able to share the joy over the birth of her nephew . . .

'Princess Anne is paid £2,050 a *week* from public money, tax free. For that, we are entitled to expect a lot.

'And we don't even get a smile.

'She has earned herself a new title: Princess Sourpuss.'

Oh dear, *Poor* Princess Anne. But when the press and public have digested their new discovery, I hope that they will settle down, like me, to loving our Sourpuss Princess. Why on earth should she be anything but a sourpuss, if that is her nature? The great embarrassment of her previous image, while the press and broadcasting people were tacitly agreeing to protect her, was that we were expected to revere a nondescript young woman who was plainly neither very intelligent nor very charming. Now, at long last, we learn that she is not nondescript at all, but a genuine and unmistakable eccentric. For my £2,050 a week, I would much prefer to see her scowl. Her smile, though no fault of her own, is rather a horrible thing. We have been living with it now for over 31 years, and it added nothing to the good cheer of the nation. Her scowl, on the other hand, is sincere and genuine and immensely enjoyable, making a huge contribution to the Royal Family showbiz package.

3.7.82

*   *   *

The Duke on Housing

We will not see the report of his inquiry into British housing until Prince Philip presents it to a grateful nation on the centenary of the famous Royal Commission on Housing for the Working Classes of 1885. That Commission produced a searing report which stirred the consciences of all our great-grandfathers with its account of overcrowding and poor sanitation – the famous Inhuman Conditions which can still be found by dedicated quarriers in places like the Gorbals, Merseyside, Newcastle and South London, wherever the improvident, incapable or slatternly congregate.

Oddly enoug, I had just received a similar report from my younger daughter about living conditions among Oxford undergraduates in digs. She returned from a short, but obviously agreeable visit with a harrowing account of rooms which were a foot deep in dirty socks and underpants, coffee mugs festering in every corner, blocked lavatories shared by the multiple occupants of a boarding house which would have made any

25

Royal Commission weep except that the occupants were all middle-class, all from well-to-do homes, some even connected to the peerage.

After leaving Oxford these people will go to live in identical squalor in London, often five or six of them in a two-bedroomed basement flat. An enormous amount of attention has been paid to housing for the working class in the past hundred years, and prodigious, unimaginable sums of money have been spent on it. It is not time for a Royal Commission on Housing for the Younger Middle Classes?

It was once fashionable – at any rate before the Thatchers arrived on the scene – to remark that Prince Philip had one of the most difficult and possibly disagreeable jobs in Britain, at any rate among white collar workers. There was always an element of conscious perversity in this judgment, a calculated affront to the underdog's snarl, *'It's all right for some'*, which measures human happiness in cash terms. But I remember thinking that for an opinionated man – and the Prince is unquestionably a highly opinionated man – the restraints imposed by being Royal Consort might prove irksome. It was in recognition of these restraints that we – the great British middle class – refused to envy him his £180,000 odd pocket money on the Civil List, his mortgage-free residences in Pimlico, Windsor, Norfolk and Aberdeenshire, his use of private aeroplanes and the royal yacht. It was also, of course, in recognition of the fact that his privileged existence, although inflated out of all proportion, mirrored our own much smaller advantages over the common herd of those less fortunate than ourselves, and somehow even sanctified these little differences. Just as we set a good example by not being jealous of the Duke, so the common cry of curs had no business to be jealous of our little comforts and treats: our occasional glass of wine with our meals, our robustly built Volvos and our little holiday cottages in the Dordogne or wherever.

The report of this committee under the Duke's chairmanship will not be with us, as I say, until 25 July, but already enough has been leaked to tell us what sort of line it will take. One might have guessed from a study of its members, knowing that among well-mannered English committee folk the 'moderate' left always prevails.

The committee published a summary of its evidence. Prince Philip, in his preface to it, appeared to accept the committee's conclusion, that the 'inequities' of tax relief on mortgage interest payments were in part responsible for an alleged failure to 'generate finance' for new and improved municipal housing for the lower classes – i.e. the working classes and those who for one reason or another are not actually working. Anybody who studied the matter from the other end of the telescope – that is to say from the Treasury's point of view – would know perfectly well that this is untrue. Any money 'saved' (i.e. seized) by the Treasury by

26

the ending of mortgage interest tax relief would immediately be swallowed up by public employees in the never-ending inflation of public sector consumption. What the Duke's committee is advocating, in fact, is an increase in both taxation and public expenditure in the vague hope that this might result in more council accommodation – at a time when the elected government is pursuing a policy of selling council houses, with enormous public support.

So much for the Duke's impartiality in political matters. But what is interesting from this point of view of the middle classes is the means by which his committee reached the unwelcome conclusion that mortgage relief should be ended. It revealed the startling discovery that 'the allowances against tax for those borrowing for house purchase are worth more to the highest rate taxpayers than to those with lower income; and more to those able to afford a large mortgage than to those able to buy a cheaper house. Many of those presenting evidence felt the impact of these concessions to be inequitable.'

Coo! But it is that use of the word 'inequitable' which gives everything away. I wonder if the Duke knows what it means. Equity is not the same thing as equality, or his own position would be the most inequitable thing imaginable. It has nothing to do with equitation. You see, your Royal Highness, higher tax payers are people who pay more tax. Their taxes help provide housing for lower tax payers. But higher tax payers need houses, too. The middle classes want middle-class housing just as much as the working classes want new and improved working-class housing. Unlike many workers, the middle classes have to pay for their houses, which are more expensive. But they cannot do that if the Government grabs all their money and gives it to the working classes.

Perhaps Prince Philip sincerely believes that everybody except himself and other members of the Royal Family should be equal. It is a position which others have held before him. God is widely thought to take the same view of the human race, but God is somewhat less vulnerable to public opinion. The middle classes decide what public opinion is to be, and the middle classes will ultimately decide whether or not the Government needs an alternative opposition in Buckingham Palace.

29.6.85

*   *   *

Princess Fairytale

I am under intense pressure to say something rude about Mr Nigel Dempster, the distinguished gossip columnist of the *Daily Mail*. So, I imagine, have most other journalists in the country been under pressure, and it will be interesting to see which of them succumb. The pressure does not come from proprietors or 'international combines', as the Left would have us believe, but from those hidden manipulators of the press: wives, children, daily women, people who come to dinner, visiting French aristocrats, mysterious Russian counts who stay the weekend and leave without paying their gambling debts ... in other words, from public opinion.

The Greatest Living Englishman, as Mr Dempster is almost universally known among his colleagues (in fact, as we all know, he was born in the Antipodes and snatched from a dingo's jaws to be educated at Sherborne), has Gone Too Far. While commentators have generally felt free to be as offensive as they like about Princess Anne and even to hint that Princess Margaret may not be quite so much fun as newspapers patriotically insisted she was for many years, the Princess of Wales remains sacred – at any rate for the time being.

And so she jolly well should, of course. If she had been paid modelling rates for the use of her photograph in the world's press, she would be in a position to buy Buckingham Palace with all its resident pooftahs, Soviet agents and corgi dogs. She has appeared day after day in even the dullest newspapers to illuminate our lives and give us hope for the future. In the years we have known her she has kept more newspapers alive than Diana Dors, Jayne Mansfield and Marilyn Monroe ever did between them.

Gloomily, we decided she would almost certainly go mad before very long. Apart from the fact that she was plainly a nervous filly, and few young women could reasonably be expected to survive the strain of so much exposure, there was the metaphysical dread that in representing Britain's Youth and Hope for the Future she was in fact representing two somewhat parlous entities.

But she does not seem to have gone mad, and until Mr Dempster's amazing revelations (or shameless inventions, depending upon one's attitude to the complicated creative process behind what is known in the trade as a Dempster-truth) the fairytale seemed stuck in the lived-happily-ever-after groove. Now, according to Dempster, the Prince of Wales has become 'desperately unhappy'. The Princess has become a 'very wilful and spoiled girl. Suddenly, getting this enormous power, having people curtsey and bow to her, doing everything she wants, she's become a fiend. She has became a little monster.'

So speaks the Greatest Living Englishman. The *News of the World*, which decided (probably quite rightly) that this was the most interesting thing which had happened all week, devoted most of its front page to denouncing him: ' "FIENDISH" DIANA What a Load of Rubbish,' it shouted across the top of five columns, with the inevitable photograph of our beloved Princess over the caption 'FIENDISH – or fabulous?'

A Buckingham Palace spokesman was credited with the statement that the Princess was 'very upset by these stupid comments', although other newspapers had been able to elicit only the comment 'Ridiculous'. Wasn't 'ridiculous' the word used by a Buckingham Palace spokesman to describe rumours of an attachment between Princess Anne and Lieutenant Mark Phillips? Alas, after that painful episode, nothing a Buckingham Palace spokesman can say will have any effect but to encourage rumours to the contrary.

What, then, of Dempster? A few years ago, he announced that the Prince of Wales was secretly betrothed to Princess Marie Astrid of Luxembourg. For many years afterwards I stoutly maintained that this was indeed the case, that the two had almost certainly married in secret, that Lady Diana Spencer and her various predecessors in the Royal engagement stakes were no more than red herrings. Now that Dempster-truth has been replaced by the equally enjoyable Dempster-truth of the Fiendish Princess. To the great question of the day – whom should we believe, the Palace spokesman or the great journalist? – I would suggest the best answer is 'either, or neither, according to taste, but preferably both'. But perhaps this needs explanation.

The *News of the World*, in the course of its front-page comment on this burning issue, attributed two possible motives to the GLE before concluding that 'this must be the greatest howler of all time for the balding, 41-year-old columnist'. The first was, quite simply, that he had gone mad.

'Marathon Jogger Nigel Dempster who carries the dubious distinction of being Britain's top gossip columnist, seems to have run right round the bend.'

The second is not spelled out so clearly.

'Or would he have us believe that Someone in a High Place is stirring up trouble for Princess Diana, the shy and lovely girl who has won the hearts of millions?'

Presumably this obscure Someone in a High Place is not the *Mail*'s proprietor who could have no possible reason to stir up trouble for the Princess of Wales. No, we are intended to wonder whether Dempster could possibly have been fed this strange information by Princess Margaret. The unflattering suggestion is plainly that Princess Margaret (of whom Dempster recently wrote a biography) is so jealous of the Princess of Wales that she is whispering this poison into Dempster's ear. But nothing which Dempster has said or written, so far as I know, suggests that this is the case. It is all speculation and vile Fleet Street gossip. Dempster, in other words has himself been Dempstered. And to the question of whether or not we should believe it, I should make the same reply as before, that we should either believe it or not as we choose, but preferably we should do both.

We could not go on as before, mutely adoring the Princess of Wales. All relationships require incident and development. At very least, Dempster has provided an incident – gossip columnist attacks Princess Fairy-tale, nation rises in anger. At best he has greatly enriched our Royal fantasy experience by introducing this element of creative doubt – half belief, half disbelief – in the identity of the main characters. Is the Princess of Wales a spoiled and petulant young lady, or is she the enchanting natural person she seems? Is Princess Margaret an evil, jealous woman or is she right in what she says? Did she say it anyway? If so, why?

I would like, on the same basis, to propose various other explanations for Dempster's behaviour, always on the understanding that there is no reason whatever to suppose he had any particular motive at all. The first is frustrated rage over the Prince of Wales's refusal to marry the young Luxembourgeoise whom Dempster had choosen for him. The second is that he is in the throes of a courtly love for Princess Margaret (whom he believes to be 'obsessed by bi-sexuals') and is merely doing what he supposes will please her, though she has never given him the slightest encouragement.

This last is the explanation I prefer. Everybody in public lives, to a greater or lesser extent, in a world of make-believe. Dempster, with his lonely, pure hopeless passion for the Queen's sister, has himself melted into the mists of legend, fantasy and make-believe. He is the last of the troubadours. Long may his songs be heard.

18.12.82

2

BRITS OLD AND NEW

The Educated Man and Mrs Williams

'It is also true that Mrs Williams holds a number of views which on *The Times* we do not share. She is an egalitarian, and we are not. She wants to abolish private education, and we do not. She believes in a wealth tax which we believe would depress business investment still further. Yet *The Times* must take the rough with the smooth . . .

'Why, though, would we still say that this somewhat indecisive woman, of middling intellectual attainments, and mistaken views, would make a good Prime Minister?'

The magnificent leading article which appeared in *The Times* 10 February 1981 to support the idea of Shirley Williams as Prime Minister was not, of course, signed, but every syllable in it glowed with the high intelligence, the fairness, the humour and the humanity which have been glowing there 14 years from the noble brow of Mr William Rees-Mogg. There were the same measured style, the occasional striking phrase – 'The two old parties are widely seen as having failed, as being two grimacing skeletons of political despair' – even a little joke about leadership of a reduced Conservative party resolving between Mr Terry Higgins of Worthing and Mr Jerry Wiggins of Weston-super-Mare, although the giggle was quickly stifled: 'Not a bad choice, all things considered.' And from all the benignity and quiet patriotism, there came a stern warning at the end: 'Beyond the quality of the leader and the form of the electoral system, there is the question of national unity. Mr Foot divides the nation; so does Mrs Thatcher ... But the nation believes in its own unity, and may take a terrible revenge at the next election on those who represent division.'

It was a masterpiece, although I cannot claim to have been entirely convinced by it. Mr Rees-Mogg's sublime view of his fellow countrymen takes no account of Original Sin. He overlooks – perhaps he is even unaware of – the malice, the hatred, the ancient, irremediable grudges and resentments of the North East. He hears their voices at Blackpool and Wembley, he sees ignorance, sloth, stupidity and vindictiveness parade themselves with all the arrogance of power and he looks to little Mrs Williams to save us all: 'The British have lost confidence in themselves. None of their leaders talk to them in their own true language, a language of good nature, of friendliness, of fair dealing, of balance.'

Of course that is what we would all like to believe. What could be more agreeable? But has Mr Rees-Mogg ever actually been up North and tried to talk to Glaswegians, for instance, in a Clydeside or Gorbals pub, in their own true language of good nature, friendliness, fair dealing and balance? Or steelworkers in Rotherham? Or miners in south Wales? Obviously these bitter, unpleasant, moronically stupid people are not typical of a majority of Britons, but it is precisely Mr Rees-Mogg's passive or 'wet' approach to them which has allowed these previously caged Calibans to impose their unpleasant and destructive preferences on the country.

Let us look a little more closely at the love-object, described as being 'a somewhat indecisive woman of middling intellectual attainments and mistaken views.' Of all the crimes and disasters perpetrated by British governments since the war, whether by omission or commission, I feel the only one to compare with Mr (now 'Lord') Stewart's murderous

31

policy in Nigeria (which all the Gang of Four supported) is the imposition of comprehensive schooling. Quite apart from its exacerbation of class antagonisms – even in calm backwaters as Somerset, middle-class or hard-working children of any class are regularly beaten up as snobs – it has removed any prospect the working-class child might ever have had of improving himself, escaping from the miserable proletarian rut which the 'workers' create for themselves wherever they have the upperhand.

By the time Mrs Williams arrived in September 1976, with her background of St Paul's and her degree from Somerville College, her much vaunted 'personality one can relate to', it was plain to everyone except the blindest ideologues and fanatics in her Department that the whole comprehensive idea had been an atrocious mistake. It was not too late, then, to rescue a large part of an education system which had once been the pride of Britain, which produced most of the Labour Cabinet and represented the ladder out of the vicious circle of stupidity, ignorance and inertia for generations before theirs. Instead of which this somewhat indecisive woman threw herself into the battle to end all selective education with the fanaticism of an Ayatollah. The comprehensive system is her monument, and so long as there is breath left in my body I shall seek to punish, torment, humiliate and ridicule this loathsome pig-headed woman for the damage she has done her country.

It would be easy to explain that, in a nation which is rapidly dividing quite sharply (despite his own perception of it) into wets and nasties, one instinctively sides with the wets. But it is not for his wetness that I love him. I love him partly, no doubt, for his scrupulous fairness, his benignity, his ability to understand and respect other people's opinions, his sense of his own absurdity, his courtesy and simple good manners. These qualities of patience, fairness, moderation and high intelligence undoubtedly add up to a sort of wisdom even if, in combination, they generally produce the wrong answers. More than anything else, I love him because he writes in the beautiful clear English of an honourable, educated man. *The Times* was rubbish before he joined it and will almost certainly be rubbish (although of a different sort) now he has gone. It is too early to condemn the appointment of Harold Evans, but not too early to express misgivings. If, in the months that follow, footling diagrams or 'graphics' begin to appear illustrating how the hostages walked off their aeroplane into a reception centre; profiles of leading hairdressers suddenly break on page 12; inquiries into the safety of some patent medicine replace Philip Howard's ruminations on the English language; if a cheap, flip radicalism replaces Mr Rees-Mogg's carefully argued, honourable conservatism and nasty, gritty English creeps into the leader columns where once his sonorous phrases basked and played in the sun; if it begins to seem that one or more beleaguered outpost has fallen to the barbarians, we should reflect that there never really was an England which spoke in this language of good nature, of friendliness, of fair dealing, of balance. It was all a product of Mr Rees-Mogg's beautiful mind.

28.2.81

*   *   *

Norman and Judy

'There is no such thing as the average British family,' we read as the introduction to a series of articles in *The Times* designed to establish exactly such a concept. It might have added that any idea of an average or mean in human affairs is bound to be absurd, not to say vile. But Norman and Judy – two genuine citizens, so far as one can judge from their photographs – were chosen by *The Times* as representing this average British family, as near as can be. They live in a pleasant three-bedroomed semi-detached house in a village called Chilton which the author of the piece, also called Judy – Judy Froshaug – thinks is in Oxfordshire, although on the map it looks to me as if it is in Buckinghamshire. Norman motors every day to work to his insurance office in Reading, about 20 miles away. He earns £9,000 a year.

Are these typical things to do? I do not know. What makes them slightly less typical is that they have three children, rather than the standard 2.13 or whatever. This deviation from the norm plainly caused them much heartsearching: 'Their family was planned,' writes Mrs Froshaug. 'Both agreed on two children – sex immaterial – though Judy knew she wanted three after Johnny and Anna had arrived. Norman had to be convinced . . .

'Judy remembers feeling a little guilty when Simon, their third child, was on the way . . . "it was at a time when the Department of the Environment and the press were constantly on about three being poverty everywhere, and I did wonder if I weren't being selfish for a bit."'

It is news to me that the Department of the Environment concerns itself about these things, but from her reference to the press I assume that Norman and Judy are readers of the *Guardian*. If so, this is not a very average thing to be: I estimate that only about one in a hundred of the adult population reads the *Guardian*. But it is undoubtedly a typically British assumption that any extra pair of hands born into Britain means less work, less prosperity for everyone else.

The more we read about Norman and Judy, the less they seem to be average. They are a pair of model citizens, freak goody-goodies, being held up to teach us how we ought to think and behave. Thus they are both committee members of the local parent-teacher association, Judy is

33

a governor of the school. Both are members of the local church and Judy teaches at Sunday school. Norman runs the Saturday morning swimming club and is secretary of the parents' badminton club. Nor are the children much less active. Johnny, aged nine, belongs to the Cubs and the St John's Ambulance, learns the piano and cello as well as swimming; Anna, aged seven, plays the piano, goes to dancing class and has already joined something called the Girls' Brigade; even Simon is swimming at five.

I do not for a moment wish to claim there is anything ridiculous about all this. It is admirable, admirable. Moreover, we should be reminded as often as possible that by no means all Britons are as idle and useless as our economic performance might indicate. Many, perhaps most, may spend their Saturday mornings in bed rather than running the swimming club. But it is good to be reminded that there are other citizens who are completely different, who are, as Mrs Froshaug puts it, 'always on the go'.

What *is* absurd is to pretend that they are average Britons, or that theirs is the typical marriage. They scarcely ever quarrel. As Judy puts it: 'Sharing everything and discussing everything is totally important to us. Life is too short to be falling out all the time.'

Perhaps it is the fault of their interviewer, Mrs Judy Froshaug, that they also seem unbearably smug. Pure virtue is never easy to make attractive. There they stand proudly in front of their pleasant semi-detached abode without a shadow of discontent apparent in their lives. Norman has a dark moustache and beard, wears heavy-rimmed spectacles, looks a trifle overweight. Judy, who trained as an occupational therapist, looks thinner, sharper, ever ready for a totally important discussion.

I am not quite sure what it means to be an occupational therapist, but I suspect it has something to do with the great boom area of our domestic economy which revolves around care of the handicapped. Nothing wrong with that, of course, it is an admirable thing to do, although so many young people nowadays seem to want to earn their living in this way that soon there may not be enough handicapped people to go round. No doubt they will share them out somehow.

Whatever is involved in occupational therapy, I feel sure it is something to do with the Department of Health and Social Security. A faintly worrying thing about Norman is that although Insurance might reasonably be described as a caring profession, he does not actually seem to be employed by the DHSS. In every other way, of course, he is a perfect citizen and ideal husband.

The children go to state schools of course. Even if they could afford private education, they say they wouldn't. 'I think you get a better all-round education at a good state school,' says Judy.

Education, we are told, is all-important. The one thing that annoys them is the Government's pruning of education. Judy describes it as 'terribly shortsighted. Our children *are* the future, after all, though if I were old or sick the cuts in social services would worry me even more.'

Would they just? Plainly, Norman and Judy are not just model citizens, but model products of the Welfare State. But is it really true that Johnny, Anna and Simon are the future, rather than those dear little kiddies in Toxteth – Kevin, Patrick, Ham and Joshua with 20 convictions for robbery and assault between them. Bernadette and Kissie, available for anyone with a Crunchie Bar? Will spending more money on their education really make it any better? Norman and Judy obviously think so, and I suspect that they will be voting Social Democrat at the next election like everyone else.

Like everyone else. What am I saying? I am not going to vote for them. Practically nobody I knows intends to vote SDP. It is unlikely that more than a fifth of the electorate will do so. Judy and Norman are *not* Mr and Mrs Average Briton. They are just another pair of unrepresentative freaks, like the rest of us. I pay £9,100 a year out of taxed income to educate four children, but at least I do not pretend this is a normal thing to do. Why on earth should the future lie with their children rather than with my own or anyone else's? Mrs Judy Froshaug does not tell us their surname. Possibly she has a good reason for this. I suspect it is Galtieri or Cvünk, Finkelstein or Pissupski. We must *not* be brainwashed into accepting this gloomy couple as average Britons. Far more people take the *Daily Telegraph* every day than have ever taken the *Guardian* and *Times* combined. Britain is not yet a collection of Normans and Judys.

8.5.82

*   *   *

YITS and WAPS Abroad

Among their various dirty or disreputable habits, I imagine that most *Spectator* readers still read the *Sunday Times*. So, I have to admit, do I – mostly, because it is there but also because just occasionally perhaps once every four or five weeks, it has something worth reading in it: an interview by John Mortimer, a review by Paul Theroux, or an article on some part of the world one knows nothing about. This should not interfere with our image of the *Sunday Times* reader as combining in his unsavoury person all the distressing attributes of the New Briton: he is white and overweight, flip, cynical, ignorant and boastful; untrustworthy in business matters, over-confident in conversation yet infinitely gullible in his cynicism, insecure in his boastfulness. He eats bad food greedily and is loud in his praise of nasty wine. He wears his hideous moustache in a downward-turning bow and invariably says 'No way!' when he means 'I think, perhaps not'. His wife is even worse, with a terrible underlying seriousness which turns everything it touches to dust. Both are planning to vote for the Social Democratic Party next time round.

Sometimes these horrible people can be rattled by questions about their fatuous and dishonest political opinions; sometimes they can be baited by irreverent or even rude references to their class origins. But on the whole it is best to leave them well alone. Nothing but boredom and misunderstanding result from any social contact with a *Sunday Times* reader. Which is why it is vital to read the colour magazines at this time of year to discover where the brutes are planning to go on their holiday, and take evasive action.

France, India, Hong Kong, America, Sri Lanka, Egypt, Romania and China have drawn the short straw this year. Of these Egypt and Sri Lanka are the saddest. A Nile cruise taken with my wife the spring before last was one of the pleasantest experiences of my life, without the trace of any *Sunday Times* reader in sight. I have never been to Sri Lanka and until this Sunday it remained one of the few places left I still wished to see. In fact I had half planned a visit in the spring. Now it will be full of New Britons. Like Cambodia and Vietnam, Uganda, Mozambique, Angola, Spanish Equatorial Guinea, Iran and, to a lesser extent, Laos and Burma, I have left it too late.

The article on France is possibly the most disturbing. Surely the New Britons do not want to spend much time in France? It is a place to be motored through at full speed on the way to the Spanish coasts or Costas as old Spanish hands call them. We who motor down to the South every year know exactly the roads they will take, the places they will stop, even the hotels they will stay in, and avoid them all like the plague. Now these filthy people are being advised to take their time, ambling along the minor roads and looking for bargain meals among the fortified towns of the Midi. One of the recommended routes even takes them to within 40 miles of my own house in the Aude, and recommends them to eat *cassoulet* in Foix. God help us. We all believe in the freedom of the press and nobody more passionately than I, but ... but ... but ...

As Shakespeare said, power without responsibility has been the pre-rogative of the harlot through the ages. What possible reason can there be for encouraging *Sunday Times* readers to eat *cassoulet*? It is not so much a question of seriously damaging their health as actually killing them. Most doctors don't eat it. No way. If they try to jog or hold a Fun-Run after it they will almost certainly explode. Their moustaches will turn green, their beards will drop off and they will foul their track-suits. Their Lifespan will turn sour and in their delirium they will forget their dental hygiene. But even by the special standards of 'committed' journalism, I do not see what is to be gained by sending these panting, farting, greedy brutes to remote and friendly French country taverns and little-known market towns in the Languedoc. If the press does not put its own house in order, it must increase the danger that some unsympathetic government of the future ...

Although, as I say, I suspect that most readers of the *Spectator* still take in the *Sunday Times*, if only through general inertia, I fear that comparatively few of them also take the *Daily Mirror*. This is a pity, as it is a much better newspaper and more intelligently written. Even its politics are in many ways less objectionable. One of the great hazards of travel in recent years is that one must not only avoid the hideous New *Sunday Times* Britons who will be coming into their own during the course of the Year of Information Technology 1982 (perhaps they will rejoice in the acronym YITs) but also our beloved workers spending their bloated redundancy payments and unemployment entitlements in an age which seems to have become an extended workers' playtime. Workers at Play or (WAPs) are generally easier to avoid than yits because they do not, on the whole, take their cars with them. But the waps are fanning out like a global pack of beagles, and it would be as well to know where they are heading.

Mr Paul Hughes, travel editor of the *Daily Mirror*, lists 19 places to be avoided at all costs, from the Spanish Costas at £150 a week ('favourite with those who want family fun, cheap wine, sandy beaches and certain sunshine') to Australia at £850 for a fortnight ('a great country with great people. Enjoy yourself on the trip of a lifetime') In America, avoid Florida ('Allow two days to see Disneyland and don't let the kids drag you away') and New York ('It's all you ever thought it was only more so'). In North Africa, avoid Morocco ('the most exotic country near to Britain. Kasbahs, Arab markets, snake charmers and spicy food – young children might get tummy upsets') and Tunisia ('very good value'). Avoid Scandinavia ('great for family hols in log cabins'), Amsterdam ('great for lovers on a mini-holiday'), Italy ('great night life. Excellent range of hotels from cheap and cheerful to posh and plushy'), Hawaii ('worth going just to say you've been') and Greece ('ideal for youngsters on rucksack holidays. Fares and accommodation cheap').

And so it goes on. Avoid Hong Kong, China, Yugoslavia, Madeira, Corsica, the Caribbean and Canada ('all the wildlife and adventures you can take') too. One of Mr Hughes's most alarming recommendations is the South of France: 'Britons have all but taken over the topless beaches from the French jet-setters. Excellent value for rent-a-tent family camping holidays. Coach and tent, £100 a fortnight.' No doubt their bleached bones will still be around next year.

Where on earth is left? Only one of Mr Hughes's recommendations

37

receives my unqualified blessing, where he urges his readers to try Alaska: 'The frozen hell weather makes you feel brave just walking along the street. Glaciers and icebergs are all around. Fascinating for adventurers. £314 for eight nights.' If only the *Sunday Times* had the same flair. Next year, I hope *all* newspapers will concentrate on the joys of Alaska. That is what I call responsible journalism

9.1.82

*　　*　　*

Class War in MI5

When I came down from Oxford in June 1960, after only a year there and without a degree, my father said there were only two possible professions for young men in my situation: teaching or spying. Since I was under no illusions about my suitability as a teacher I wrote off, at his suggestion, to his old friend Sir Roger Hollis, who was then Director-General of the Security Services. He replied, civilly enough, that I was too young for his branch of the Service, but recommended me to the Foreign Office people from whom I heard in due course.

The history of my attempts to join MI6 must await another occasion. Suffice to say that although I was reasonably convinced I had spotted a Soviet agent on the selection committee and still feel bitter, when I think of it, about a former friend who testified to the investigators that my chief characteristics were my indiscretion and irresponsibility, I do not feel, in retrospect, that the Secret Intelligence Service was making one of its gravest blunders when it declined my offer.

I remember one incident with particular shame. Whatever may be claimed about subsequent developments, it was quite plain in the autumn of 1960 that the Foreign Office was already looking for candidates who were both classless and left of centre. Accordingly, that is what we were all desperately trying to be. During a committee discussion about Africa, I had expressed misgivings about the future prospects of a newly independent African state. Afterwards, the invigilators asked me if this meant I thought Africans were innately inferior. Not at all, I replied cleverly, just that they were better at different things. What things in particular, asked one of my tormentors – probably the Soviet agent – did I think Africans were better at? My brilliant young mind raced. A mental seizure. I could think of nothing. 'Well, climbing trees,' I said weakly.

I had no further contact with Sir Roger Hollis until, in retirement, he came to live fairly close to us in Somerset and supported the wicked scheme for building a golf course in the Quantocks, which I was instrumental in frustrating, but I often saw his brother Christopher – one-time Conservative Member for Devizes and resident poet of the *Spectator* –

38

who was my godfather. From my father's *Diaries* Roger seems to have been quite a convivial fellow – 'a good bottle man'.

Not the sort of person I would expect to be much impressed by the Soviet Union. True, Burgess was a bottle-man, too, but there is all the difference in the world between an Oxford bottle-man and a Cambridge bottle-man. Nobody who knew Tom Driberg at all well could have been in much doubt that he was a Soviet agent. Tom was not a man who liked being laughed at, but he always pretended to be immensely amused whenever I accused him of spying for Russia. It never seriously occurred to me that he was drawing money from MI5, too, although rereading the reference to him in my introduction to *The Last Word; An Eyewitness Account of the Thorpe Trial*, (Michael Joseph £6.50) I see I must have guessed subconsciously. In any case, one had only to reflect on his sexual preferences to spot that he was an obvious candidate for one or other of the British Intelligence Services. It is my contention that what caused Roger Hollis's downfall was an inability, in dealing with 'people like ourselves', to distinguish between those who came from Oxford and those who came from Cambridge. But before pursuing this argument, I must repeat an anecdote which acquires a certain poignancy in the light of last week's revelations, that Sir Roger was – and in some quarters still is – seriously suspected to having been a Soviet agent.

About 15 years ago I heard a funny story about John Wyndham (later Lord Egremont) that when he was Macmillan's private secretary in Downing Street (or possibly Admiralty House) he would sometimes, late at night, decide to play a little prank. He would telephone the Director of Security Services (in fact Hollis) at his home in Campden Hill Square and as soon as he got through would shout down the telephone in an assumed accent: 'Aha! Villain! I know your secret!' – and ring off. After he had played this joke a few times, the Security Service put a tab on the calls and traced them to the Private Office of the Prime Minister. Red faces all round and a tremendous wigging from the PM.

This excellent story came to me from a source which left me in no doubt whatever as to its truth, but which was too private for me to use. But five years or so later I wheeled it out to illustrate an article I was writing for a French – or possibly a German – newspaper on the English sense of humour, or some such rubbish. Rather to my surprise, it was picked up by a hack on the *Sunday Times* who telephoned a few weeks later to say he had checked the story with Lord Egremont – something I would never have dared to do – and Egremont had denied it with the most extraordinary vehemence. At the time, I attributed this to the discernible assumption of the upper class that they have an absolute right to tell point-blank lies to the press (the same trait, I imagine which explains Lord Home's denial that he was told about Blunt in 1964, which he has had to stick to ever since and which continues to cause general confusion. Hollis certainly told him and if Home were half a man he would admit it). The latest revelation – that Hollis was indeed suspected of having a guilty secret – not only explains Egremont's vehemence but may throw an unexpected light on his sense of humour.

To understand Roger Hollis's downfall – and the continuing vendetta against him – we must go back to the atmosphere of the Sixties. At the time it was not so much fashionable as obligatory to believe that the country's salvation lay in the hands of the new 'classless' generation of upwardly mobile working-class folk who were just about coming into their own, many if not all with vicious chips on their shoulders.

In the aftermath of Burgess, Maclean and then Philby, the duffle-coat brigade within MI5 saw its main chance. All the old-timers were suspect, most particularly those from a public school background. As Director-General, Hollis was constantly irritated by requests to investigate his friends and trusted colleagues. He refused them permission to tap his deputy's telephone (Graham Mitchell – Winchester and Magdalen, Oxford) and discouraged them from blackening the name of my poor cousin Guy Liddell, another deputy director who died as long ago as 1958. In both these instances he was unquestionably right. How many other colleagues he protected from harassment by these ambitious young creeps we shall never know, but by the time Blunt's turn came round his reaction must have been more or less automatic, and this time he was wrong. The lean and hungry new boys smelled blood, and this time they were right. The leader of the pack made himself so objectionable that Hollis, in exasperation, sacked him; he was re-hired by the rival firm MI6, put back on the interservice counter-espionage committee which is apparently known in Fleet Street as the Fluency Committee and, from the moment of Blunt's final exposure in 1964, Hollis was doomed. His greatest error was to have mistaken a soft-faced Cambridge homosexual for one of us. It is not hard to see where Chapman Pincher's information came from, or that the renewed hounding of Sir Roger is a simple continuation of the class war within MI5.

At least it all proved a useful diversion from the launch of the Social Democrat Party. For the future, we are told in *The Times* (which, in its own words, has itself 'given wider ventilation to the raw material') of the search for a new kind of classless spycatcher: 'A wider social mix in its intake is being sought ... A suspicion of left-wing activities, arising from a *Daily Telegraph* style view of the world, is not judged an especially bad trait as at present MI5 regards the far left as a greater threat to the nation's stability than the far right.'

Those who are groping their way towards an understanding of Times New English will deduce that MI5 is particularly anxious to recruit lower-class lefties. Which just shows how times have changed. Few, if any, intelligent children of the middle class are remotely drawn to the Soviet Union nowadays. But there is something oddly comforting in the knowledge that MI5 is once again trawling in precisely those waters where the future traitors will be found.

4.4.81

3

THE WORKING CLASSES

Workers' Power

By all accounts, the working class is busy creating a sort of hell on earth for itself: rubbish lies uncollected in the street, old-age pensioners are mercilessly raped whenever they venture out after dark, dying like flies in any case and their corpses left unburied, everybody in work is on strike and the rest are unemployed. Perhaps this is all a pack of lies. Perhaps merry, red-faced women are to be seen happily scrubbing their doors, making their amusing jokes in rhyming slang and everybody is as happy as the proverbial sand boy.

Of the two versions I think I prefer the former because I happen to have seen the sort of hell the workers create for themselves if they are left to their own devices in places like Liverpool, Birkenhead and Kirkby New Town. But my point is that it is really no business of ours any more what they get up to in these places. The working class, for the first time in its long history, is now the master of its fate and the captain of its soul. We may wish it joy in its new power or not, as the case may be, but the most important thing is to ensure that it never becomes the master of *our* fate or the captain of our souls – that it never succeeds in dragging us down with it. For all of us that means arranging our lives in such a way as to place least reliance on the continued good will or even the intelligently self-interested participation of these people and to put ourselves, so far as possible, beyond the reach of their spite. And when one takes a step back from one's initial reactions of panic and horror at the phenomenon of 'workers power', it is surprising how nearly all of its applications are directed against the workers themselves.

Some applications appear to have no direction at all. Thus it would be easy to grow indignant, and waste inches of column space on the National Union of Teachers' present campaign against racism and sexism in children's books: illustrations must show at least one coloured child, and girls should not be seen in such womanly occupations as helping mother with the housework, the union urges. One could write pages of sarcasm about this, suggesting that Winnie the Pooh be recast as a Golliwog, demanding that Wendy be acted by a boy, Bulldog Drummond be sent to Casablanca etc. But the important thing to bear in mind is that the NUT is just making noises – impertinent and bossy noises, perhaps, but for all the effect they will ever have it might as well be blowing bubbles.

Similarly, I read in the *Daily Telegraph* that my own union, the National Union of Journalists, is agitating to abolish the Press Council and replace it with a statutory body with powers to enforce its own drivelling code of Left-Wing Conduct. One could easily become alarmed by this, even panic-stricken to the extent of deciding to go in oneself and organise the Moderates, if one had not taken that essential step backwards. Of course they are just blowing bubbles, like so many other people in this country. To take them seriously would mean joining their little game and blowing bubbles oneself. Do those bossy, under-occupied twerps seriously imagine that anything they may decide will make the slightest difference to whatever I think, say or write? No doubt they would control the entire press and reproduce it in their own wet and unsavoury image if they could, but they can't. The union is there to sue employers on our behalf when we are sacked and to lend dignified substance to any spontaneous moods of frustration, over-tiredness or general hooliganism which may visit two or more journalists on one newspaper at any given time. Everything else is soap, water and halitosis.

In the context of the class war, where we began this treatise, it is not possible to claim that all manifestations of workers' power are equally benevolent. In the course of any 12 months we too are liable to be inconvenienced by a train strike or two, a postal strike, an interruption in supplies of petrol or heating oil. Practically nobody is unaffected by a power strike. Some of us may be mildly distressed by the mountains of garbage. All I beg is that we do not lose our sense of proportion. The important thing to remember is that however much we may be inconvenienced, the working class suffers far more. Imagine the plight of the single pregnant old-age pensioner with three babies under 18 months unvisited by social workers and stuck on the top of a tower block during a lift strike, aggravated by a firemens' strike as the crackling flames rise higher and higher . . .

It is by such reflections as these that we may learn to bear our own smaller afflictions. Those of us with a modicum of civic responsibility may even learn to welcome them with a smile and sincerely pray that they continue, at any rate until the election. The time has not yet come for us to take our pick handles, whistles and tin helmets to the barricades and start bashing the 'workers'.

17.3.79

*   *   *

Social Security

Ladies I meet in London sometimes say what a convenient thing it must be for me to have as many opportunities for airing my social conscience and simply Doing Good. Sometimes I detect a note of rebuke in these approaches. There are so many evils in our socity, are there not, so many injustices, so many things which need putting right? Like the case of George Davis, now languishing in prison for one armed robbery he plainly did not commit.

The case of Albert Thorogood, sent down by Southend magistrates for refusing to work, strikes me as entirely different. Albert's only crime is that in twenty-five years he has worked for thirty-three weeks, drawing £12,000 in social security benefits during that time.

A little arithmetic will show that in the 1,257 weeks he has not been working, he has averaged £9.47p a week, scarcely a princely income, and a great deal less than it would have cost to keep him in prison. Social security rates may be too high at the present time – I do not know – but they certainly haven't been throughout the twenty-five years of Albert's retirement. In appealing to the Queen to grant this blameless man a free pardon and state pension to save him the trouble and indignity of collecting it every week, I do not expect her to follow my economic arguments to the effect that after twenty-five years on the dole Albert should be hailed as a hero of British Labour and presented with a gold watch, although I know she tries to follow everything I write. Instead, I would simply appeal to her sense of British fairness, whether it is right that those of her subjects, who are of a philosophical or contemplative turn of mind should be persecuted in this way.

The economic case for arguing that they also serve who only sit back and draw their social security entitlements is much more complicated, and so is the case for suggesting that Albert Thorogood should be held up as an example which large sections of the working class could usefully follow. At this point, in fact, I would advise all housewives and intelligent women of both sexes to switch off and turn to the crosswords.

Addressing a lunch to celebrate the bicentenary of Smith's *Inquiry into the Nature and Causes of the Wealth of Nations* at the Institute of Economic Affairs last week, I mentioned a few of the political obstacles in the path of any liberal economic system, not least of which are the two great forces which have emerged within the democratic process, the forces of stupidity and idleness. I did not mention the third great force, of envy, since this was a friendly, non-political occasion.

Until recently, liberal economists had to assume that at any rate a majority of human beings were rational and inspired by intelligent, material self-interest. The trouble was always that while this assumption may once have been true, any application of free market principles was liable to produce areas of such depraved and unredeemed squalor as were repugnant to the peace of mind or humane consciences of the well-to-do. Liberal welfarism may have blunted the self-help potential of the working class to some extent, but the arrival of one-man-one-vote, socialist welfarism and the doctrine of redistribution has plainly directed it into other' channels altogether.

If I am right, then it might seem that both Adam Smith and Samuel Smiles are up the creek without a paddle. It is at this point that we turn to the benign form of Mr Albert Thorogood, forty-six, his loyal wife, Kathleen, fifty-five, and her son Jesse, eighteen, all of whom appear to live happily on the dole and only ask that they should continue to be allowed to do so.

I made a reasonably close study of the *Inquiry* for the purpose of my address, and while it may seem impertinent to speak on behalf of someone unable to do so for himself, I feel it is a reasonable guess on my part that if Adam Smith were alive today he would agree with me that, in a technological age, vast sections of the working class have become an economic anachronism. By this, we would not mean that they should be sterilised, murdered, or deported, merely that they should not be encouraged to 'work' if they do not wish to do so.

The average industrial wage is now apparently £70 per week. A new machine may easily enable one man to do the work of five. One does not need to be a very clever mathematician to see that he, his firm and the nation as a whole will be better off if one of the other four moves to a new machine while three retire on £25 a week national assistance than if all five hang around the machine reading comics and cracking dirty jokes on £70 a week each. The problem is to convince enough of those earning £70 a week that redundancy can be Fun, even on £25 a week.

At this stage in the argument, I have always tended to fall back on pleas for the free availability of some cheap, harmless, euphoriant, appetite-reducing drug, possibly a derivative of betel, or cannabis, or *qat*, which would sort out those who prefer to work and grow rich from those who are happy to cultivate their own gardens, whether interior or out of doors.

But Mr Albert Thorogood has shown that this unacceptably radical solution is not necessary. Instead of being locked up in some airless dungeon, he should be feted throughout the land, taken to every working men's club in Britain and bought pint after pint of beer, have a statue put up to him outside the Workers' Educational Association headquarters in Upper Berkeley Street.

I think Mr Thorogood may well be right: many working men on £70 a week do not have a more enjoyable life than he does. Recently, much against my better judgment, I had to buy a new gramophone. The old one had stopped working after twenty years – that is to say, it continued to go round and round, but it no longer made any noise. I was shown machines costing up to £500 and £600, their controls winking and flashing like the cabin of a Concorde airliner, their reproductive systems characterised by a fidelity which puts Queen Penelope herself to shame. This, I was told, is what the working classes spend their money on when times are good.

Are they all mad, or have they just got peculiarly sensitive ears? These same people won't have a bottle of decent wine in their houses from one year's end to another; they allow their wives to cook filthy meals every day, whether from laziness, ineptitude or the fashionable sexist conceit of our times. When I did a nationwide survey of working wives for a down-market women's magazine twelve years ago, I was told time and again that they were working so that they could buy expensive frozen food instead of the fresh stuff. Oh no, the working man's life is horrible, horrible.

6.3.76

*   *   *

Two Nations

Liverpool

Living as one does, or tends to do, in rather a large country mansion surrounded by its own meadows, lakes and wooded pleasure grounds, I sometimes find that the normal satisfaction a man might be expected to feel in the elegance and superiority of his own appointments is marred by a certain nervousness. Wherever the class war is being fought, it has not yet reached the Taunton area, but even in West Somerset we hear – or imagine we hear – the rumble of distant guns. My neighbours take refuge in bizarre, violent and sometimes unpleasant political attitudes, most of which seem to involve the killing or imprisonment of large numbers of their fellow-citizens. Even the mildest of them demand the instant appointment of Enoch Powell to a position somewhere between that of wartime Prime Minister of England and Chancellor of the German Reich in the same period.

In Liverpool, for instance, there is a substantial body of opinion which

45

appears to regard him as a Catholic left-wing rebel from the Labour Party (but not so left-wing as to be unrespectable) whose chief concern is to ensure that the department of Liverpool Corporation responsible for mending windows and unblocking lavatories in council estates does its work promptly.

How on earth, it might be asked, do I know what people are thinking in Liverpool? It is a fair question. Nobody even told me what a beautiful city it was – and still is, despite some of the vilest modern buildings in Europe – and in thirty-six years I had never so much as visited it before this week. It just seemed a good place to start if I was going to involve myself more thoroughly in the class struggle to which we should all be dedicating ourselves.

What had alarmed me in my view of the class war was that all the gunfire seemed to be coming from the other camp. Whether out of wetness or, as I prefer to believe, natural sanctity, the middle classes were taking all the punishment, not only in taxes but also in the war of words and ideas. The first task in my lonely but undeniably admirable campaign was to seek out and confront this class animosity at its root. It is for this reason that I have spent my time since returning from France trailing round the slums of Manchester, the twilight areas of Birkenhead and docks of Liverpool with a merry crew of assistants and researchers. My role has been to taunt the unemployed in pubs, lecture slum-dwellers in their pitiful homes, insult dockers at their place of work and generally make myself useful in an understanding of this delicate problem.

My efforts have been surprisingly unsuccessful, although there was an excellent moment in a pub. An unemployed electrician whom I had been taunting with the reminder of how much richer I was leaned forward and said: 'What are your qualifications? I know exactly what your qualifications are. You bent over in the showers to pick up some soap at Eton and Harrow, like all the rest of them.'

But my most surprising discovery so far has been how little class animosity exists where one might expect to find it most. Certainly, it is not that people up here are especially polite. They are not at all polite in the conventional sense, and far franker than their equivalents in my part of the country. But they have an indomitable goodwill, a friendliness, a refusal to believe that anyone can dissent from their own conclusions and attitudes which I found almost impossible to overcome.

Among the dockers, it is true, this absence of class animosity may have been a temporary phenomenon. Insult and goad them as I would, I could only draw the tolerant, contented purr of cats which have suddenly found their cream ration doubled. But among the unemployed and poor the lack of class animosity was not the result, as might be supposed, of the sort of political apathy which is well known to afflict starving Africans and Indians. On the contrary, many of them were vocal and militant, but all their militancy was directed to securing better service from the Liverpool Corporation and more benefits from the Department of Social Security. Such animosity as existed – and was very strong indeed in places – was all directed against faceless bureaucrats in these two departments, who are regarded at the same time as the universal providers and class enemies of the entire human race outside.

It was only then that I saw the extent of the gulf which divides the English. No doubt people are friendlier in the North and conditions are also worse. For most of the unemployed there is not the slightest prospect of employment even if they wanted it very much indeed, which some of them do. But those who are employed have exactly the same attitude, that if a window is broken they will wait three months for the Corporation to come and mend it. In the course of time they will pester the Corporation offices with telephone calls and personal appearances, they will take days off work to organise a petition and even a demonstration, they will expend twice the money and twenty times the energy needed to mend the window themselves, but they would sooner live with a broken window for the rest of their lives than mend it themselves. If anybody doubts the truth of this, I can take him on a tour of estates in Manchester, Liverpool and Birkenhead which will prove the point.

Nearly everybody I have met up here has been extraordinarily nice, but the two most dynamic people I have met were both fully (and independently) engaged in teaching their fellow-citizens to claim whichever of the forty-one state benefits were available to them. They are not idle or reluctant to help themselves; the only difference is that self-help means forcing the Council or corporation to help you.

17.4.76

*   *   *

Wetness of the Middle Classes

Montmaur, Aude, France

Over all M. Mitterrand's deliberations in these first heady days of power – whether or not to introduce a wealth tax, by how much to improve the lot of the worst paid – there hangs a grisly spectre of modern Britain, now reduced by over-emphasis on social welfare and 'workers' rights' to a nation of unemployable, semi-imbecile football hooligans.

I could bore on for hours with anecdotes about the extraordinary superiority of the French working man over his English counterpart. Like many, if not most, English families of the middle class we have always preferred French motor cars, reckoning that even if British cars worked, which they are widely believed not to do, everything about the British car industry is so profoundly offensive to reason and good taste that one might as well give one's money straight to the Labour Party.

Eighteen years ago, as an elegant and rich young married couple, we decided to import our own solution to the servant problem, capturing a wild young Catalan peasant girl in this region. She was a small hairy thing, in appearance something between a monkey and a very large spider, called Lolita. We grew very fond of her, of course. As soon as we had brought her to our agreeable London home in Chester Row and let her out of the cardboard box with holes punched in the side she started working and never seemed to stop. After a few days it grew harder and harder to think of things for her to do, and after a week she exclaimed incredulously to my wife: *'Mais, Madame, vous avez peur de me commander'*. So it proved. After three years she was as lazy, as overpaid and as discontented as any English girl, with many of the airs and graces of a Norland nanny, and had to be sent home.

Which illustrates as well as anything else why Britain is in such a terrible mess. If I am right, the main reason why a large part of the British working class is unemployable is that an equally large part of the British professional and managerial class is unfit to employ anybody. We cringe and prostrate ourselves in front of our employees. We smirk and touch our forelocks and lose no opportunity to ingratiate ourselves, but we are simply not competent to impose the conditions which would make employment worthwhile.

Just supposing I am right in this and it is the wetness (or social guilt) of the middle classes rather than the inherent laziness or bloody-mindedness of the lower classes which has led us into this *impasse*, we might care to subject next week's deliberations of the TUC conference in Blackpool to class analysis along these lines. Left to themselves, the lower classes have produced what they call 'an alternative economic strategy' of such overwhelming and self-evident fatuousness that one has to be a very wicked man or a very foolish one indeed even to pretend to take it seriously. Everything about the TUC programme is either blatantly dishonest or blatantly moronic, most being a mixture of both elements. Invest North Sea Oil revenues in industry and vastly increase welfare spending? What on earth do they think happens to North Sea revenues now? Every single element in the programme – from defence and foreign affairs to domestic fiscal policy – is a recipe for more or less instant disaster: hyper-inflation, economic collapse, mass unemployment, civil war and national subjection. Yet it is plainly the best these oafs can do.

Next week's conference, even more than the Notting Hill Carnival, may be seen as a festival of all that is most fatuous and infantile in contemporary Britain. Equally, it may be seen as a monument to the failure of Mrs Thatcher's government to reduce the unions – and with them the major forces of anarchy and despair – to their proper role in the nature of things. Mrs Thatcher's failure to recognise and channel the enormous tide of popular resentment against the unions which brought her to power in May 1979 will probably be judged the worst of all the failures of post-war British governments – certainly far worse than her failure to honour Mr Worsthorne,[1] for which she may incur the greater odium in her own lifetime.

There are those who argue that the unions are no longer the major problem, that she has effectively defeated them by allowing a proportion of their existing mischief to run its course. Certainly there are very few strikes, and if the effectiveness of industrial policy is measured by days lost in industrial disputes, she has done magnificently. I have even heard rumours of a Japanese-owned car factory in Wales where productivity is higher than in Japan, although I would like to see it before believing in it. Until I have seen it I will stick to my prejudice that although modern Britain can excel in a few things – banking, insurance, even medical and scientific research – it can survive only in those things requiring least assistance from the sour and spoiled section of the community we still call 'the workers'.

5.9.81

*   *   *

Horrors of Prosperity

Is it very wicked to rejoice in our country's present discomfiture? Even the most fanatical Tories or free marketeers can generally show a few crocodile tears to accompany the sincere indignation they feel at being excluded from influence and attention. The whole language of politics is geared to treating anything as good which is conducive to general prosperity, anything as bad which is detrimental to it. One often finds whole passages of political rhetoric – from both sides of the political fence, and from journalists as well as politicians – which assume that this pursuit of prosperity is the only and supreme Good. Preservation of the countryside, protection of old buildings, survival of the arts, defence of freedom? Prosperity must come first, enshrined in the Tabernacle of Average British Living Standards.

Am I alone in rejoicing every time a fat face appears on the television to tell us we must all reduce our living standards still further? My reason for this perverse emotion, why I cheer when the newscaster mournfully

1. Mr Peregrine Worsthorne, a journalist and political commentator, for whose public recognition Waugh campaigned.

announces that inflation is getting worse and groan when he brightly claims that oil in the Forties Field is more copious than formerly imagined, is not simple puritanism. It may come, in part, from malicious glee at the discomfiture of politicians, but far more it comes from a profound disillusionment with what is nowadays meant by prosperity. They do not mean, these politicians, that hard-working middle-class parents, like myself will once again be able to send our children to public school, drink good burgundy at luncheon and even employ a butler to pour it out for us. They mean that the working classes will have more of everything they like: fish fingers, over-cooked meats, transistor wirelesses to take out of doors with them, caravans and motor cruisers to fasten behind their cars and choke up the Somerset lanes in summer. Television advertisement for all these disgusting things will be longer and more lavish, television companies and newspapers will compete with each other in attracting the affluent proletarian market. Feeling stronger and more self-confident, the political wing of the Labour movement will renew its vindictive campaign against any remaining outpost of middle-class values with the certainty of success wherever battle is joined.

There are two components in any conviction that further enrichment of the uneducated working class and impoverishment of the educated middle class will bring about the end of civilisation, or at any rate of anything we recognise as civilisation. The first, obviously enough, is sorrow at the passing of a culture with which, by birth, upbringing and conscious choice, we identify ourselves. The second is revulsion from the proletarian culture which threatens to replace it.

Cynics will fall upon the first component as the explanation for everything. We are resentful at the attrition of privilege, they will say, and react in petulant spite with these impotent, ivory-tower political attitudes. As I say, this is only part of the truth. In fact I have observed very little attrition in whatever privilege may ever have attached itself to my person, just as I have observed very little decline in my own standards of living. Occasionally, it is true, my wife will announce some lunatic decision of the sort that we can no longer afford Marmite, but I generally manage to talk her out of it. No, I am honestly convinced that of the two components I have listed, it is revulsion from the noise, smells and spiritual devastation of the proletarian culture which is the stronger motive force.

Which makes it rather poignant, somehow, that the only bulwark we have in this country against the rising tide of world prosperity should be our wonderful British trade unions. Responsible commentators often judge it imprudent nowadays to place the blame for our economic plight where it obviously belongs, on the intransigence of the unions, but the surliest unionist can scarcely complain if I give unions the credit for their splendid work in maintaining our traditional decencies.

50

There can be no serious doubt, although it is fashionable to talk about the incompetence of management, that overmanning and other restrictive practices among the workforce are mainly responsible for the fact that there is no investment in British industry. There can be no serious doubt that this drying-up of investment explains why British industry has lost its competitive edge, and why there can be no increase in real wages, outside a handful of fringe racketeers like hospital laboratory technicians and television crews. There can be no doubt whatever that these over-manning agreements and other restrictive practices are imposed by the unions with all the enormous power put at their disposal by obliging governments and with all the obstinacy which comes naturally to people of limited intelligence who find themselves engaged in argument. Thank God, we must all say, for the trade unions.

23.10.76

*   *   *

Society's Fault

'It is the little people, the nobodies like me who are always in the wrong. They are always the same, these so-called society people. They have money and everything and they can do no wrong. They think people like me are rubbish.'

Thus Mr Philip Derek Jennings, 26, otherwise known as 'Bouncer', explaining to police why he had cold-bloodedly murdered two middle-class women and raped one of them – crimes for which he was sentenced to 30 years imprisonment with two others. All three of them came from Yorkshire, although they had travelled to Cheshire for the occasion and were apparently affronted by their victims' middle-class accents.

I suppose it would be judged tendentious, as well as provocative, to identify Mr Jennings as the authentic, clarion voice of the North East. I have written about the North East before on these pages, often at great length and in a very caring sort of way, but I cannot say that I have uncovered evidence of any widespread habit of murdering people for sociological or phonetic reasons. In that respect at least, Mr Jennings and his two partners, Steve 'Puss' Anderson, 24, and Paul 'Spiderman' Hebel, 31, were untypical of the North-Eastern working class from which they all sprang. Even the *Daily Mirror*, which usually tries to see the under-dog's point of view – pointing out that these three professional criminals were 'from the other end of the social spectrum, unemployed and short of cash' – seemed to feel they had gone too far and stepped out of line: 'The three monsters of murder mansion were caged for life yesterday', it reported, without any trace of regret, explaining that the 'depraved trio' had trapped and sexually tormented two helpless wives before ruthlessly executing them: 'The Guy Fawkes Day savages ... pleaded guilty at Chester Crown Court to their horrific crime.'

There can be no doubt about it, Bouncer, Puss and Spiderman had gone too far. Nobody was going to pay too much attention to their class grievances, under the circumstances. I seem to remember an occasion about 12 years ago when the wife of a former Director of the Mirror Group Mr (now Sir) Alex McKay suffered a similar fate after being kidnapped by two Pakistani brothers.

There are occasions in life when one catches a glimpse of the perverse, under-side of human nature in all its incomprehensible futility, when cosy ideas about social disadvantage somehow seem less relevant. Even the 'Evil Men' of *News of the World* headlines retreated, rather than advanced, when we learned that the murdered corpse of its deputy chairman's wife had almost certainly been fed to pigs on an Essex farm. Mrs Alex McKay, Mrs Ann Carryer and Mrs Christine Blood were all called upon to pay a price which few of us, mercifully, are called upon to pay, for the fact of being better off. One can take refuge, if one likes, in indignation that anyone should be required to pay the price, or we can honour them as token sacrifices on the altars of envy, 'underprivilege' and lower-class resentment, but that is to evade the real point. The main question is whether or not we should surrender before the undoubted fact of this resentment.

In actuarial terms, there is no case for a surrender since the proportion of rich people who are kidnapped or raped and murdered on grounds of envy or class resentments is infinitesimal even in Italy and so tiny as to be non-existent here. If we allowed our social attitudes to be decided by the fate of three of four rich women who have been unlucky over a period of 12 years in the country we might as well walk around in deep-sea diving suits against the dangers of another Flood. But in this context one must make the point that Mr Jennings's attitude is not so unusual as its bizarre expression might suggest. While Bouncer, Puss and Spiderman must certainly not be mistaken for typical members of the North-Eastern working class, still less for typical readers of the *Daily Mirror* or *News of the World*, still less again for typical members of the British public, their social attitudes are not so very dissimilar from those freely advertised in public life.

Perhaps I am alone in finding something poignant in the words which Mr Jennings used to introduce his remarks about 'the little people', already quoted. When he was chided by a policeman for his cruel and beastly behaviour to the two women, Mr Jennings said: 'Murder, what is murder? There are people who have murdered thousands. What about Amin? We are talking about only two women. It is the little people, the nobodies like me who are always in the wrong ...'

One needs to be a student of proletarian dialectic, I suppose, to appreciate the finer points of this argument. Never mind the casuistical question – what is murder? – or the specious claim that the murder of two women is somehow justified or made negligible by the fact of larger numbers murdered elsewhere by other people. Never mind the choice piece of proletarian erudition which names Amin as one of the great murderers of our time, excused from punishment on class grounds.

The chief characteristic of Bouncer's speech is surely its indignant self-righteousness. This is all the more remarkable because one might have thought he was on a particularly sticky wicket, having forced the two women to strip and dance naked in front of him before tying them up, raping one and murdering both in a peculiarly unpleasant fashion. In a properly conducted sociey, he seemed to think he would have a perfect right to behave in this way. His victims were the people at fault. 'They are all the same, these so-called society people. They have money and everything and they can do no wrong. They think people like me are rubbish.'

Of course, it is all society's fault that Bouncer, Puss and Spiderman found themselves in the dock. That goes without saying. But Bouncer goes further than many social reformers in the field, and further than most people are prepared to follow him. Perhaps because his case is such a hopeless one, perhaps because he seems to reduce social determinism to its ultimate absurdity, I feel a sneaking sympathy for him. Although I have never yet been tempted to bind, violate or murder anybody whose accent or social attitude affronted me. I find my television set comes in for a certain amount of battery and assault at Parkinson[1] time . . .

But I am not sure that militant apathy is the best response towards these 'little people'. The risk of being oppressed by their philosophy is much greater. Of the original depraved trio, the three monsters of murder mansion, one is now dead. Poor Puss was compassionately allowed to take matches into his cell and burned himself to death in the small hours of Saturday morning. Unlike Bouncer and Spiderman, he seemed to be suffering from an old-fashioned conscience. But I am not sure that it is an adequate response to say 'good riddance'. Puss should not be forgotten so easily as that. He merely broke ranks from the army of 'little people' who are everywhere, resenting our better fortune and hating us for it.

Personally, I doubt whether abolishing differences of wealth would make the slightest difference to their sour natures, but I feel we should all decide for ourselves whether or not the enjoyment of greater wealth is worth the attendant odium and risk. I think it is. No doubt the police

1. Parkinson: a Yorkshire television personality.

can look after Bouncer, Puss and Spiderman, but the rest of us have an interest in ensuring that no sooner has one of these 'little people' crept out of his philosophical hole in the ground than he is knocked straight back into it.

26.7.80

*   *   *

A Model Briton

Some years ago I decided that Britain was becoming rather an unhappy place and probably needed a hero. It was obviously a waste of time suggesting a clean-limbed public-school sort of person with finely chiselled nostrils who had distinguished himself by some conspicuous act of bravery.

A proper hero must belong to the people who idolise him, rather than appear as something admirable and freakish on a pedestal. Leadership need not feature among the hero's qualities and usually doesn't. What is more important is that people should identify with him and, through general adulation of the love-object, vicariously bolster their own self-esteem.

At any rate the person who caught my eye as a possible hero for the British people was called Mr Albert Thorogood. He was imprisoned by magistrates in Southend for refusing to work, and in the course of his inquisition it emerged that he had been drawing the dole with very few interruptions for over 25 years.

There were several reasons why he seemed to qualify as a Hero of British Labour. In the first place nobody – or practically nobody – in Britain likes working. He alone had the honesty and perseverance – the sheer bloody guts – to face up to this national characteristic and see it through. In the second place he really appreciated not having a job, and this seemed a splendid example to all workers in the technological age. Although, as I say, nobody in this country much enjoys working, they all expect to have a 'job', and it is this expectation which is ruining the country.

But my campaign failed. The forces of hypocrisy and make-believe were too strong. No statues were put up to this blameless man and his admirable family in the public squares. The Queen, to whom I addressed my petition on Mr Thorogood's behalf for a free pardon and state pension to save him the trouble and indignity of collecting it every week, turned a deaf ear. Mr Thorogood, who must now be 52, with his wife Kathleen, 61, and now a pensioner, and Jesse, 24, disappeared from view.

Now, a new Hero of British Labour has emerged. This time I do not even have to launch him but can jump on the bandwagon of the popular newspapers. 'PORTRAIT OF A CHAMPION', screamed the *Daily Mirror* across a two-page centre spread, subheading the excellent article by William Marshall: 'Fat, boozy, toothless . . . and £50,000 a year.'

'He is wearing a blue cotton shirt that hangs straight down over the ramparts of his belly and his trousers sag around his ankles. There is something brave and defiant and undefeated about this ruffled figure. He asks for a beer and fumbles for another cigarette.'

Those who watched Jocky Wilson winning the Embassy world professional darts championship on Saturday night's television will recognise the poetic accuracy of Mr Marshall's description. 'Jocky, who has no teeth to adorn his ever-smiling image, says "I lost my dentures not so long ago during a darts match. They fell out when I got too excited and smashed on the floor. I don't think I'll get another set. People like me the way I am. They didn't fit anyway."'

Before long, one realises that Jocky Wilson is the nicest person to emerge in public life for a very long time. 'I have been described as fat, boozy and toothless. That's pretty accurate. I don't mind because when people are slagging me off they're not slagging anybody else. I need seven or eight vodkas to keep my nerves in a proper state so that I can play at my best.'

As he correctly discerns, people like Jocky the way he is. The Darts Championship Fancy is obviously an agreeable, relaxed section of our society, unlike football fanciers, and includes many of the nicest people in Britain. Apparently many of the contenders for the title looked rather like him, although the English finalist, Mr John Lowe lacked what must only be described as Jocky's charisma - the unmistakable stamp of divine favour. But the cult of Jocky Wilson now extends beyond the Darts Championship Fancy. He has attained what Mr Albert Thorogood never quite managed, the status of a national hero.

He is 31, with three children, formerly penniless and unemployed, and not, by any standards, a pretty sight to look at. On top of that, his Scottish accent makes him virtually incomprehensible to most Englishmen, which may well be a further recommendation. The English lower classes have always been suspicious of anyone who seemed over-articulate. Verbal communication is more oppressive to them than the written word, because it requires an instant response.

But there are two main differences between him and our Lost Leader, Mr Albert Thorogood. In the first place, Jocky Wilson, unlike Albert, is supremely good at a particular skill. Never mind that it is a skill of derisory importance. There might be an elitist undertone in a man's ability to kick a football more accurately or run faster than anyone else, but there is none in his ability to throw three darts over a couple of yards. In the second place, Jocky is rich, earning £50,000 a year and being driven round by a chauffeur as a result of his useful knack.

55

It would be nice to think that he was admired chiefly for his skill. I am rather afraid that he is admired chiefly for his luck: 'Listen. How lucky can a guy get? Here I am making all this money doing something I love, chucking three darts into a board. I feel guilty because everything is so good.'

Jocky has everything needed to make him the new Model Briton. Above that, he is a good example to us all, showing us how to turn leisure into something pleasant and profitable. I am not suggesting that the Queen appoint him to the Order of Merit or make him a Knight of the Garter, although on this occasion I rather fear she might. It is enough that the nation should join in a single gasp of admiration for this mild and magnificent man.

23.1.81

PART TWO

THE GENERATION WAR

4

YOUTH

Shirley Williams's Achievement

Many middle-aged men nowadays must dream of revenging themselves on the young. It is not just that the young are so ignorant and rude. Their worst crime is to be so conceited. For two decades it has been fashionable to talk about the generation gap as if it sprang from some failure on their part. Weighed down by bourgeois and materialistic considerations, if not by simple snobbery, the middle-aged were unable to make the great imaginative leap necessary to communicate with the young.

Young people were by definition idealistic, uninterested in materialistic things, untouched by colour or class prejudice. Their attitude to sex was healthy and natural, uncoloured by hypocrisy or religious guilt. They were interested in employment, which gave them an opportunity to help other people – the old, or kiddies, or deprived folk generally – but they were definitely not interested in joining the wage-slave rat race, buying themselves a semi or equipping it with labour-saving devices. Wages were less important than fulfilment. If they drank at all, it was only in moderation. They preferred the subtler, more peaceful satisfaction of cannabis. Young people ruled the earth, and anybody over thirty must cringe before them.

As for the kids, they were if anything even better. They were never happier than when redecorating the home of some senior citizen, voluntarily, in their spare time. Of course they were too intelligent to be impressed by older people and, being naturally classless, they were sometimes slightly impatient of snobbery when they met it. But, by and large, kids were wonderful.

Then Shirley Williams arrived on the scene – or, to be more exact, the first Harold Wilson government arrived, with a huge apparatus of educational theory. The primary purpose of state education was no longer to inculcate the rudiments of reading, writing and arithmetic in those whose natures made them unreceptive to anything more advanced. Still less was it to introduce a finer taste of the discipline necessary for any sort of social existence. The purpose of education was not even to prepare children for a classless society where nobody could look down their noses at anybody else – it was to create such a society. At whatever cost to the conventional values of education, the joys of engineering came first. Every valley must be exalted at whatever cost to the hills and mountains.

When Mrs Shirley Williams arrived as Secretary of State at the Department of Education and Science it was already perfectly plain that the great Comprehensive experiment had been a disaster. Like socialism, it simply did not work. Huge schools, with little or no supervision of the teachers, let alone the pupils, were open invitations to truancy and violence. In the four years since the Labour government was defeated there has been plenty of time to take stock of the havoc which was wrought on an entire generation by this silly woman's opinions. For at least seven years I have been pointing out that a substantial proportion of young Britons – I would put it at about a third overall, perhaps a quarter in the south and a half in the north – are completely unemployable. They not only lack the discipline necessary to acquire the most rudimentary skills, they also lack the necessary will to please. They are a lost generation without even the resources to amuse themselves.

My own observations, which must coincide with the experience of anyone prepared to take a look around, have generally been treated as a quirky, slightly perverse obsession of my own. Kids were still the kindly, idealistic people of *Blue Peter* and similar propaganda films. Now at last the truth is beginning to emerge, that the hopeless generation of louts and bores which Mrs Williams has produced is not only completely useless to anyone else but also harmful to itself and deeply unhappy.

A brilliant series which ran all last week in the *Daily Mirror* was called 'Bloody Kids! who do they think they are?' Put together by Keith Waterhouse, it echoes every sane person's awareness of what has happened and is continuing to happen to a substantial minority of Britain's youth. It is also, I fancy, to be read as a cry of pain from someone who is certainly the best and possibly the wisest commentator in the business. If the rest of my piece is taken up, for the most part, with quotations from his work, I hope he will interpret it as an act of homage rather than as one of simple plagiarism. I cannot, alas, reproduce the horrifying photographs which accompanied the text.

This is Heather Smith, 17, unemployed, of Gateshead, Tyne and Wear: 'I like being a skin because I like fighting ... Sometimes they come looking for us, sometimes we go looking for them. We always beat them. There are about fifty of us in the SHAM (Skinheads Are Magic) Army and no one can beat us ... I drink snakebites (lager and cider). They make me drunk quicker. I like getting drunk ... I never had a job ... I was supposed to go for an interview last year but didn't turn up. It doesn't worry me.'

Stacey Ottwell, 15, a schoolgirl of Derby, is more moderate in her approach to violence: 'Pointless violence, no. In a good cause, yes – like a demo for more jobs.'

No doubt Stacey is teacher's pet. Nigel Connelly, 19, unemployed, of Newcastle may have been less pliable: 'It's just another game, isn't it? You can't let anyone push you around now, can you? ... I've started fights a canny few times when I'm, drunk ... Mostly I have been provoked, but a couple of times it has been completely unprovoked. It doesn't give me a conscience. I'll do it again, probably.'

Most of them drink – 'I usually get into fights when I'm pissed up' (David Webster, 17, skinhead, Plymouth) – but there is a certain debate between drinkers and those who get their satisfaction elsewhere.

Darren Kemp, 16, Woolwich: 'I get £32.32 a week and spend £10 of it on drink. Cider – I just like it. Beer makes me sick. Got the money, can't spend it on much else.' Andy Butlin, 18, unemployed, Glasgow: 'I spend £16 a week on glue, it's £3 for a pint and I buy a pint and a half every other day. I sniff every day ... I'm in the house all day – my dad drinks and he just annoys me.'

On sex, there was a healthy difference of opinion between members of the idealistic generation. Thus Ray Hillyard, an unemployed punk of Plymouth, says: 'Load of crap – not interested.' Wayne Munden, 17, also unemployed of Worcester, says: 'I wouldn't get married. Girls are there to be used when you want them.'

Danny Newbury, 18, a fruitpacker of Bolney, Sussex, is more idealistic: 'I believe in sex. I was just over 14 when I started. You learn about it in school and that influences you a lot. They show you all these books and pictures and you think I'll try that. But I prefer spending my time on my bike.'

Chivalry survives among the men – 'I've a lot of respect for them, especially if they don't drop their knickers for two or three weeks' (Jeff Strange, 19, unemployed, Bedwas, South Wales). Paul Higgs, 19, unemployed, of Mid-Glamorgan, carries his chivalry to extremes: 'I've never had sex with a girl friend, it would be too embarrassing like just to ask her.'

Above all, there is the perennial problem that teenagers are misunderstood. Thus Fiona Peace, 19, unemployed, of Leeds: 'Teenagers are misunderstood. Many people think we are all dreadfully promiscuous. I'm not easy to sleep with ... I keep a list of boys I have slept with. I don't star-rate them – I don't think that's fair. My list has the boy's name, then how many times we have done it – not the exact number, but whether it was once or twice, numerous times or infinite.'

Perhaps the real difference is that we listen to their callow and idiotic opinions. That, too, I feel can probably be blamed on Shirley.

7.5.83

*   *   *

Marrying a Younger Woman

'The pressure to conform – to do certain things that you don't find pleasant – certain things that you find downright insulting to your own personal integrity – is really too much, too much.'

Thus spoke Mrs Margaret Trudeau to a *Daily Mail* reporter called Roderick Gilchrist in New York, explaining why she had abandoned her role as First Lady in Canada to come to New York with a Rolling Stone.

'I'm just protesting in a very nice, quiet, hopefully – um, nice way. For the time being I'm devoting myself to my photography. And to my own pursuit of my own self. I would like to do something instead of a passive role of smiling and supporting. I would like to take a more dynamic role of being myself – whatever that is. And that's not in terms of public image, that's in terms of private image. It's in terms of art.'

Many people seem to be troubled by the stirrings of an artistic impulse nowadays. I don't suppose there has been a moment in the world's history when more people felt themselves to be artists, or when less art was produced. Not that I've got anything against artists, of course. As Enoch sometimes says about the blacks, it is a question of numbers. But while the world waits on tenterhooks to discover whether it is Mick Jagger or his matchstick-thin, spiky-haired guitarist Ron Woods who is playing Byron to Pierre Trudeau's Lady Caroline Lamb, I can't help wondering why I am not more stirred by Trudeau's predicament. Like most young men of my generation, I was anguished by the spectacle of the young Melbourne when the absurd, club-footed, nail-biting figure of Lord Byron appeared on the scene, as described by David Cecil:

'There limped into the room a self-conscious youth, with a handsome, sulky head, fidgety movement, showy, ill-fitting clothes, and a manner compulsively lacking in the ease and naturalness usual in a man of his rank ... But is was not Byron she cared for: it was his reputation, and still more the idea of herself in love with him. Beautiful, brilliant, seared with the flames of exotic passion, and the most lionised man in England, he was everything she had all her life been seeking. Here at last was a hero worthy of such a heroine.'

Nobody can doubt that Mick Jagger (or possibly his wafer-thin guitarist Ron Spikes) is today's exact equivalent of Lord Byron. It is only when one begins to identify the other two characters in the drama – Mrs Trudeau with Lady Caroline Lamb and Pierre Trudeau with her husband, William – that there are difficulties. Possibly these may explain the general lack of sympathy for Trudeau – I would hate to think it was a hardening of the heart with age which makes me chuckle every time I think of his anguished French-Canadian face.

Where the women are concerned, we must remember that although their behaviour has much in common, the fiendish Lady Caroline was not only notorious for her nastiness in London's easy-going society at the beginning of the last century; her extreme egotism was considered pretty well unique. She was one of the earliest products of a permissive upbringing recorded in British social history – victim of a foolish, self-indulgent mother, Lady Bessborough, and the Devonshire House set, with whom she spent much of her childhood. From her earliest appearance in polite society, she was recognised as a freak. Known as 'the little beast' by her in-laws, her devouring egotism drove her to an extravagance by which she might draw attention to herself – the wearing of trousers, fits of ungovernable rage in which she would scream and tear her clothes and which soon came to be recognised as symptoms of lunacy.

Like Lady Caroline, Mrs Trudeau has suffered from insanity, although her visits to a lunatic asylum are nowadays described as a period of psychiatric hospital care to relieve a condition of severe emotional stress. Like Lady Caroline, she comes from a privileged, politically powerful background, being the daughter of a former Cabinet minister. Like Lady Caroline's (real or illusory) affair with the poet Byron, Mrs Trudeau's (real or illusory) entanglement with the Rolling Stones has been conducted in the brightest glare of public attention, to the maximum possible humiliation of her husband.

But the enormous, unbridgeable gap between them is that whereas Lady Caroline was universally seen as a freak and a monster, Mrs Trudeau is seen as a typical, healthy child of her generation. If she has been inside a psychiatric hospital, so have a large proportion of women in her class and age-group. Her egotistical ravings, with which I opened this article, are the familiar small-talk of innumerable middle-class London dinner parties.

Now let us compare Pierre Trudeau to the young Melbourne, or William Lamb, as he then was. The similarities are obvious. Both became prime ministers at one time or another, both were liberals and both saw their wives go mad and run away with at least one notorious philanderer within six years of their wedding. There the similarity ends. Unlike Melbourne, a simple Whig, Trudeau was a 'new wave' liberal who first drew attention to himself as Minister of Justice with proposals for abortion and homosexual law reform. Unlike Melbourne, Trudeau was already prime minister and a fully mature man of fifty-one before he married, however well preserved his ripe old carcase may have been. At the time, you may remember, we all grew misty-eyed about our own fifty-four-year-old bachelor prime minister, Teddy Heath, and wondered if at last he would pull his finger out, if that is the right expression.

Whereas Melbourne, at twenty-seven, was only six years older than his fiendish bride, Trudeau could give his 'flower child' twenty-six years. Now of course there may be something very beautiful and romantic in the idea of this idealistic young woman with her flat tummy, firm, high breasts and wholesome expression, giving herself to a wrinkled, walnut-coloured prime minister of fifty-one. We must be careful to avoid any temptation to sexual jealousy, must we not? So many men of that age have wives who leave their dentures by the side of the bed and read Doris Lessing into the small hours.

Nevertheless, he chose to marry into a young generation which, despite its present flat tummies, high, firm breasts and wholesome expressions, has few inner resources and whose particular ethos puts no premium on duty, loyalty or sacrifice at the expense of self-fulfilment. Any of us could have told him that six years and three babies later his wife would be dissatisfied, more self-obsessed than ever and most probably mad. It was just a question of the price he was prepared to pay for cutting a little dash – one more reminder of the glorious fact that sex makes fools of us all.

19.3.77

*   *   *

Unwanted, Angry Policemen

The expression 'unwanted, angry kids from Handsworth' used by Mrs Shirley Williams to describe the products of her own education system surely deserves a place in the vocabulary of contemporary social studies. She was comparing them, because they were mostly black, with the UAKS of South Africa, although the UAKS of Handsworth were protesting chiefly against police attempts to enforce our unenforceable drug laws. The UAKs of Broadwater Farm, Tottenham, by contrast, although they were also, for the most part, black, were protesting about the death of a respected local figure who had apparently died of terror during a police raid on her home.

But the phenomenon is by no means confined to Britain or to blacks or to the products of the Labour government's disastrous comprehensive experiment. In America, original home of youth worship, hatred of teenagers is breaking out in a rash of local curfews, from the suburbs of Washington to Newport Beach, California, by which all teenagers have to be off the streets and shut up at home by ten o'clock at night. This is not so much to protect their morals – universally agreed to be non-existent – as to protect the rest of America from the sight of them. As Mr Mike Hart – a city councillor at Newport Beach – puts it: 'Kids who don't have money should go home. What business do they have standing out there at night?'

It would seem that 40 years of Doctor Spock have finally succeeded in producing a generation which is not only so ignorant and undisciplined as to be unemployable, but also so unpleasant and aggressive as to be unliveable with. The problem is now to contain the amount of nuisance which they can create for the rest of us. Even a nationwide teenage curfew – I would suggest eight o'clock as a more suitable hour for them to be home – would have only limited effectiveness, since by general agreement it is the 20-25 age group which is the worst of the lot. And the attitude of parents, when shut up with their unwanted, angry off-spring from eight o'clock onwards, might prove electorally significant.

One solution much canvassed, especially among retired majors in Somerset, is to reintroduce National Service. This would solve at a stroke not only the problem of indiscipline but also those of employment and housing, since they would be taken away from the parents to whom they cause so much irritation and anguish. The reintroduction of National Service is an obvious vote-winner and the only serious objection to it is the one put forward by Alexander Chancellor: do we really want to train this generation of UAKs in the use of weapons?

Sir Kenneth Newman suggests gassing them and shooting them with plastic bullets which seems, on the face of it, quite sensible. I have often thought that metal-tipped stockwhips might be useful in riot control, although the French experience suggests that nothing is so effective as the baton charge with pick handles. The problem about arming the police is that they, too, belong to the generation of unwanted, angry kids for the most part, and although there might be some philosophical comfort for the middle-aged in the spectacle of the UAKs divided into two camps, bashing the hell out of each other with knives, shotguns and HK sub-machine guns firing 650 rounds a minute (possible from police helicopters), it offends the most elementary ideas of fair play that one side in the squabble should be given such an advantage.

Recent events have convinced me that the police, in their officially approved new methods of policing the ghetto areas, as well as in the cowboy attitudes of the younger metropolitan constabulary, are as responsible as the black UAKs for the state of war between them which is liable to break out in serious rioting at the drop of a hat. This is a hard thing to say of a force which is dedicated to preserving the peace, which comprises the thin blue line between our comfortable, secure existence and the horrors of anarchy, and which is made up for the most part of sincere and humane men doing an unpleasant job. But unless one is prepared to examine what is happening among the new intake of 25-year-old policemen roaring around the big cities four-strong in their 100-mph cars with sirens screeching, one is liable to misjudge the mood of the nation very seriously indeed, as I believe Mrs Thatcher has done.

It was only after police had bagged Mrs Cherry Groce, the Brixton housewife, that we learned that the armed raid on her home was one of 50 carried out by the police in the Lambeth district this year. Many of these were in search of drugs, like the one on Mrs Paula Belsham in August, graphically described in the *Observer*. It is only when they manage to shoot a baby or a housewife or terrify a fat woman to death that we learn of these violent police swoops, but they are happening the whole time. They undoubtedly strike terror, but do they do anything to discourage crime?

I was not present at Blackpool to judge the exact quality of the applause which greeted Mrs Thatcher's promise of a blank cheque to the police. It will mean they buy more helicopters – I gather the Metropolitan Police already have three Bell 222s costing over £600,000 each and capable of crossing London in a quarter of an hour at 170 mph – and more 100-mph cars with which they will be able to scream through the streets looking tough and macho, jumping out four strong to bundle off some unfortunate drunk who has been reported over the wireless for insulting a community policeman. More and more UAK school-leavers will be hired at wages which climb to £18,000 after a few years, more and more private houses will be violently broken into by gangs of frightened, armed thugs claiming to represent the forces of law and order.

Soon, by my reckoning, there will be little to choose between these gangs of young policemen and the gangs of young blacks, except that the young blacks are more localised. Both will be feared and hated by everybody else and I feel that the Tories if they identify themselves with one particular gang of unwanted, angry kids will be making as big a mistake as Labour if it identifies itself, like Bernie Grant, with the other.

Helicopters and 100-mph cars do little or nothing to prevent crime or even to bring criminals to justice, if the clear-up rate for notifiable offences is anything to go by. Armed police do neither, and I have not yet heard of a single case where a policeman's life has been saved by carrying weapons. All these things can do is to teach us which gang of UAKs is on top. Perhaps we should be grateful to the West Indians for taking up so much of their aggression. Otherwise I feel they might turn it on the rest of us.

19.10.85

*　　*　　*

Father Christmas Day

Mr Tom Hunt, a scrap dealer in the east end of London, came briefly to prominence last week when his 15-year-old son, Graham, was sentenced to ten years for robbery and manslaughter of a little old lady of 85. Although she was only four and a half feet tall, and weighed only six stone, he and two other boys left her tied in a cupboard after they had beaten her up and robbed her of her life's savings of £600, so that when she was found nearly a week later she was dead. The boys cheerfully owned up to various other assaults and robberies, all of elderly people. The fathers of all these were interviewed in the press and asked if they were not shocked at the severity of the sentences. Two of them said they were deeply shocked, but Mr Tom Hunt was reported as saying:

'I spoiled that boy. I gave him everything he wanted. It's my fault. If he wanted a new bike he had one. If he wanted money, I gave it to him. I wasn't surprised at the sentence. I thought he'd get 14 years.'

One of the great consolations of life in socialist eastern Europe at this time of year must be that under socialism there is never, *never*, anything to buy in the shops. Once you have bought a few extra tins of mackerel and a couple of those interminable wooden dolls which fit inside each other you have done your Christmas shopping. Half of the women of England go mad at this time of year from the pressures of it all, and I wonder whether this absence of anything to buy in the shops under socialism may not explain why so many otherwise sane middle-class women are attracted to the Workers' Revolutionary Party, Socialist Workers' Party, Communist Party and all the rest of that gloomy rubbish.

The rest of us, poised for our annual orgy of Christmas shopping, might ponder the words of Mr Tom Hunt before we lash out on ever more expensive presents for children. My wife and I have 25 children between us who seem to expect Christmas presents – nephews, nieces, and godchildren included – and there must inevitably come a moment of doubt, when we wonder if we are doing the right thing. Quite apart from the terrible suffering of elderly victims – they broke three of Mrs Rosa Lewis's ribs before gagging her and leaving her tied up in the cupboard to die – there is the fact that one does not particularly want any of one's children, nephews, nieces or godchildren to spend ten or 12 years of their young lives in prison.

'I know what they did was serious, but you don't associate such long sentences with kids of 15,' said the father of Simon Marius, another of the three. Nor, of course, do you normally associate kids of 14 (as they were then) with a sustained campaign of torturing and robbing old people in their homes. Life is full of surprises. The third father, Mr Alf Vinyard, attributed his son Georgie's behaviour to the leniency of juvenile court magistrates on the lad's earlier appearance before them. Even if he is right – and my own experience of life, such as it is, does not convince me that heavier penalties necessarily act as greater deterrents to crime, although I agree it stands to reason that they should – few of us are in a position to do anything about it unless we happen to be juvenile court magistrates. Whereas all – or nearly all – of us are faced with the problem of buying enormous numbers of hideously expensive children's presents which will join a mountain of similar presents on Christmas Day. If Mr Hunt is right, the nation's elderly and infirm had better look sharpish and keep their doors locked in the weeks after Christmas. But the normal dilemma remains: should we, as responsible adults, acquiesce in this general corruption of the young?

The idea of Christmas as a specifically Kiddies' Festival seems to be of very recent origin. The present-giving ingredient in Christmas festivities derives from the ancient Roman feast of Saturnalia, held on 17 December and later extended for a full week when no work was done, presents were exchanged, many forms of moral laxity were permitted and slaves were allowed to be impertinent to their masters. But there was nothing much for children on these genial occasions. I suspect that children crept into the Christmas idea – perhaps it would be more accurate nowadays to talk of the Father Christmas Idea, and Father Christmas Day – with the decline of religious belief: religion was seen as a fairy story for kiddies, evoking happy, sentimental memories of one's own childhood when one believed in it all and honestly thought Father Christmas came down the chimney. So now Christmas has become quite simply an orgy of presents and sweets for kiddies, when grown-ups mince around waiting on them and trying to look sweet too.

None of which would matter much if it only happened for one day, but having stretched itself from the last week of November until the end of the weekend after New Year's Day, our new form of Saturnalia threatens to spread through all the year. Perhaps the nastiest expression of the Christmas season, or Father Christmas season, is to be found in the new $11\frac{1}{2}$p stamp, which seems to have been circulating for about three weeks already. This, we are told, is the design of Samantha Brown, aged five; it shows a grinning Father Christmas waving his arms charismatically. Miss Brown won the *Blue Peter* competition held last January, and it obviously expresses everything that Christmas means to her.

I do not want to spoil Samantha's moment of glory. I am sure it is much better than anything I could have done at her age. But the fact remains that it is a five-year-old's painting and five-year-olds' paintings are things to be admired extravagantly and then put in a drawer. Quite apart from the shameful ugliness of this particular design, there is something profoundly sick about a country which uses them to advertise its own warmheartedness.

And in a sinister way – or so it seems to me – Samantha Brown's disgusting little scrawl threatens to invade our national identity. The Father Christmas Idea has already overtaken large areas of public life, whereby public administration is seen as a matter of handing out goodies with a happy smile while the rest of us – the kiddies – clap our little hands and think how sweet we are. Mrs Thatcher's government is judged by its failure to hand out big enough parcels with a happy enough smile on its face. Men and women go into politics for no other reason than the pleasure of handing out other people's money in this way.

There is little or nothing we can do about it, of course, in our own little circles of influence, but I would like to leave one thought in the minds of *Spectactor* readers. Father Christmas has absolutely nothing to do with the nativity of Our Lord. He is a filthy foreign importation. The presents he gives are usually rubbish. Many, if not most, Father Christmases are male homosexualists in disguise. Sadly or not, there is a strong anti-homosexual drive among the nation's youth. Children have always enjoyed pulling Father Christmas's beard and humiliating him in other ways. If we could divert the nation's kiddies from the elderly and infirm for a moment and teach them to persecute any and every Father Christmas they see, we might eventually succeed in driving the brute from our shores. It may not be much, but it is a start.

12.12.81

*   *   *

Hatred of Children

The English are famous throughout the entire civilised world for their hatred of children. My own guess is that we hate children even more than we hate the old. Until I have had time to start a Gerontophile Information Exchange I will be unable to test this hunch, but I am prepared to bet that public reaction will be much less extreme.

If I am right, the violence of the public reaction against paedophiles should be seen as a cover-up – not, heaven knows, for any sexual attraction towards children on the part of the general public – but as a sign of the guilt they feel for disliking children so much. I have often observed how the English, who shut their parents away in retirement bungalows and old people's homes as soon as the opportunity presents itself, yet feel constrained to make little mooing noises of appreciation whenever an old age pensioner is wheeled onstage during a children's pantomime or other

67

public entertainment. So it is with children. In order to understand the present phenomenon I am afraid we will need to analyse it by social class.

Members of the upper and upper middle classes (we, gentle readers, the Beautiful People) have always got rid of our children by sending them to boarding schools. We have usually known that a small but significant proportion of the teaching staff of these establishments is paedophile. Such stirrings of guilt as we might have felt at this inhuman treatment were subdued by the reflection that the education was better and we were making enormous financial sacrifices to send our children off in this way. Those parents who were prepared to face up to the matter – I am amazed by the number of my contemporaries who assure me that homosexuality has now disappeared from the nation's preparatory and public schools – accept that there must be some consolation in the miserable life of those who choose to look after children.

Which may explain the fairly tolerant attitude towards these unfortunate people which has grown up in our bourgeois society. It does not extend to child rapists or violators or pre-pubertal girls, but if the boys end up buggered that is accepted as a small price to pay for the opportunity to develop their whole characters etc which separation from parents must bring.

The lower middle classes have never been able to send their children away, of course. Their method of showing dislike for their children is to refuse to talk to them, to dress them in hideous clothes called anoraks and romper suits, to turn them out of the house or dump them in front of the television set as soon as they come in; and, if they give the slightest trouble, to stuff their mouths with sweets until their teeth blacken and fall out to lie like rabbits' droppings all over the fitted carpet in the television lounge. If ever parents of the lower class feel the slightest guilt about this inhuman treatment of their children, they overcome it by giving them huge sums of pocket money to buy even more sweets until their bodies and legs disappear and they have to be taken to school in special aluminium wheelbarrows designed by Lord Snowdon and supplied by the Welfare.

But however much one may sneer, snarl or hoot at these people one must also admit that they can't send their children away and actually have to live with them. So one can see they might feel indignant at any suggestion that their children should also be buggered.

1.10.77

* * *

68

Potty Training on the NHS

Recently, I met a beautiful young lady at a party. She was elegantly dressed with gold bangles, tinkling around her slender wrists, richly coiffed and perfumed. When, in my gauche and middle-aged way, I asked her what she did, she replied (although her expression was coarser) that she helped children to defecate.

She is a child psychologist in a small unit attached to one of the London hospitals. They can only take twelve children at a time, and there is a four-month waiting list. Most of her time is spent sitting on a 'pretend' lavatory next to a child who sits on a real one. She makes straining noises and gives whatever other forms of encouragement seem appropriate. I do not know how much she is paid for this employment, but if one judged by the richness of her apparel it could scarcely have been less than £3,500 a year.

The reason for this epidemic of constipation among London children, as she told it to me, is a strange one. It appears that progressive mothers nowadays make a point of congratulating their children whenever they go to the lavatory. It is vital, they feel, that children should not be ashamed of their excretions, or think of them as something dirty. So whenever little Johnny goes to the lavatory, he is forbidden to flush it afterwards until Mummy (or Jessica, as she is probably called) has had a chance to inspect and praise whatever he has produced. In really progressive neighbourhoods, they even ask the neighbours in and have a general discussion about it. These children's shit shows threaten to eclipse the traditional Tupperware parties of Neasden and Mortimer Crescent, NW6.

All of which could only add to the happiness of the nation and, through spreading happiness, reduce the tremendous Health Service load of neurotic housewives requiring tranquillising drugs. Unfortunately, however, a complication has arisen. One of the less happy characteristics of children brought up by progressive methods in small families is that many of them become vilely unpleasant, consumed by a whining selfishness which may, indeed, be the best preparation for life in the welfare state. As soon as these odious children hear praise on every side for their nasty little turds, they decide that they must be worth keeping. Before long, they become dangerously constipated, and since laxative or aperient medicines have long been labelled unprogressive, their mothers have to send them to these psychological units where they can be helped towards a less negative attitude.

So here we have a new load on the National Health Service, and a new function for government. In the bad old days, of course, parents generally assumed responsibility for potty-training their infants, but if the state can't take over that sort of job nowadays, what on earth is the state for?

I can just imagine the scenes of jubilation at the Department of Health and Social Security when the news came through that potty-training had landed on its in-tray, despite flanking movements from the Department of the Environment (public hygiene and sewage section of the ministry for local government) and the Home Office which claimed, rather forlornly, that wilful constipation probably belongs to the general department of crime and punishment. Let us be thankful, at least, that this delicate business has been kept away from the Department of Education and Science. No doubt there are unpleasant, left-wing ways of doing these things but my greatest fear would be that no child entrusted to its care would ever be able to evacuate its bowels again.

I once wrote a novel about a clergyman with an anal fixation which tickled me at the time but I now know *it is dangerous ground, dangerous ground*. By reducing the whole vexed question of public expenditure to this one example of enlightened public administration, I risk the accusation that I, too, am infected by the dread disease. But one story this lovely young lady told me stays fixed in my mind. Taking one of her patients for a walk, she chanced upon a dog's mess in the middle of a zebra crossing. The child immediately threw a tantrum, mistakenly supposing that the turd was his own and had somehow escaped without his noticing it. Before she could stop him, the child had scooped up the dog's turd and was trying to stuff it through his own trousers.

When one discusses things like public expenditure cuts in the abstract, I think it important that we should occasionally descend to the particular. Are we really prepared to countenance the sort of society where children become so confused about their bowel function that they shed bitter tears of jealousy every time they see a dog's mess? Constipation, whatever the fashionable doctors say, can be very dangerous, resulting in massive haemorrhages and uncontrollable internal abscesses. Of course they can always give the little darlings some syrup of figs, but that, too, in its way, would be an admission of defeat.

31.7.76

*   *   *

In Praise of Punks

Unexpectedly, *Saturday Night Fever* has arrived in Taunton. Goodness knows what the Senior Citizens were supposed to make of the film which has taken America by storm, but I was warned to turn up at the beginning of the whole programme if I wanted a seat. Unfortunately, when the bogus mid-Atlantic accent of the Seychelles tourist 'B' movie gave way to the genuine Brooklyn accents of John Travolta I found myself unable to understand a word of what was happening. To judge from their anguished adjustments to various deaf aid systems my companions had the same difficulty.

What little I did understand struck me as almost entirely meretricious. Travolta and his upwardly-mobile girl friend (whose name I did not catch) looked far too cute to represent the frustrated juvenile working class of any country. The film was designed for middle-class voyeurs. They may be a little vicarious excitement to be derived from contemplating these working-class youths who, stuck with a boring, ghastly job as befits their intelligence, aptitude, ambition and readiness to exert themselves, manage to let off steam by dancing on Saturday nights. Perhaps a few middle-class fans can take a little of the working classes' pleasure from these activities to add to their enormous battery of existing pleasures, and without experiencing any of the discomfort or frustration which give rise to the original Saturday night fever. I do not know. But the chief satisfaction which a middle-class audience seeks from it is surely the same as clients may seek from a massage parlour – to be soothed. Cute little John Travolta is perfecly *happy*, is he not?, with his ridiculous job, unpleasant environment and ludicrous recreation. Let us lie back and admire the robust vitality and honesty of the working-class culture, untroubled by such moral confusions as can haunt the bourgeois mind. We may even feel the additional thrill of compassion, that great show business mainstay which supports diversions as far apart as the Thalidomide Bonanza movement and the Spanish bull-fighting industry.

I am the last person to sneer at those who seek comfort in massage parlours, but my objection to this sociological massage is that the relief it affords is illusory. Real-life Travoltas are *not* cute and they are *not* content with their lot. With the advance of technology, those of them who are still employed will be in a position to demand that the world readjust itself to their liking. Those who are unemployed will be left on a scrap-heap whose worst features will be determined by their own intellectual, moral, cultural and educational limitations.

Which is why it seems to me that while Travolta is a phony show-biz projection, the English punks may have had something genuine to say. For all I know they may still be saying it, but it is in the nature of human society that nobody can go on saying the same thing for long. In either case, it does not discredit what they said or how they said it. Both contain an enduring truth about the human condition which transcends any momentary self-awareness among the lower working class.

In fact I have never seen a real-life punk, even on television, and have never been a particularly close student of the phenomenon, largely through a class antipathy which punks would undoubtedly reciprocate in no uncertain terms. Although a few middle-class trendies, drop-outs and

71

other inadequates tried to latch on, it was noticeable how the genuine punks went out of their way to make themselves too disgusting for the dilettante, weekend or Travoltaist groupie to follow. They remained essentially and exclusively working-class although few, if any, of them worked. There were no thrills of compassion to be derived from watching them and very little reassurance, except of a rather disreputable kind. But a book, *In the Gutter*, describes their behaviour and attitudes very well. It is written by a handsome if elderly (by punk standards) and inescapably middle-class journalist called Val Hennessy.

She traces the punk idea to the satirical invention of *Private Eye*'s visionary show business correspondent, Mrs Maureen Cleavage. In 1964 – twelve years before anyone applied the word 'punk' to music – the *clairvoyante* Mrs Cleavage introduced the Turds: 'The Turds are something new. Irreverent, greedy, short and acned, there is a trendy look about them that sets a '60s pace, as up-to-date as next year's Courrèges Underwear ... The leader of the group, Spiggy Topes, explained: "Actually we don't have a leader. In our eyes, all Turds are equal". The Turds like everyone else in the world are classless and horrible ...'

This might form the prospectus of one of the better known Punk Groups today: Sex Pistols, Throbbing Gristle, Erect Nipples, Dirty Macs, Stinky Toys. The interesting thing is that the Turds in 1964, were largely modelled on the Beatles and reveal how punk elements were discernible even in the early stages of the great proletarian musical culture. But where the major theme in 1964 was proletarian triumphalism, it is now proletarian defiance.

'Life stinks, I'm not talking about Devon or the Isle of Wight, I'm talking about concrete jungle-land, council estates.'

'Our estates where we live are terrible. I tell yer, the Prime Minister came round our flats at Rotherhithe and all the old girls was out polishing their door-knockers and waving union jacks and making out they was happy ... I want to be able to say when I was young NO ONE told me what to do.'

The interesting thing about Sid Vicious, Johnny Rotten, Victor Vomit and the rest of them is that they would probably agree with my thesis that one reason – not the only reason but possibly the main one – why these council estates are so terrible is because such horrible people inhabit them. 'We're ugly,' 'We're horrible,' 'We're evil,' they cry, and their desolation is compounded when former proletarian heroes – the Beatles, the Rolling Stones – betray them:

'This is what it was like, right? If you wanted to see the Who, or Bowie, or Dylan you had to queue for days to get a ticket. You'd go to the Isle of Wight and there's mud everywhere and no bogs and people pissing all over your sleeping bag and everyone's starving hungry, and getting ripped off 50p for a hard-boiled egg ... Then, afterwards, the Stars zapp off in their Rolls-Royce with all their beautiful trendy pals while we have to hitch home. And it's *us* who've paid big money for the tickets and made them the rich, untouchable bastards they've become.'

'Can you see Princess Margaret shaking hands with Johnny Rotten?' asks one fan admiringly. 'Can you see ANYONE shaking hands with Johnny Rotten?'

At times in Mrs Hennessy's admirable book one sees touches of a genuine philosophical nihilism, as when the magazine *Sniffing Glue* urges its readers to stop reading it – 'no, I'm not mucking about, I'm being honest and it hurts'. At others, one sees nothing more than cretinous cynicism:

'Sex? We ain't against it but we don't know what all the fuss is about, you've done it all between the ages of twelve and twenty. What is it when you work it out, a mucky dribble ... ' At others, again, a touch of pathos shines through the brittle defiance: 'All punks are working-class and proud of it, except we're not *working* any more, seeing as how there's no jobs and the ones we're offered are a load of shit.'

When John Travolta dances his nimble feet tread the most elaborate measures. When the punk bands play, the fans pogo. This pogo is the punk dance. 'They leap up and down yo-yo like, sweat pouring down their faces, herded together and crushed against the stage.' No doubt they give off a very ancient and fish-like smell on these occasions. Perhaps the whole of Christian and liberal humanist philosophy was an elaborate curtain to give these Calibans self-respect and prevent them from looking in a mirror. Now the curtain has been removed, they might as well jump up and down.

29.4.78

*   *   *

Mothers and Daughters

'She was silent within my embrace and I stroked her hair, there was a tangle at the back, in one of the flaxen fronds that fell and parted around the nine-year-old hollow apricot neck.'

So Polly Devlin sets the scene for a 'moment of truth' with her nine-year-old daughter, to be shared with two million or so readers of the *Sunday Times* as they sit around burping and farting after their Sunday breakfasts. Next in the series of 'Conversations with my daughters' is promised for this week. If nothing more dramatic crops up, I hope to discuss the series week by week, as it appears, but she has certainly given us plenty to think about for the present.

The drama begins when, during a row with her mother, the daughter picks up a postcard on which she has previously written 'I love you', crumples it up and throws it in the wastepaper basket. Daughter Devlin then leaves the room, Mother Devlin rescues postcard from wastepaper basket like some lawyer collecting evidence. Re-enter Daughter Devlin:

' "I don't love you," she said, "any more. What will happen?" '

' "Nothing will happen," I said. '

' "What will you do?" '

' "I'll be sad for a while," I said. Was that the right answer? "But it will be all right. We'll love each other again. I'll rescue it." ' '

Was that the right answer? Mother Devlin reveals that her natural reaction had been to scream at the girl, kick her and hit her. Would that have been better, she asks.

It seems to me she has several problems to face. The first concerns her daughter's hair. Flax is not something of which I have much experience, but I imagine it to be a coarse, fibrous substance of yellowish grey colour when untreated. If it covers her daughter's head in fronds, or leafy branches, tangled at the back, I should recommend a powerful shampoo. The very least Mother Devlin might do is to set the girl a good example by brushing her own hair thoroughly. As it appears in the *Sunday Times* photograph it might provide a friendly shelter for half a dozen sparrows, a colony of bats and even some flying foxes, but it is scarcely a good example to any daughter with hair problems.

The hollow apricot neck sounds more serious. I do not know whether Mrs Devlin is suggesting that her daughter's neck has the colour or the texture of an apricot, but in either case I would suggest that it is a matter for the family doctor, if not a specialist. All necks, I suppose, are hollow to the extent that they contain a trachea and an oesophagus, and there need be nothing to worry us there, but if her daughter's neck seems somehow hollower than most, she might be well advised to consult her doctor once again, if only for reassurance. It is not the sort of thing which comes right after an aspirin or two, or some syrup of figs.

On the great postcard question, my own reaction would have been one of mild annoyance at the waste of a postcard. One should try to discourage children from scribbling on every available surface, even if they write twee little messages like 'I love you'. Perhaps the *Sunday Times* provides postcards free to its female employees for this purpose, but even so the finances of Times Newspapers are not so strong that they can afford to throw away these important documents. What will the *Look!* pages use for their Christmas number? Even so, I feel that to scream, kick *and* hit the girl would have been an over-reaction. A short lecture on the perils of waste would surely have been enough. But Mother Devlin was not going to let the matter rest there. She decided to take the opportunity for a long lecture on child relationships and reproduction, for later publication in the *Sunday Times*:

' "If your love isn't very strong, or is very new, or you can't trust the person you love, or trust their love, which is much the same, then you can *really* hurt or be hurt – you can do a lot of damage. But the love between a mother and a daughter is old and very deep, even though you're young. Because remember before we knew each other to look at, we knew each other: you were inside my body – nothing could be closer than that." '

No doubt this advice was well-intended. Mother Devlin sincerely hoped to bring them closer together by reminding her daughter that she, the daughter, was once in Mummy's tummy. She expected, and by her own account received, an affectionate and grateful reaction along the lines of, 'Gosh, thanks, mum. Now I understand why we are such good friends.' Perhaps modern children genuinely react in this way to such reminders, but I should have thought it was the ultimate snub or put-down for a child to be reminded of where it comes from, far worse than being asked to stand up when grown-ups come into the room, or even than being told that children should be seen and not heard.

It is also, or so I should have thought, the ultimate self-indulgence for a mother to be constantly reminding her offspring that they were once foetuses, inside her reproductive system. The truth is that once children are born they have a character and identity of their own. Modern mothers having once given birth must simply learn to belt up. The nightmares which children used to suffer from being told that a long red-legged scissor man would cut off their thumbs if they sucked them must pale into insignificance beside this constant injunction to get back into their mother's womb. I can well believe that Mrs Devlin's daughter is odious as well as stroppy, that her cute little ways and leafy branches of matted, fibrous hair hide a calculating brain, but this is no way to put her in her place.

Nor do I think it is a very good idea for journalists, when short of copy, to take up acres of newsprint with discussion of their children. Both Sir William Rees-Mogg and Captain Simon Raven have been criticised for this in their time, but at least they refrained from harping on the biological aspect of their relationship. They did not feel it added to their parental authority to remind their lads that they were both in their times, one of 75 million or so spermatozoa swimming around which happened to have won the race – a sort of glorified *Sunday Times* Fun Run – to the ovaries of their dear mothers. One may marvel, as a parent, that any child of one's own can ever win any sort of race, but that is food for private thought, part of the wonder of creation. It would be extraordinarily offensive to tell one's children that they were once carried around in one's testicles and must therefore realise how close they are to one emotionally.

My own anxieties about the Devlin household do not end with the children. After the two of them have – by Mother Devlin's own account – bored each other stiff in this moment of truth, we learn that Daughter Devlin 'trotted out to the garden, accompanied by a large mewling cat and terribly overweight dachshund'.

This information raises so many questions that we must leave them for another week. Broadly, they are: 1) why did Daughter Devlin trot? 2) why did the cat mewl? and 3) why was the dachshund overweight? This last question may require immediate action. Is Mother Devlin not aware that it is extremely cruel to allow dogs to become overweight? As founder of the Dog Lovers' Party of Great Britain, I think I may have to draw this to the attention of the appropriate authorities. Nor do cats mewl, when going out into the garden, unless they are in pain. When we add to this the evidence which we have already discussed about the condition of Daughter Devlin's hair and neck, I think it may well be time the Devlin household received a few visitors.

16.10.82

*　　*　　*

5

THE OLD

Against Cheaper Tickets

Of all the problems besetting our poor, battered country, I should have thought that one of the least urgent was the problem of moving its old people about. Anybody who travels a certain amount by train as I do will realise that old people are constantly on the move. In every compartment they can be seen flashing their false teeth from behind their Senior Citizens Railcard, exerting their special brand of dumb appeal to make one carry their suitcases and budgerigar cages for hundreds of yards to where their sullen relatives are waiting to collect them. Those with motor cars usually head for Somerset to drive in an endless convoy, very slowly in the middle of the road, round and round the country lanes as they await the awful moment of judgment when they will meet their Maker face to face.

Are these journeys really necessary? I should have thought that old people had a better chance of discovering that serenity of mind which is the hallmark of dignified old age if they tried staying in the same place. People would then visit them and listen to their wise saws and present instances, pretending not to notice the lean and slippered pantaloon or the gentle slide into second childishness and mere oblivion.

Old age holds many terrors in a godless generation, but immobility is surely the least of them. As a race, we are perfectly foul to our old people, turning them away from the family, and telling them they much prefer to be independent. Perhaps there is an awareness of this in the guilty, sentimental noises we all make whenever anyone mentions old age pensions. It is an observable fact that the greediest and most ruthlessly grasping trade union leaders are always the ones who make loudest noises about the old.

A document published by Age Concern, the National Old People's Welfare Council is ominously entitled *Your Rights*. It tells old people how to claim all the myriad cash benefits to which they are entitled in addition to their basic retirement pensions; it guides them through the extra weekly allowances under supplementary benefit, rent and rate rebates, attendance allowances, tells them how to avoid charges on the national health service, how to acquire wigs, fabric supports, teeth and eyes, legal help, income tax allowances and even, as a last resort, how to apply for the Death Grant (full rate £30, reduced rate £15):

'If the person who has died was aged 87 (or 92 for a man) before 5 July 1975 *no* grant will be paid. If they [*sic*] were aged 77 (or 82 for a man) before 5 July 1975, only the reduced grant will be paid.'

All you have to do is to call in at the local social security office with your death certificate. 'You should also take your marriage certificate and a written estimate of the cost of the funeral.'

But I can't help feeling that this is the wrong approach to the dreadful spectre of death which haunts us all, or at any rate nearly all of us. We buy off the dead and dying with extravagant bribes and tell them to go to the local social security office. A final chapter of the gruesome booklet is devoted to Travel Concessions, urging the advantages of the Senior Citizens Railcard 'to any man aged 65 or more and any woman aged 60 or more living in the United Kingdom provided you can give proof of your age.'

Why, just look at my teeth, you fool, or cut me in half and count the rings in my trunk. But it's no good pretending they can get to heaven on a Senior Citizens' Railcard.

Problems of old age can't be solved by putting old people on some sort

77

of British Rail merry-go-round and hoping that under the stimulation of constant movement they will forget their falling teeth and hair, their ungrateful children, their problems of forgetfulness and incontinence and personal hygiene. We need an entirely new policy something to inspire hope and gladness, a sense of belonging and of usefulness. It is simply not enough to shut them in a train and wave them off from the platform. Quite apart from the cruelty involved there is the consideration that other people – wage-earners, wealth-producers or what you will – have to travel by train as well, and it is rapidly becoming impossible with all these subsidised old people being pushed around, backwards and forwards, for no reason at all. A humane transport policy would try and discourage them from travelling, adding a premium on the price of any ticket sold to a woman over sixty, a man over sixty-five. This would nominally be in recognition of the additional nuisance they are likely to cause to their fellow passengers, but in fact it would be to encourage them to stay at home and acquire a little dignity.

So it was with great excitement that I turned to the article in last week's *Spectator* by Timothy Raison, MP, which promised an alternative Conservative transport policy. The obvious response to Age Concern's distressing pamphlet called *Your Rights* would be a Central Office pamphlet called *Your Opportunities*, teaching these people how to shell peas, slice runner beans, top and tail gooseberries – even, with the aid of diagrams, how to pluck and clean a chicken. There are a thousand and one ways in which old people can make themselves useful and valued members of society if they have a mind to it. Stuffing them with money and keeping them on the move is not the answer.

But what prospect of an alternative society does Mr Raison offer, where in his vision of the old sitting in quiet dignity at home over these broad beans and *gros point* tapestries while trains run freely with their cargoes of happy, young people on wealth-producing missions? First, he quotes Sir Reginald Wilson (former Chairman of the Transport Development Group) in what he describes as 'the best analysis of the fundamentals of Transport that I have ever read.' This is what Sir Reginald said: 'Birds have wings, and human beings have always aspired to a comparable freedom of movement.'

Well, yes, allowing for a little poetic licence. This is what Raison deduces from Sir Reginald's flight of fancy:

'There is still a vital need to make this mobility available to old, handicapped and young; but this is surely the direction in which we should all be pointing.'

No, no, no. Apart from the disgusting suggestion that there is *any* direction in which we should all be pointing, there is absolutely no vital need of this sort. Rather the reverse. He demonstrates once again the bankruptcy of the two-party system. Conservative and Labour now lob the same discredited ideas backwards and forwards as if the government of this country was a friendly tennis match in an old people's home. Can't he see we have *tried* giving the old people wings and teaching them to fly, and the result that is they are all utterly miserable? He should motor past Taunton post office at 9.20 on a weekday morning when the old people are queueing outside for their social security hand-outs like dope-addicts outside an all-night chemist. He should listen to their comments and reflect on the sort of society we will have in a few years' time when old people are in the majority. Movement is not the answer. We need an alternative vision.

16.7.77

*   *   *

Uses of the Elderly

There is an old woman who lives in a neighbouring village to ours in France called Mathilde. She is a widow whose only son died: she now lives in retirement after a lifetime of service as cook in a private house. She has only two teeth, but they are very large and obviously quite useful. The rest of her body is in excellent shape, as far as one can tell, although it is only fair to say that her face is not such as invites the eye to linger over her body, speculating about its less accessible parts.

Mathilde supplies us with the livers of geese and ducks, lovingly fattened throughout the early autumn and slaughtered with many a merry cackle towards the end of November. In the cold winter months, when her English equivalents are burning each other to death in horrible residential centres administered by the local authority, she makes crocheted bedspreads of delicacy and antique charm.

Most of these are given to her nieces, of which she has a huge supply, but just occasionally she can be persuaded to do one for money. When the delicate matter of payment arose, my wife at first suggested that it should be at an hourly rate; but she had not taken into account the hours involved. It transpired that if we paid Mathilde one franc (12p) an hour, the bedspread would cost 500 francs (about £60) in labour costs alone. Everybody agreed that this was far too much, and Mathilde herself, who is a deeply religious woman, was appalled at the idea. So we fixed the fee at 250 francs and left it at that.

It goes without saying that Mathilde is the happiest woman alive. She distils her own *eau de vie* which she wisely does not drink herself, being of religious turn of mind, but offers to guests. She rides her *mobilette* to market in Castelnaudary every Monday, and generally returns with a

79

green plastic bowl, a five-kilo bag of boiled sweets or some similar trophy. She lives surrounded by nieces and cousins; she has a position in her village, and her moustaches are admired for miles around. In terms of social usefuless, she is worth a charabanc load of teenagers, twelve young married couples, half a dozen factory workers and a battleship.

Is she, I wonder, the same breed, the same species as the Archbishop of Canterbury is talking about when, after much agony of spirit, he chooses to remind us of the traditional Christian doctrine that there are circumstances in which the old or incurably ill may decently be left to die?

On every other occasion this vain and foolish man has chosen to open his mouth, his words have fallen like the proverbial cowpats in a field: his ludicrous suggestion at a Lord Mayor's Banquet (of all places) that the better-off might like to forgo a proportion of their income to improve still further the housing of the lower classes – presumably he has never heard of progressive taxation; his preposterous Call to the Nation, suggesting we start a Great Debate on what sort of society we wish to be – even *The Times* now admits that his seed like Onan's fell on stony ground, if I have not got my biblical references mixed.

It would be a terrible thing if, in the course of his maunderings about the old, he suddenly hit a fertile patch. Nothing Dr Coggan said could possibly be held to condone geronticide. He was, as I say, just droning along, opening and shutting his mouth like a goldfish which has suddenly, miraculously learned to speak. His words had no application whatever beyond the pleasure it gave him to utter them. But *just suppose* somebody imagined he was really making a point, what point could they possibly imagine he was trying to make? Obviously, he must have been dropping hints: just as the Church of England has been having a long, hard look at its previous doctrine on the sanctity of human life in relation to unborn babies, so the time has now come for it to have a long hard look at its previous attitude to old people, many of whom are incurably insane, not to say incontinent, unpleasant and greedy ... Can old people be said to have immortal souls, and if so, does it really matter? A large part of the Christian message is surely that many of these people will be much happier after they are dead. Living standards are much higher in Heaven, so are old age pensions, and there are more facilities, of course, for looking after the old ...

All I do know is that if I were an old age pensioner at the present time, I would be beginning to think of ways to make myself scarce.

Poor things, they could hardly make themselves scarcer as it is. The secret, smouldering hatred of the English for their parents requires that we, alone of all civilised nations, tuck them up in retirement bungalows and old people's homes, as far away as possible from the family. Then, to appease our consciences, we make sentimental noises about them at Christmas time. As a result, they are not only miserable but also idle and useless.

The notion that retirement should be spent in idleness, that people are only happy when they are idle, may be an inheritance from our wicked system of primogeniture, as I believe, or it may be a subtle form of punishment reflecting this secret hatred of the old. In either case, it is plainly a waste of time to urge people to change their attitudes to work and old age at a moment's notice. But it might be prudent for old people to try to make themselves a little more useful in the difficult times ahead.

There are a hundred things they could do if they had a mind to it, even hampered as they are in this country by false teeth that don't fit, ridiculous spectacles and surgical trusses. They could shell peas in the summer, clean shoes, baby-sit. We would sooner employ young people to babysit, of course, but it is not good pretending they are very reliable nowadays. Quite often, one reads, young people murder children left in their care. Many old people still have useful skills, like plucking chickens, cleaning rabbits, darning socks. In the year of the beaver, it might be a good idea to give us a sight of them.

15.1.77

*   *   *

PART THREE

IDEOLOGICAL WAR

6

POLITICS

Britain's World Role

June 1 [1978] was Biafra's national day, being the eleventh anniversary of the declaration of Biafran independence on 30 May 1967. That month also, by unhappy coincidence, marks the tenth anniversary of the fall of Port Harcourt to Federal Nigerian troops in the civil war and the imposition of the siege which with British and Russian support was to last for twenty months, eventually bringing about the Biafran collapse and surrender on 12 January 1970.

The exact number of deaths in that time is known only to God. More moderate Nigerian partisans put it at 600,000. Lady Hunt, Nigerian wife of the British High Commissioner in Lagos throughout most of the war, seemed to be favouring the lower range in a recent letter to the *Spectator* defending her husband who, since his return from foreign parts, has been elected the Brain of Britain. Rather than descend to one of those unseemly arguments about exactly how many Jews were murdered during the Holocaust, one might examine the figures issued by the relief workers in the field. On 14 July 1968 the International Committee of the Red Cross in Geneva estimated that 3,000 people were dying daily in Biafra – nearly all children and old people, suffering from protein-starvation. On 3 August, they upped this figure to 6,000 and continued to publish estimates throughout the war which at one time reached 10,000 a day.

Now it is quite possible that the International Committee of the Red Cross got it wrong. Those dour Swiss officials might even have been influenced by a desire for cheap publicity. But at times when it is not in conflict with the desires of the British government – as, for instance, when it might have reported on the victims of the Katyn wood massacres – the ICRC is generally thought a fairly respectable body. And however much one may doubt the ability of any foreigner to count corpses properly, the fact remains that the British government had no one in Biafra to do the job any better. So however many people actually were dying the best information available to Mr Wilson's government at that time was that first 3,000 a day were dying, later 6,000 and finally 10,000. And it was on the basis of that information that his government persisted in supplying arms and support to the Nigerian war effort and using diplomatic pressure to obstruct relief to the Biafran side.

My purpose in wandering down memory lane is not to re-open old wounds or apportion blame yet again between the Biafran and Federal sides. There seems little doubt that after the surrender the Nigerians were able to restrain their troops from gross slaughter, however oddly they behaved in other respects, and it must certainly be admitted that the Biafrans used the fear of genocide – however rational such a fear might have been in the light of previous events – to bolster their own morale, if that is the right expression. Few people, I suspect, will be celebrating the anniversary in Enugu, Nsukka, Onitsha, Umuahia, Aba, Owerri, Calabar or Port Harcourt. But I feel we should not forget it in England.

I became involved in the Nigerian civil war at a fairly late stage, in the summer of 1968, when I was sent as the *Spectator*'s political correspondent to report on conditions inside Biafra, already reduced to an enclave of the heartland around Aba, Owerri and Umuahia. My trip was a brief one, ten days all told, just long enough to convince me that the place existed, that the Biafrans thought they were in the right and thought they had been unjustly treated by Britain, that they were determined to fight and that reports of mass starvation had not been exaggerated. Thereafter I covered the story, and watched the unfolding pageant of events, exclusively from the Westminster and Whitehall end.

It would be idle to pretend that my interest was not coloured by the things I had seen and heard in Biafra, or by my admiration for the Biafrans. One could not listen to the well-rehearsed arguments for continuing British policy in the Nigerian civil war with quite the same equanimity having once seen its results and knowing that the results were growing more severe with every week that passed. Having said that, and making every allowance for a certain failure of imagination among the British official and political classes (many of whom came from humble homes and poor educational backgrounds) whereby one or two million Africans dead might represent no more than a statistical concept, something to be played around with on a computer, a tribute, in some way, to their own responsibility and importance in the world – making every allowance, as I say, for all of that – I can only testify that the episode has burned itself into my memory.

It has entirely shaped my subsequent attitude to politics and politicians, journalism and journalists, the House of Commons, British democracy, the British people and its suitability to have any particular role in the world, to the Labour and Conservative parties and to a strange collection of individuals with nothing else in common but that they supported the Federal side: John Mendelson, the 'left-wing' Labour MP for Penistone who died last week; John Cordle, Tory businessman and adviser to John Poulson, who resigned his seat recently; Frank Giles, dapper Old Wellingtonian foreign editor of the *Sunday Times*, who still seems to be with us; Michael Foot, once so much admired and loved, now Lord President of the Council; Sir Alec Douglas Home, now 'Lord' Home of the Hirsel ... the list could be continued for a long time.

But the chief insight I gained during that unhappy period was into the mentality of people who seek power. One was always aware of their vanity and absurdity, but this was my first glimpse of their ruthlessness, or of the lengths to which they will go if they think they can get away with it. Harold Wilson was not a wicked or evil man, like Hitler; just an unprincipled opportunist. Michael Stewart, his disastrous foreign secretary, was not even an unprincipled man; just an obstinate and foolish one. Yet between them they urged and assisted for twenty months a policy which involved starving to death anything up to 10,000 children and old people every day.

They, it is true, are the real villains of the story, along with Mr Donald Tebbit, of the FCO, Mr Ronald Burroughs, of MI6, and Mr Maurice Foley who briefed one of the 'impartial' observers, Major Ian Walsworth Bell, to give what assistance he could to the Nigerian forces. But what of the whole army of FCO information officers, junior officials, Labour party and journalistic lick-spittles who supported them? What of the House of Commons, which divided three times on the issue and each time gave Mr Stewart a mandate to continue his policy?

The last time it was debated before Biafra's collapse was on 9 December 1969, when the war had already lasted two and a half years with the best available estimate of two million dead. The chamber was sparsely attended until the Division Bell rang, when 254 voters (including six Tories) appeared from nowhere to swamp the 84 Members of all parties who had decided to vote against the government. The Tories had advised abstention; Labour put on a two-line Whip. It was a motion for the adjournment, with no question of confidence being involved, no very serious embarrassment for the government if the vote had been lost. I do not think that 84 Members prepared to vote against such a policy is a very impressive figure – nor will I have any confidence in the respectability of our public affairs until the men responsible for it have been brought to justice. But above all I thank God that Britain no longer has sufficient power or importance to influence events in many other parts of the world.

3.6.78

*   *   *

The Workers' State without Vodka

It is no earthly use pretending that any problem in Britain is anything like as serious as the drink problem in the Soviet Union. For Soviet citizens not prepared to hijack an aeroplane – they are nearly always repatriated by the weasel democracies of the West in any case – the only effective escape from the horrors of state socialism and the Russian winter has always been found in a bottle of vodka. The equivalent institution in this country would probably be television, which saves us from the need to talk or think or do anything. Under socialism, needless to say, television is so boring, so rigidly controlled, so parsimonious with information and so full of lies that its only effect is to drive people back to the vodka bottle. But to understand the enormity of Gorbachev's drive against drunkenness in Russia one must try to imagine some crazy intellectual among politicians in this country – Enoch, perhaps – proposing that the only way for Britain to recover its soul, for our kiddies to be saved from delinquency, vice and drugs, was for the television stations to be closed down, cable television to be banned and videos impounded.

Even as I write I hear the cheers going up in a thousand *Spectator* homes. Of course, a ban on television is exactly what is required to save the new generation of Englishmen and Englishwomen. Let our children learn again to be children – blow blackbird's eggs, tickle trout, torture the neighbour's cat etc. Married couples might even rediscover the simple pleasures of sexual intercourse. A total ban on television is the sort of thing which would be passed in half the undergraduate debating societies and loudly supported in every saloon bar in the land. Nevertheless, we all know it is unthinkable. So long as any vestige of democracy remains, so will television.

In the Soviet Union, of course, there is no vestige of democracy, but the whole system of oppression by the Party is kept going by two big Lies, and it will be interesting to see how these two Lies stand up to this determined assault on the one institution which sustains them. The first and immensely the less important of the two Lies is that of the Virtuous State. Communism aspires to create the sort of society where drunkenness and crime will wither away because their social causes have been removed. State socialism requires occasional assurances that things are moving in that direction. Nobody who looked around the Soviet Union and saw half the workers dead drunk half the time would be much impressed by that claim. Now Mr Gorbachev' demonstrates that the way to stop socialists drinking is cut off their supply of drink, rather than to re-educate them or create the sort of ideal society where nobody wants to be drunk. Perhaps he plans to cut off supplies now, then create his ideal society, then let anyone buy as much as he wants so that the world can see how nobody wants to buy it.

I suspect that this Lie of the Virtuous State was never of much interest to anyone in the Soviet Union, except at the Wolf Club or Brown Owl level of Komsomol training. The second Lie is more important because it is the one which the Party bureaucrats in their less secure moments genuinely believe to be the force keeping the country together, and keeping themselves in their positions of privilege and power. This is the lie of the Worker's State – a society run by and for its workers.

For reasons which many may find hard to understand, the privileged and great of the Soviet Union are no less terrified of revolution – what they would call counter-revolution – than our own privileged and great in the West. In fact, to judge by the enormous resources devoted to tracking down and punishing the first hint of subversion, they are considerably more nervous. To this end, the myth of the Workers' State is sustained by one vital concession which capitalism can never make, a more or less total security of employment. Unless workers do something which is actually High Treason, like going on strike, they are almost impossible to sack. They are given extremely cheap housing, if of a quality and size which would be illegal for pigs in this country, and have a rudimentary health service such as might be described in an article by John Pilger about collapsing Liverpool.

But what really keeps the show on the road is vodka. Factory production is so bad and planning so incompetent that workers have precious little else to spend their money on; in any case it is all they want to know about. Take that away and their blunted, brutalised brains will be capable of only one thought – that they have not got the single thing they really want.

Gorbachev hopes that without vodka they will work harder, and produce more goods which they can then buy with the money that they would otherwise have spent on vodka. Anybody who lives outside that accursed, groaning slave empire, can see perfectly well that he has got everything in the wrong order, he is attacking the symptoms, not the cause. It is socialism which leads initially to incompetence, idleness, poverty and vodka. Vodka then leads to further poverty, idleness, incompetence – and socialism.

At present, when he goes impulse-shopping, the Soviet worker has a choice of two articles which are unrationed and in plentiful supply: he can buy either a curious, ethnic doll with other, smaller versions of the same doll inside it; or he can buy tinned mackerel in various sizes of tin. Otherwise he must queue, often for long periods, and often, no doubt, in working hours, thereby adding one more unit to his work place's statistics for absenteeism, no doubt attributed to drunkenness. Since it is considered no disgrace in the Soviet Union to be drunk (except by increasingly alienated authorities) the Soviet worker may well claim to have been drunk when in fact he was queuing for razor blades, or lavatory paper, or some other unimaginable luxury.

I often think it strangely suitable that vodka should be the national drink of Russia – the dullest and most brutish way of imbibing alcohol which mankind has yet invented. But after the armed forces and the secret police, I should judge it the chief pillar of the Soviet state. I wonder how Mr Gorbachev hopes to keep his workforce placid when its incentive to work is in the form of plastic flowers and Dralon curtains. Opium is presumably ruled out by the requirements of the Virtuous State. Perhaps he will try religion.

5.10.85

*   *   *

A Political Sex Fantasy

Isn't it time we had a decent sex scandal in Britain? Washington is plainly in for an enjoyable summer, as disgruntled secretary after disgruntled secretary comes out with her exclusive account of sexual adventures on Capitol Hill. In Britain, it looks as if we have nothing but a few race riots to look forward to in the long, dead month of August when law courts and Parliament are in recess. And if the blacks aren't prepared to get off their backsides, we shall just have to look into the sky and pretend to see flying saucers ...

Perhaps British politicians are less venal than their American equivalents, or British secretaries more discreet. Or perhaps both have succumbed to the general torpor. But it is a sad fact that no scandal has much chance of getting off the ground in Britain unless some reference can be made to it in Parliament or in the courts, where reporting is privileged. A secretary may have been gang-banged by the whole Government Front Bench and even the Opposition Front Bench, too, poor woman, but not one of our brave, crusading newspapers will mention the fact until she says it in court, or somebody brings up the matter in Parliament.

In several years of sitting through every important debate in the House of Commons, I never consciously heard anyone tell it a word of truth; I never once checked on an answer to a Parliamentary Question without finding it either gravely misleading or a straight lie. But then I never uncovered any sexual scandals, either – or none to which I was prepared to give serious credence – and this discouraged me after a time. As a natural romantic, I had hoped to find the House of Commons like a cornrick where every sheaf lifted will reveal a family of rats fighting, eating and copulating with each other and dashing for cover when exposed to the light of day. Instead, I found an assembly of dirty-minded but torpid and inadequate drunks.

Nothing could be more depressing than to discover that our parliamentarians are almost as sexually torpid as their idiotic public image seems to require. My intention, believe it or not, was the entirely benign one of trying to prove that politicians are really human, against all the evidence. I am convinced, as I have often explained, that a huge majority of Englishmen and Englishwomen find sexual disclosures about politicians funny, not shocking, although if one can succeed in making a few people genuinely indignant about such matters it only adds to the entertainment for the rest of us. The glory of our democratic system is that such disclosures still destroy a politician's repulsive career in a way that proven association with crooked business enterprises does not.

But it is no good living on past shock horror sensations. If we are to enjoy any political sex scandals this summer, we shall have to invent them ourselves; there will be no help from those sluggish, overpaid ranks in the House of Commons.

Oddly enough, I have been working on the outlines of a political sex extravaganza for some time, without ever having the opportunity to write it. No doubt the plot, when explained, will prove too preposterous for any West End impresario or mogul of Independent Television, most of whose minds are on higher matters. No audience will invest much credibility in it either, so resigned are we all to the gloomy proposition that our political leaders are sexless as well as incorruptible. But since nothing else has happened this week for me to write about, I suppose I might as well set it down.

The hero is a youngish, fairly idealistic politician – I suppose we had better make him Labour – who falls from grace just once. Although he is already married, he embarks on an affair with a lady from work. The affair only lasts a comparatively short time – about two years – but he makes the mistake during this time of taking his lady friend to Russia with him, where he is visiting on business, not one but three times. During the first of these visits, they are photographed in compromising circumstances by agents of the Soviet security police at a hotel where they are both staying.

The plot, as I say, is a preposterous one – anybody who knows anything about politics will know how absurd it is to suggest that a politician could ever have an affair with anyone who was not his wife – but this is the least preposterous part of it. Those who have made a study of such matters assure me that the KGB take infinite pains, and every single applicant for a tourist visa to the Soviet Union – even half-witted students or journalists on a Thomson package tour – is made the subject of a KGB decision on whether the applicant should be recruited, compromised or merely neutralised (that is, prevented from seeing anything unsuitable). The risk of a politician visiting Russia with a lady friend being made the subject of such attentions is so great as to be a virtual certainty, and where repeated visits are involved, it is more than a certainty.

At any rate, our hero comes back from the Soviet Union to discover that the KGB have the screws on him, and the only person in England who knows this is his lady friend. Fortunately, she remains loyal to him, and in fact stays by his side like the proverbial limpet long after their sexual passion has run its course. But the knowledge undoubtedly gives her a certain moral purchase.

His career progresses, as politicians' careers are wont to do, and in time he finds himself the leader of his party and eventually (why not?) Prime Minister of Great Britain. As the former lady friend approaches a certain age, her influence becomes unsettling. The demands she places upon his loyalty become more strenuous, and the threats more overt. Eventually he inexplicably resigns, his last actions in obedience to her demands leaving a noticeable question mark over the whole episode.

The truth finally comes out when, in a fit of hysteria, either the politician, or his lady friend – or possibly both – institute libel proceedings against a brave, handsome, much-loved journalist who has guessed their secret. In the final court scene it is revealed that the former Prime Minister has been an agent of the Soviet Union – albeit an unwilling one – throughout his entire period of office.

Are there any takers for this preposterous fiction?

19.6.76

*   *   *

The Power Urge

Taken by a friend to the dress rehearsal of Peter Hall's magnificent *Coriolanus* at the Olivier theatre last week, I have since spent my time urging as many people as possible to go and see it, even buying tickets for them. It was not a play I had thought about much since studying it for 'A' level nearly 30 years ago, when it seemed tremendously boring. One could not sympathise with the hero, or find his mother anything but disgusting, his wife irritating, his best friend a fool. Although it contained some fine polemic against the working classes, such people did not threaten one's life or comforts in those days as they do now; in fact, to the extent that they infringed at all, they appeared as friends and supports in life's struggle. It was inappropriate to describe them as a 'common cry of curs' – and also rather rude when, in many cases, they had not enjoyed one's own advantages.

Although I passed the examination, and have the certificate to prove it, I never understood the play until seeing Ian McKellen's memorable performance last week. The play's message is very simple, and even more relevant to modern democratic society than it was to Tudor England: that politics is not a suitable occupation for a gentleman. If that message could be generally accepted by all intelligent people in the country it would have a profoundly beneficial effect not so much in discouraging gentlemen from dabbling in politics, since very few are tempted to do so nowadays, but in giving the rest of us a more accurate perspective of politics and politicians.

In fairness to the great British public, it has never shown a tendency to put any exaggerated trust in politicians. But until it accepts that the urge to power is a personality disorder in its own right, like the urge to sexual congress with children or the taste for rubber underwear, there will always be a danger of circumstances arising which persuade ordinary people to start listening to politicians and would-be politicians, and taking them seriously. It happened in Russia, of course, and in Germany, and may even now be happening in Central America for all I know or care. The important thing is to prevent its happening in England.

Where Peter Hall's *Coriolanus* is concerned, the contemporary relevance is emphasised by an extraordinary physical resemblance between Ian McKellen and Lord Lambton, Mr Heath's former Under-Secretary for the Royal Air Force. The actor even wears dark glasses at the beginning of the play. Of course the parallel is misleading. Lord Lambton was anything but a Coriolanus figure. At a time when most intelligent people had decided that the only acceptable or honourable motive for going into politics was the remote chance of becoming an earl at the end of the day – not just for our own honour and glory, but for that of our children and children's children – Lord Lambton started on the slippery slope as the elder surviving son of an earl, a dead cert for the earldom if he played his cards right and stayed alive. Then he threw it all away to further his ludicrous political career. If he had been asked to flaunt his scars in the market place, he would have shown the brutes his appendix scar as quick as a flash. For those of us who have the misfortune not to be born earls, or with any prospects of an earldom, his behaviour is hard to understand or forgive.

Few people would criticise Mrs Thatcher's Government on the grounds that it has too many gentlemen in it, let alone toffs. The extent to which genuine toffs have disappeared from public awareness may be judged by the way that some newspapers even discuss the second Lord Gowrie, Mrs Thatcher's swarthy 'art' expert, as if he were one. Politics, as I never tire of saying, is for social and emotional misfits, handicapped folk, those with a grudge. The purpose of politics is to help them overcome these feelings of inferiority and compensate for their personal inadequacies in the pursuit of power.

Power, I imagine, is all that democratic politicians have ever been interested in. Those who do not suffer from this urge may have difficulty in understanding it: they may even be reluctant to believe in its existence. Among the lower classes it is generally supposed that politicians are in it for the money, but I believe that they are wrong, and we should all study this phenomenon of the power urge. It seems to cause far more unhappiness than happiness.

The yells and animal noises which the nation listens to on the radio programme *Today in Parliament* have nothing to do with disagreements about the way the country should be run, or how much fuel should be given to old age pensioners at Christmas time. They are cries of pain and anger, mingled with hatred and envy, at the spectacle of another group exercising the 'power' which the first group covets; alternatively, they are cries of alarm and anger as the group in 'power' sees its territory threatened. Old age pensioners are mad if they think anyone actually cares about their wretched coal.

Until one understands this one will never understand the confrontational nature of democratic politics. Unless I am wrong, Labour Politicians would be just as happy to charge old age pensioners double price for their coal as Mrs Thatcher would be to pour the stuff down their throats in unlimited quantities absolutely free. The only thing that any of them is really interested in is the chance to make decisions and see them put into effect – to press a button and watch us all jump.

15.12.84

*   *   *

British Infertility

Since time immemorial, May Day has been honoured with pagan rites and dances, propitiatory sacrifices and uncouth symbols, all suggestive of sexual intercourse and fecundity. It was banned in 1644 at the beginning of the Puritan Terror and remained banned until the Restoration, when Charles II put up a huge 134-foot maypole outside the old church of St Mary-le-Strand, where it stood for fifty years. Its original purpose would appear to have been frustrated again now the day has been officially designated as a Festival of Idleness to celebrate the Second International of 1 May 1889, the federation of socialist parties which eventually, on Lenin's insistence, committed all socialist parties to the class struggle and the inevitability of social revolution.

The Second International was founded at a congress in Paris, but Britain's workers might have had difficulty in getting abroad because baggage-handlers at Heathrow were threatening a strike, as they usually do on days of national holiday. This time they were protesting about police interrogation of a baggage handler over alleged thefts from baggage. Was it to protect the rights of baggage-handlers to pilfer from baggage that Wat Tyler marched on London? But it did mean that any British worker who felt like celebrating the Second International by being international in Benidorm had to think again. Nor could he visit many public places at home, since all the major state-owned galleries, museums and gardens were closed down in the galloping epidemic of idleness which has marked the progress of workers' power in Britain.

But it is not my intention to demonstrate yet again how the loathsome stupidity and short-sightedness of workers' leaders must inevitably create a society in which workers are poor, miserable and repressed. I merely wish to draw attention to the removal of any association with fertility from these gruesome May Day celebrations. Recently I wrote about the collapse of the birthrate in Britain. The social consequences of this development are, of course, exacerbated by emigration which represents a solid drain of the healthier and more qualified. But it is no use pointing this out to the Government, since there can be little doubt that the modern administrative mind does not welcome such people. Emigration is the result of deliberate government policy aimed, through the tax and education systems, at producing a malleable population of government employees, second class citizens and welfare fodder.

But the social planners of the future are going to find themselves horribly frustrated if there is nobody left to plan, and I really think the Government might address itself to the problem of the collapsing birthrate. Since writing about the phenomenon I have done some research into the various ordeals and humiliations attendant on childbirth in the Welfare State, and my conclusion is that it is a miracle any English woman has a baby at all.

In the first place, there is a vast army of social workers and health visitors waiting to harass, patronise and insult the expectant mother. As fewer women have babies, so the army of experts in supervision grows and a friend who returned home from having a baby recently was visited by five separate government officials to remonstrate with her for not taking the baby to a welfare clinic. When she eventually sent the baby round in charge of her *au pair*, the clinic responded by sending a doctor to her house on the assumption that she was insane or gravely ill. A further stream of welfare visitors continued to arrive to demand that she breastfeed her infant and insult her for declining to do so, until she discovered a wonderful and little known form which applied for permission to look after her own baby. This provoked a return of all the bossy and embittered spinsters – mostly, she suspected, lesbians – who had been haranguing her about the benefits of breastfeeding. They were very cross indeed that she had applied for permission to take responsibility for her own child, implied that she was plainly incapable of it, lacking their experience of what happens when things go wrong, and let it be known that she was being very rude to them personally, in applying for this permission.

But few mothers put up such a fight. The sister of a friend who had a baby recently was visited by another of these white-coated lesbian ladies who said she wanted to see the baby smile. The baby took one look at her and screamed, so she came again the next day at the same time, which happened to be feeding time, so the baby screamed again. Next day the council sent round its chief expert in baby-smiling techniques who brought every sort of gadget known to human science to make the baby smile and the same result. As she left, the chief council baby-smiler looked worried. 'I am sorry', she said, 'but your baby will have to go down on the files as being socially unaware.' Goodness knows what sort of handicap this will prove when the poor little thing eventually has to apply for a job in the welfare service.

A third young mother of my acquaintance decided to do everything she was told to do, and regularly takes her baby to the clinic for inspection and discussions. First the baby is stripped and examined, then it is put through a series of humiliating tests. Then a lesbian stands in front of the baby and builds bricks while another lesbian stands behind and rings a bell. When the baby showed more interest in the brick than the bell, the second lesbian said she was afraid the baby would have to go on the files as being deaf. It was only by taking the matter to the local Infant Deafness Appeals Tribunal that the mother managed to have its hearing officially restored. At another clinic, she was asked whether the baby was talking yet. The baby was only ten and a half months old, so the mother replied that although it made many interesting noises, there was nothing that could really be described as conversation.

The interrogating lesbian then put on a stern expression. 'You've got to talk to *her* you know' she said. 'It's no good expecting baby to talk if you don't talk to *her*.' There followed a long lecture on Talking to Baby which my friend, an intelligent educated girl of proper middle class background, had to take on the chin.

The trouble may be that the lesbians are too early. In time, when we are thoroughly proetarianised, they will be able to treat all citizens as if they were ten-year-old halfwits. Perhaps mothers of the new, cowed working class will learn to enjoy this treatment and start having babies again. But it seems a bit of a risk and what distresses me is the wetness of Fleet Street in the face of the existing peril. Whenever a baby is murdered by its parents, every newspaper in the land sets up a wail for stricter and more effective welfare supervision. In fact babies have been battered since time began and it is very sad, but the only thing to do about it is to send the wretched parents to prison when the bodies are found. By treating all parents as potential baby-batterers, they simply ensure that nobody has babies. I hope Mrs Thatcher will restore May Day to its original, pagan function.

6.5.78

*　　*　　*

Death of Lucie Gates

On 31 May 1979 Miss Linda Gates was a 28-year-old spinster living alone in a council flat in Welling with her three children – a boy of eight, a girl of six and a second daughter, Lucie, aged two. She was obviously not a very competent mother, and her interpretation of her role had produced no fewer than 108 complaints to the various welfare authorities who concern themselves with other people's children. In the course of seven years the three children were treated in hospital 35 times, but not for injuries attributable to brutality.

The flat was regularly visited by police, social workers, health visitors, the NSPCC, home helps and the WRVS. Conditions were generally described as filthy, but at various care conferences which were held within the Bexley welfare authority it was decided that, with help, the Gates family would be better off as a family unit. Then, on the fateful night of 31 May 1979, Miss Gates decided to go out and visit a pub. According to her father, Mr Basil Gates, Miss Gates never drank, but visited pubs for the country and western music she found there.

While Miss Gates was listening to this music in a pub six miles away, an electric fire fell upon two-year-old Lucie Gates, inflicting injuries which proved fatal. In her defence, Miss Gates said that she had arranged for a girl who lived nearby to come in and keep an eye on the children, but the girl had stayed at home and watched television. She was sentenced to 18 months, suspended, and her surviving two children were taken into care. At her trial, the Recorder posed the question: 'Did society, through its social services, having taken on the burden of responsibility for little children and a strikingly incompetent mother, fail to implement its purpose or not?'

Many of us might suppose that the answer to this question was obvious enough, but no sooner were the words out of the judge's mouth than a committee was set up to find the answer. It produced not one but two reports, adding up to 600 pages. The first, of 350 pages, was written by the chairman, Mr Arthur Mildon QC, and took one point of view. The other, of 250 pages, was produced by Mr Colin Smart, a senior social services administrator from Tyneside, Miss Susan Douet, described as a 'child health area nurse' from West London, and Dr Rosemary Graham, described as an 'area specialist in community medicine' from another health area. This took another point of view, but both agreed in criticising welfare services, social workers and the police for allowing the thing to happen.

Other opinions have been canvassed and expressed. Miss Gates's neighbours, far from blaming the welfare services, seemed to blame Miss Gates. They have chased her out of the neighbourhood. An unnamed neighbour was quoted in the *Daily Mirror*: 'You either have children and are responsible for them, or you don't have them. It's no good social workers being blamed for something you should be doing yourself.'

Her father also rejected criticism of the social services contained in the two reports: 'They can only work with the money and the people they are given,' he said. 'I blame the government for cutting the money.'

The nation sits in judgment. We have three possible villains: the social services of Bexley; Miss Gates; and the government. Let us start with the last suggestion, that more money should have been spent on the problems of Miss Linda Gates and her family, that a better class of person should be employed in the fields of social work and health visiting.

My first reaction, on studying the narrative of events set out above, was that Miss Gates seemed to have created an enormous amount of employment, in one way or another. Not only had she been visited regularly by representatives of at least three branches of the government and two voluntary services, she had also provided further employment (over and above the call of duty) to her local hospital service, to the judiciary and legal professions, culminating in two years' work for a QC (presumably between other jobs, but just think what the fee must be for a 350-page opinion from senior counsel) and three others. If the Welfare State awarded medals for job creation, Miss Linda Gates would qualify as one of its heroines. I imagine (although we are not told so) that she was unemployed herself throughout this time. This would seem to add lustre to her role as Bexley's biggest job-creator. But is there the slightest reason to suppose that if more money had been spent on her the outcome would have been any different? Apart from introducing a PhD into the household of every forgetful or incompetent mother in the land on permanent watch, there seems to be no way of spending more money usefully on people like Miss Gates.

The second suggestion, that Miss Gates was to blame for the accident, speaks for itself. She was found criminally culpable. One may doubt whether any deterrent would have been created if she had been sent to prison to persuade other incompetent mothers to be more competent. It was the easiest thing in the world to pass a law saying that no child must ever be left unattended, quite another to enforce it by locking the Miss Gateses of this world into their council flats for 24 hours a day with their three (no doubt delightful) children.

Which leaves only the social services to carry the can for failing to avert an accident which must, I suppose, be seen as avertible. Nobody can claim that the social services ignored the problem. They were seldom out of the flat. The worst that can be said is that faced with the choice of removing the children from their mother or letting them stay with her, heavily supervised, they made the wrong decision. They must have decided that there was something better than a sporting chance that if left at home the children would not suffer an appalling accident.

In the event, the gamble failed, but I am quite prepared to believe it was the right decision for them to have taken. It depends on how many Miss Gateses there are around. If, as I imagine, there are at least several hundred of them in every public health area, then it does not stand to reason that every child at risk can be taken into care. There is all the difference in the world between parents who are violent or sadistic and parents who are merely neglectful or incompetent. If every child of every neglectful parent is automatically taken into care for fear it will fall into the washing machine, it will not only be the thin end of a very nasty wedge but will create the certainty of greater misery for more people than it might avoid for a few. The fact that so few children do, in fact, come serious croppers and so many survive owes practically nothing to the efforts of the welfare services, however well-intentioned, and nearly everything to ordinary human instincts for survival.

In other words, the gamble may not have paid off in the case of Lucie Gates, but if it has paid off in the case of 5,000 other Lucie Gateses who would otherwise have been forcibly removed from their parents, then no one has blundered. The final lesson of Lucie Gates must be that since the welfare services are unable, with the best will in the world, to do anything about the various imperfections in human nature which led to the tragedy, they should not try to assume such responsibilities. Their role should be reduced rather than increased.

But those of us who are constantly irritated by the size, cost and pretensions of the social workforce should never be tempted to use Lucie Gates as a stick to beat it with. To blame social workers for Lucie Gates's death is to play into their hands, suggesting that they might have been able to do anything useful about it. They could not – and should not have been allowed to pretend they could.

20.11.82

*   *   *

Illusions of Poverty

The day before the Post Office closed for its long winter recess, I went to buy my weekly supply of postage stamps in Taunton. This is one of my few outings nowadays. Others claim to divine what the lower orders are thinking by conversations with London cab drivers, but I have never been able to understand a word they say. The Taunton Post Office queue is my only contact with these engaging people, most of whom, I notice, are very, very old.

There are two topics of conversation. One is the level of prices, and the inadequacy of their various pensions, benefits, rebates and bonuses to grapple with the problem. The lady standing in front of me this time had just paid 95p for a hamster, which did indeed seem a lot of money when you think of what hamsters used to cost, although I could not help wondering what she wanted a hamster for at her age, or why she should expect me, the only tax-payer present, to pay for it if she did want one.

The other topic of conversation is medicine, but I shall not worry readers with any of the horrifying things I learn every week about the nation's health. For my own part, I am convinced that if medicine were not free, we should have none of this morbid preoccupation with the intestines. But nobody ever asks for my opinion, and after various attempts to interest them in my own ailments and in my brutally in-adequate War Office pension I have come to accept that they will never take me to their hearts as one of themselves, at any rate until I am sixty-five and have lost all my teeth.

Only two counters are now open in the Taunton Post Office, and there are seldom fewer than fifteen or twenty old age pensioners in each queue. Notices on the wall exhort 'Please take a child benefit claim form'; 'Rent rebates – Are You Getting Yours?' After some thought, I chose three pamphlets for my morning's reading. They are: Leaflet W11 Free Milk and Vitamins; Leaflet F151 Family Income Supplement; Leaflet P111 Free Prescriptions. I ignore Child Interim Benefit for One Parent Families (a CH1B Leaflet) and Equal Opportunities: A Short Guide to the Sex Discrimination Act on the grounds that I could see no obvious advantage in them. Leaflets W11, F151 and P111 similarly let me down, as I already have free prescriptions and can find no way of entitling myself to free milk, vitamins or a Family Income Supplement. Disgraceful. But I feel sure I could do something with Rent Rebates, if only I paid a rent. Over 37,000 GLC tenants already get a rent rebate, as the pamphlet proudly announced, and 'RENT REBATES ARE NOT A CHARITY – if you are a tenant (or about to become one) you have a legal right to apply for a rent rebate.' Soon, no doubt, we will be liable to prosecution if we don't apply.

The lady in front of me – the one with hamster problems – had grabbed her handful of blue five pound notes, counted them suspiciously and retreated with groans and snarls to her lair, or possibly to the Senior Citizens' Rest Room behind the car park. As I approached the counter, it occurred to me that I was the only customer whose business had anything to do with the post, and also the only one that morning who actually paid anything in. All the rest were collecting – most of them between eighteen and twenty-three pounds, so far as I could count, but one or two much more. A swarthy, dishevelled young man (not black – just swarthy, and almost certainly of English stock) collected £70, an obviously mad young woman about £55. And the queue behind me was much longer than it had been when I joined it at 9.30.

Now I do not resent that thirty or forty people should be maintained in the style to which they are accustomed on the proceeds of my earnings. In point of fact, the taxes I pay in a year would scarcely keep the Taunton Post Office going for a day at its present rate, but that is the Government's problem, not mine. But it does occur to me that anyone who talks of poverty as a widespread or important phenomenon at the present time is talking through his hat. And there is a whole generation of creeps and bores, many of them earning almost as much as I do, who can talk of little else.

The basic welfare sustenance level, so far as I can see – and if poverty has any meaning, it must refer to people at this level – is now appreciably higher than the level of skilled workmen in full-time employment twenty years ago. There is still some bad housing, although I would dispute the extent to which it is the fault of bricks and mortar rather than the neglect of the people who live in it; and there is undoubtedly a surviving body of those people who are too simple-minded or too proud to claim their various entitlements. It is also true that more old people die in cold weather than at other times of the year, as they always have done and always will. But to pretend that real poverty, real deprivation or discomfort exists in any substantial way is to indulge in the sort of masochistic fantasy which can only be explained in terms of emotional deprivation.

No doubt a hundred hysterical women will write to inquire how I would like to live in a damp rat-infested slum on a diet of baked beans and Kit-e-Kat. Small pockets of poverty undoubtedly remain – but they are not a large part of the social scene, and certainly not large enough to justify any major social readjustment. The rhetoric of the poverty corps may be explained in terms of deliberate lies for political ends, or it may be explained in terms of hysteria and emotional insecurity, as I prefer to believe, but it cannot be explained in terms of social analysis. And if anybody disagrees, or asks me to walk round the Gorbals on a Friday night, I can only reply by asking her to stand with me in the Taunton Post Office queue on Monday morning. A great problem of our time is not poverty but guilt, and I can think of no better cure for it.

8.1.77

*   *   *

Extending the Welfare

Nothing has changed much in the Taunton Post Office queue – they still moan gently to each other about their feet, varicose veins, operations for gynaecological disorders, and those of their friends and relations. The miseries of old age and inflation are sometimes interspersed with bitter 'jokes' about the weather. If I arrive before the Post Office opens, there is a little group of them, waiting like junkies outside the all-night chemist for their midnight 'fix'.

The conversation, as I say, does not change much, although sometimes someone has just died of cancer, or is about to do so. The only thing which has changed is the amount of money they receive. Waiting to buy my weekly £5-worth of postage stamps, I am amazed by the huge brown bundles being handed across to those in front of me in the queue. It reminds me of nothing so much as Expenses Day on the *Mirror*. We all know pensioners are terribly underpaid, but I simply fail to understand how any government can manage to hand out these wads of £10 notes to its citizens every day and hope to survive.

Last week, for the first time that I can remember, my queue had a new grievance. It concerned the case of Baby Malcolm, reported prominently in that morning's *Daily Mirror*. This was a tragic and horrible one by any account. Two young parents had been sent to jail for 12 months after their 14-month-old baby was found starving, frozen, gangrenous and filthy by ambulance men who were summoned by the mother only a few hours before the baby eventually died. Further details made the case even more gruesome, but chief among them was the fact that the family had been visited on many occasions by about ten social workers – one of them returning 48 times – to no avail.

The news reached Taunton – and, indeed, the rest of the country – after a delay of 11 months. Baby Malcolm died last February, but it is

100

the law of England that nothing can be published in the newspapers which might reflect to anyone's discredit until it has come to court, when it may be reported under the qualified privilege allowed to court reporting, with whatever comments, pithy or asinine as the case may be, which the judge chooses to utter. Any conclusions to be drawn by the general public, or any lessons to be learned, are thus delayed until the public may be informed. Malcolm's mother, Mrs Edwina Page, had employed the time in having another baby.

The *Mirror*'s own comment, after originally publishing its story under the memorable headline: 'Malcolm died as he lived. Freezing cold, starving and surrounded by social workers', was notably restrained. Inexperienced, underpaid, young social workers should not be blamed, it said: 'if they never made a mistake it would only reduce the number of failures, not eliminate them. That would depend on eliminating some of the causes of child cruelty: poverty and bad housing, health and education. That's the responsibility of the nation ...'.

In point of fact, there was no evidence that the Pages were either poor or badly housed – on the contrary, Mr Page had a good job, making £70 a week as a storeman of which he took home £56 a week to spend after tax, insurance, rates and rent on his council house had been deducted. Mrs Page was plainly not too keen on housework – the Welfare had been in to clean up her house on three occasions – but then how many housewives are, nowadays? Neither set much store by furniture, sleeping on the floor with their four children until the Welfare gave them two beds. As the Welfare did not give them any blankets, they did not buy any, with the result already mentioned. One may doubt whether, if the Pages had been given higher wages or better council housing, they would have behaved any differently. But we must not carp or quibble. The *Mirror*'s reaction is obviously the correct one to take under these circumstances. Yes, yes, we are all guilty.

This message did not seem to have come through to the queue in the Taunton Post Office as its members waited to collect their bundles of £10 notes with a patience born from a lifetime of deprivation. Their fury was directed entirely against the welfare workers. One woman gave it as her opinion that the entire welfare department responsible should be sent to prison. When I suggested, in my helpful way, that hanging was too good a fate for these welfare workers, there was a slight pause and moderation asserted itself. The compromise solution, which eventually became the consensus, was that welfare workers who fail in their duty to members of the public should be made to pay compensation to the members of the public concerned. I never discovered whether the money should come from their own pockets or the public purse, and it might have posed a bit of a problem. The normal working class reaction to any

101

mishap is that the state should pay for it, but in this case there was a distinct antipathy to social workers, as being middle-class, interfering and – worst crime of all – thinking themselves superior.

But the idea that Essex Social Services Department should pay a large sum of money to Mr and Mrs Page for having failed to prevent them from starving and freezing their baby to death struck me as a new development in the welfare philosophy of our times, and one which should be recorded and discussed. In fact, the Pages were convicted of cruelly neglecting Malcolm and wilfully neglecting his younger sister, Suzanne. Should they receive in addition a smaller payment from the welfare department for the second matter, in that it also failed to prevent them wilfully neglecting the younger child, or should payment be, as it were, by results?

On Saturday, we read of another case, in Birmingham, where a young father, called Haddon, after various visits from the welfare department, had murdered his baby daughter by smashing her head against the wall. In that case, both poverty and housing may have had something to do with it, as the unmarried father and mother – she was only 15 when her baby died – were both unemployed and living in a bed-sitter. In this sort of case, I imagine, it would not be enough for the Social Services to pay the parents compensation – both Housing and Employment should chip in, too.

Poverty, housing, health and education. These, apparently, are the causes of child cruelty, rather than brutal selfishness or perversity of nature. Personally, I do not think that health – other than mental health – has anything to do with it, unless it can be shown that these child murderers were suffering pain from an untreated toothache or varicose veins at the moment of their crime. The country has already decided more or less to abolish secondary education, on the grounds that equality is more important – so that the Pages and Haddons of this world may not be driven to anti-social behaviour by feelings of inferiority. So I think we can rule out education, as being contrary to the welfare philosophy. Only poverty and housing are left; these are comparative measurements of deprivation, rather than absolute ones, and since by no means everyone who is comparatively poor or badly housed is criminal it follows that those with criminal tendencies should be given better housing and more money than the rest.

There is a beautiful symmetry to the welfare philosophy, but I do not think it quite explains how the nanny state has bred a generation of ignorant, spoiled and useless louts who cannot be trusted with the simple human function of raising their young. No doubt we are all guilty, but not, I feel, in quite the way the *Mirror* suggests.

26.1.80

*   *   *

The Nilsen Millennium

Somewhere along the line, Dennis Nilsen seems to have got it all wrong. His father, a Norwegian soldier stationed in Scotland, moved off at the end of the war leaving his mother to cope with three children, of whom Dennis was the youngest. From his earliest years, his memories are those of a client of the welfare state. By the time he had moved on from two forms of government employment – in the army and the police force – to a third, in the Manpower Services Commission, he had emerged as such a boring and unpleasant person that nobody could bear to spend time in his company. He was a homosexualist, of course, but even with the opportunities available to him for making new acquaintances of similar persuasion through his post in the Charing Cross Road Job Centre, people found him so stupendously boring that nobody would spend more than an evening in his company. Like so many social and emotional cripples he drifted into left-wing politics and became branch organiser of the Civil Service Union, but even there his boring self-righteousness failed to secure the warmth and comradeship which he sought. So he was reduced to seeking the company of corpses as being the only people who would not walk out on him.

Other people, in the same sort of predicament, became prison visitors, but Nilsen kept his corpses under the floor-boards, retrieving them from time to time to sit them in an armchair and harangue them with his boring left-wing opinions, his grudges and grievances and the catalogue of his self-pity. Then, when the natural processes of decomposition made the corpses unacceptable company, even by his own undemanding standards, he boiled their heads, put them down the lavatory, and started looking around for a new companion. In this way he disposed of 15 young men in the course of five years, before being brought to book as a result of blocked drains in the house where he lived.

Nilsen obviously provides an extreme example of what used fashionably to be called urban alienation – the loneliness which rootless town-dwellers suffer who are too boring, too unpleasant or too unattractive in other ways to make friends. He also, perhaps, offers a paradigm for the relationship between personal inadequacies, left-wing views and bureaucratic sadism. Although I have no particular reason to suppose that Nilsen was such a sadist as one is liable to meet in the course of any dealings with a government ministry or local authority, a glance at his face assures me that he almost certainly belonged to that group. I have often speculated about the private lives of people behind desks who spend their working hours making things difficult for other people. It would be tempting to think they all have corpses under their floorboards and return home, of an evening, to harangue them. But Nilsen, as I say, is an

103

extreme example. His problem was loneliness, and the traditional solution to that is within the marriage bond. No man is so boring, or so unpleasant, or so unattractive that he cannot find an equally boring, unpleasant or unattractive woman to be his life's companion if he sets his mind to it and I have no doubt that the same must be true in the homosexual world. But Nilsen's only attempt at a homosexual marriage ended in mutual disgust; obviously he is better off in prison.

The latest edition of *Social Trends* (HMSO £19.95) reveals a dramatic increase in the number of people living alone – from 11 per cent of the population in 1961 to 24 per cent in 1983. Add to this proportion of people living in one-parent families, which has doubled from two and a half per cent in 1961 to five per cent in 1983, and one sees that the institution of the family is under serious attack.

Where abortion and contraception are freely available, the dramatic rise in illegitimate births – from six per cent of live births in 1961 to 16 per cent in 1983 – must be seen either as a deliberate flight from the institution of marriage or, more probably, a logical response to government incentives. Under the ghastly Mrs Williams's education system, children of the poor are no longer taught the old-fashioned disciplines of plasticine modelling, or how to make the longest plasticine worm. Apart from Reasons for Not Smoking, they are more or less exclusively taught How to Claim their Welfare Benefits. The first lesson in this course is to have a baby and become a single parent. There are now a million or so of them. Add to them the four and a quarter million now living completely alone, and one is plainly just beginning to be allowed a glimpse into the Nilsen millennium.

2.3.85

7

EDUCATION

The Lesson of Royalty

The most sombre lesson of the Royal Wedding concerns the future. Ever since becoming a father, more than 19 years ago, I have tried to convince my children that if they neglect their studies they will end up as roadsweepers or lavatory attendants. If, on the other hand, they apply themselves diligently enough to all the absurd and humiliating subjects in the modern child's syllabus, achieving satisfactory 'A' levels in biology, physics, 'modern' mathematics, 'Nuffield' latin, the theory and practice of positive anti-racialism, the political, philosophical and economic framework to a non-smoking policy, creative modelling in plasticine etc – then, if they are boys, they will become rich and famous like their father and grandfather before them; if they are girls, they will marry if not the Prince of Wales, at any rate a marquess, a duke or one of the better class of earls.

Even if I could think of a single unkind thing to say about our new Princess of Wales I would refuse to say it in deference to her beauty, birth and obvious amiability of temperament, but the fact remains that she has not got a single pass at 'O' level GCE and on that rock the whole ship of state looks like sinking. The Prince of Wales, in choosing such a mate, makes a statement of greater importance than if he had chosen to marry a girl of average educational abilities who was either black or working class. What he is saying, in effect – and instructing all his dukes and marquesses down to the meanest citizen in the land – is that education is no longer of the slightest use or interest to the modern Briton.

In a sense, of course, he is right. In a society where the long-distance lorry driver earns more than the university professor, the ancillary technician in hospital more than the consultant surgeon, who needs education? A chimpanzee can be trained to perform most of the functions of the 'worker' in a modern factory, and would probably perform them with better grace.

The error in this is to suppose that education prepares people for employment rather than unemployment. Present figures for unemployment are not the product of a temporary recession, still less of the Government's non-existent 'monetarist' policies. They are the inescapable and permanent result of technological progress. The greatest challenge facing our civilisation – as opposed to the dragooned and regulated societies of the East – is the challenge of leisure. Even the lower classes grow intolerably bored with television after a time. Music is already surging ahead and literature, I feel sure, will revive once it has been taken away from the Arts Council and learned to address itself once again to its readers. Education is the key to everything. If the Prince is too busy himself he should appoint a tutor to instruct his young bride in music, dancing, poetry and all the gentler arts. If Lord Goodman's health is not up to the job, I will volunteer for it myself.

15.8.81

*   *   *

105

A Horror of Elites

One recent Friday night I went to the school concert of Kingston St Mary RC Primary School. The programme was rich and varied, including a sizeable chunk of *A Midsummer Night's Dream*, violin and recorder interludes, plays written and acted by the children with a part for every child in the class, songs in English and French. There is not room here to review every item, but the one which impressed me most was a French play written and acted by Class One, aged between ten and eleven. Entitled *Le Château de Falaise* it was a satirical account of an alleged incident from the class's visit to France last year: the master in charge of the expedition, handsome and popular Mr Rodney Parish, is shown ordering a bottle of champagne in a café and becoming distinctly tired and emotional as he consumes it. The plot was not a particularly complicated one, but the French dialogue was funny, the French accents were excellent and the whole production marked by an ebullience which would probably have reminded Mr Kenneth Tynan of the beer cellars he roamed as a lad of five or six in the sad, lost days of the Weimar Republic, if he had been present.

In the event he wasn't, thank God. The Kingston St Mary annual school concert is one of those areas of our national life which do not come under his scrutiny – or, indeed, the scrutiny of many people outside a small corner of West Somerset. But it exists nevertheless, and I have no doubt that many hundreds, if not thousands, of similar events are now taking place around the English countryside, miles away from the great education debate about declining examination standards, declining intellectual vitality, illiterate or half-witted teachers, political indoctrination, uncontrollable vandalism and all the other features of the English system which come up for discussion as soon as anybody presses the button marked 'Education'.

The evening was rounded off, as always, by a little homily to the parents from the school's headmistress, Mrs Jane Tarr. Mrs Tarr is an old friend who has had the charge of all four of my children, and is one of the few living human beings for whom I have a totally unqualified admiration. When she retires in a few years' time, it will be a black day for education. Her school has ninety-two pupils, averaging slightly over thirty to the class. She points out it was physically impossible for her small staff to listen to all the children's reading, and implored parents to take their children through it. If possible she said – as, indeed, she has said every year for as long as I can remember – parents should read to their children, but above all they should talk to them, since this is the only way children learn a reasonable vocabulary. Children, she pointed out, spend one-ninth of their time at school, eight-ninths at home.

Of course, when these bright, happy children I saw gabbling to each other in French leave her care, most of them will go into the newly comprehensivised Somerset machine, and no doubt many of them will emerge as the listless, wet, ignorant, silent and incurious welfare fodder we see hanging around our university campuses, usually sucking their thumbs and reading *Beano* or puzzling over *Socialist Worker*. My reason for drawing attention to the Kingston St Mary school concert is to point out that areas of vitality survive even in the present system and there is no need to accept that what we are witnessing in education is the result of some irreversible biological decline of the Anglo-Saxon races.

Nor, when we reflect on Mrs Tarr's interesting statistic, that schoolchildren at day schools spend one-ninth of their time at school, eight-ninths at home, can we honestly decide that the degeneration of our young people into these shuffling, inarticulate oafs (who seem amazed by any suggestion that they may be capable of talking) has been achieved by left-wing infiltrators into the teaching profession. Schools simply can't have that degree of influence over their pupils. It is one of the disadvantages of television that it does not encourage anyone (apart from a few rare and beautiful spirits) to talk back to it. It turns life into a spectator entertainment, something to be gaped at wordlessly between mouthfuls of peppermint-flavoured potato crisps. But television is not peculiar to England. Other countries do not suffer from speechless goofy people – in France the generation of eighteen-to-twenty-five-year-olds strikes me as being particularly voluble – and I do not think that television can be blamed for this distressing phenomenon.

In fact, I am afraid that at least part of the true explanation may be painfully boring. If goofiness generally sets in, as I believe it does, around the age of eighteen, is confined to particular sections of society (I am not talking about the ageless and inalienable goofiness of the working class as compared to those of greater intellectual potential) and most particularly to students, is more prevalent in England, America and Scandinavia than anywhere else and is especially noticeable among children of the better-off, then the explanation which emerges may be one of blinding banality – cannabis.

If I am right, then there is comfort in the thought that goofiness is a temporary phenomenon and one which flows at any rate to a certain extent from the operation of free choice. But its effect, as I may have hinted, is to proletarianise large sections of the middle class (and the intellectual cream of the working class) by making them appear more stupid than they need appear.

The arguments of the anti-élitists, as put forward by the education correspondent of the *New Statesman*, Mr Peter Wilby, for instance, are so weak that they would not occupy the mind of an intelligent person for a moment if it were not apparent that anti-élitism is going to prevail within the state system. But it is not going to prevail as the result of Mr Wilby's arguments. They should be seen as a *post hoc* justification, or a desperate last attempt by Hampstead to jump on the proletarian bandwagon. The left has always divided into its educated and proletarian wings. So long as the voice of the educated left-wingers was heard, the Labour Party tradition of both self-education and WEA lectures survived. Since then, the proletarian wing has quite simply come out on top. Education no longer brings more money or more respect in a society where lorry-drivers, dockers or earth-shifters can earn twice or three times as much as teachers or junior doctors. The long-smouldering resentment of the working class against education and everything it stands for has now broken out into hatred and contempt at a time when the working class calls the tune in national affairs.

And that, I am convinced, is the reason for our present situation. The crowning proof that I am right seems to me that the *New Statesman*, which should, above all, be the voice of the educated left, has joined the proletarian camp, or is pathetically trying to do so with its talk of 'rigid and arbitrary divisions between the able and the less able' ... 'educational backwoodsmen who ... propagate atavistic slogans such as "academic standards"' who must be told 'firmly and finally that schools are not for the production of élites'.

The emptiness of this rhetoric is demonstrated by the simple fact that education is no longer profitable. What has happened is that the working class has taken over and in its arrogance decreed that there should be no more education. Which is not, I should have thought, a matter for re-joicing among educated people.

17.7.76

*　　　*　　　*

Disadvantaged Children

At a time of year when many of us – or many of those who are not already too old to have children at school – are gloomily awaiting their children's school reports, it is as well to remind ourselves that there are many reasons why children do badly in exams. Idleness, stupidity, bloody-mindedness, bad teaching or lack of *rapport* with a particular teacher are only the most obvious. Others might be ill-health or lack of opportunity to study at home. Nobody can seriously doubt that the child coming from a crowded, non-academic home is at a disadvantage where homework is concerned. Indeed, this amazing insight has just been confirmed in a long and expensive survey sponsored jointly by the Department of Health and Social Security, the Home Office and the Bernard Van Leer Foundation. Goodness knows how much the research cost, but the report is available at £5.90: *Parents and Children in the Inner City* by Harriett Wilson and G. W. Herbert.

Children from the poorest backgrounds (the 'severely disadvantaged') are among the most backward readers, least able to cope with school and most likely to be labelled as maladjusted, we learn. Who would have guessed it? All that remains to be decided is what should be done about this interesting truth, or whether we should simply study it in silent wonder. These same children, who will fare less well than others in any intelligence test which has yet been devised, will tend to marry into the same level of attainment and breed children of similarly inferior ability unless we – Mrs Wilson, G. W. Herbert and I – can do something about it. Apart from forbidding such people to breed, or enforcing a system of selective breeding whereby those with a particularly low intelligence quotient are forbidden to mate fruitfully with any but those from a particularly high range of intelligence, the problem – if it is a problem – seems to me insoluble. And I rather fear that such personal restrictions, even when imposed for the best reasons, would generate more resentment than the educational handicap they seek to replace. Perhaps there has been a decline in discipline in schools, but the threat of castration as a punishment for bad exam results strikes me as taking reaction too far.

Mrs Wilson and G. W. Herbert, however, are in no doubt, 'Equality of opportunity is one of the basic principles of the democratic state. To make this a reality, it is essential to eliminate poverty,' they say. Poverty, they explain, 'arises in a social system in which low wages, inadequate welfare provisions, a chronic shortage of housing and unemployment are allowed to exist.'

So all we have to do is abolish low wages, increase welfare provisions, build more houses and give everybody a job, whether he wants it or not, and *then*, perhaps, these disadvantaged kiddies will start doing better in their exams. I wonder if they are right. Poor housing conditions are, after all, only one of the many possible reasons why schoolchildren do badly. My elder son, whose housing conditions are really not to blame, does very badly indeed in almost any exam he is set. I am not, of course, denying that there may be many excellent reasons for introducing all these social reforms, but I wonder whether education is one of them – whether the same people who did badly in exams when they were poor might not do just as badly after poverty had been abolished. The underlying question is how Mrs Wilson and G. W. Herbert can be certain such people are stupid and inadequate because they are poor, rather than being poor because they are stupid and inadequate, as one might otherwise suppose. If the second explanation is the truer one, then the only solution

109

must be to take children away from their parents and swap them with children from a better background, or put all children in identically mixed state nurseries with no streaming for natural ability. Then we might have achieved the ideal of absolute equality of opportunity, but without much gain, I would have thought, in the sum of human happiness.

18.3.78

*　　*　　*

8

WAR OF WORDS - THE PRESS

Cardinal Hume and Sexy Sue

Journalists living under threat of a libel action are sometimes said to be obsessed by the plaintiff who threatens them in this way – people suggested that Richard Ingrams became unhealthily absorbed in the character and personal failings of Sir James Goldsmith when that ambitious grocery merchant was trying to have him jailed for criminal libel, although I never noticed it. But if there is any such tendency, it has a simple explanation, which may not be fully appreciated by those who employ their firm's solicitors to send out writs to unfortunate journalists. It is that the defence of even the most trivial or absurd writ involves an enormous amount of work: evidence must be taken of a wide-ranging nature about the character, standing and personal background of the plaintiff and his business; inquiries must be initiated, interviews conducted, affidavits solicited. As the result of Mr Bernard Shrimsley's[1] writ, I found myself, at the request of my solicitors, spending Easter weekend, when others were gambolling on tennis courts or croquet lawns, or posing for photographs on Brighton beach, poring over back numbers of the *News of the World* in order to cut out those passages which seemed best to illustrate its combination of ordinary salacity and prurience with occasional bursts of extraordinary Mrs Grundyish sanctimoniousness.

This was the formula which endeared it so well to Britain of the late Forties and early Fifties, when its circulation touched eight and a half million. One of the few encouraging aspects of modern Britain is how its circulation has plummeted since then, until after five years of my tor-

1. *News of the World* editor.

mentor's editorship it now stands at little over four and a half million. Later ABC figures published in January show a huge loss of 238,478 copies (or 643,860 'readers') in the six month period ended December 1979.

All of which is most heartening. If Shrimsley can keep it up, perhaps Mr Murdoch's dirty bottom will begin to itch (which is the original meaning of the word 'prurient'). But the sad result of my having spent the weekend poring over backnumbers is that I could write about nothing else, even if I wanted to. My head is totally full of Shrimsley filth and Shrimsley sanctimoniousness: Roddy's brother tells all ... My seven lovers in one week, my two debs in one bed ... Night of Terrors for a Naked Civil Servant ... Massage Girl's Dog Chewed Up his Underpants ... life and loves of Jean Shrimpton ... the Cops Made Me Strip, says Girl ...'I will beat the Flying Pickets' by Rt Hon James Prior ... The Sleeping Wife and the Stranger in her Bed ... Lolitas paid in Sweets ... Len Murray: 'Yet I believe that Britain can have a good future' ... The Head who Canes Tiny Tots ... the Hot Blood of an Ice Cream salesman ... on facing pages, Dr David Owen: 'The Way Out Left cannot be Right for Labour' and topless Celie: Girls Beware the Beastly Bogart of Bondage ... Confessions of Tracy Reed: 'His Highness the Aga Khan was my first Real Lover, But it was "Edward VIII" who made me Pregnant' ... We expose the shocking Truth about the G.A.Y.M.C.A. (*News of the World* reporters provoke five homosexual pick-ups) ... What Charles needs is a Proper Job by Paul Johnson ... Cheeky Confessions of the Wedding Photographers: 'There's no way you can walk out of a wedding these days without at least one girl lined up' (three photographers claim to have slept with brides afterwards) ... Secret of Girls Who Don't Love Men ... Our Own Olympic Games Orgies by Model Della ... Frantic Antics of Juicy Jackie and Sexy Sue ...

But nothing, surely, in the *News of the World*'s 77-year history, can beat the special Easter Number of 'Britain's Favourite Sunday Paper (the Big One)'. Christ's Resurrection was greeted by a Special Easter Message from Cardinal Hume: 'For a surprising number of people Easter still gives meaning and purpose to life.' Why, yes. Spread across some 17 columns on pages four and five is the Amazing True-Life Horror of TV Dancer: When a Witch Joined them in Bed.

'Christianity is not a political manifesto, but it does offer people inspiration for political action,' writes the Cardinal, explaining as the basis for his social gospel; 'we want to build a world fit for human beings to live in.' Of course. That explains the newspaper's main lead story on dole scroungers. 'Colour does not count, nor class, nor sex, nor talent, nor culture.' On the previous page, we had learned of two teenage Girls at Mercy of Beast with Whip; A Nigerian Beast had threatened them with a rawhide whip before raping them. 'We live comfortably in a world where 800 million are destitute and 2,000 million are poor', drones the Cardinal. On the page facing him, Middlesex prison officers complain about having to give English lessons to illegal immigrants.

After quoting 'Christ's words' that 'man does not live by bread alone' (Shrimsley should have been able to correct him there – Christ was merely quoting from Deuteronomy, of course. But I expect Shrimsley was too busy with My Love by a Runaway Churchman on page six, or a 'bad case of gang bang' on page nine) the saintly leader of Britain's five million Catholics reaches various conclusions:

'Economic commonsense demands partnership not cut-throat competition. Cooperation not rivalry. Pooling of resources, not frittering them away ...

'Christianity then sets before us a programme for action: to make a society fit for the children of God.

'No discrimination, no exploitation, no injustice. A society where the strong help the weak, where cooperation, not confrontation, is the keynote.

'It is here that economic commonsense and religious vision can meet and join hands.'

Well, possibly, if this good, unworldly man is talking about the *News of the World*. Perhaps he feels that his gag about 'cooperation, not confrontation' comes from the New Testament, too, but I think I recognise a quotation from the last Labour manifesto but two. Never mind. It does not matter that his economics are nonsense and his theology suspect. The important thing is that the whole mucky formula – of boring, sanctimonious rubbish from elderly clergymen and dirty little peeps at the Clippie who Stripped off on a Late-Night Bus – no longer works, and readers are deserting it in droves. Let that be our Easter message of hope and renewal.

12.4.80

*　　*　　*

Copper's Nark

Generally speaking I attribute the extreme unpopularity of the press in Britain to the hypocrisy of the British, their terror of being revealed for what they are. We hide our nasty little secrets behind a huge smokescreen of concern for the privacy of others, for the feelings of innocent wives and children which might be hurt by untoward revelations. We build great defensive ramparts around the absurd proposition that nobody has any business to know anything which does not concern him. Idle purveyors of information have every conceivable motive attributed to them, from the sadistic or merely mercenary to a self-righteous zeal for establishing some principle of 'the public's right to know'. Of course this ludicrous notion can be shot down as easily as the notion of a public right to work, eat, smoke opium or wear inflammable nighties.

The press, as I say, is a thoroughly good thing, adding enormously to the gaiety of the nation and even to its intellectual vitality by feeding it with a constant stream of information – some more or less true, some more or less false – for people to discuss, believe or disbelieve, approve or disapprove and fit into the pattern of their lives. But having said that I believe the press to be a thoroughly good thing, I must obviously qualify the word 'good'. Newspapermen are not like nurses, midwives, ministers of religion or Salvation Army volunteers. They do not provide a public service in the sense that firemen, policemen, even soldiers, provide one. They are not 'good' in the socialist sense of making a selfless contribution to the social structure, only 'good' in the sense that entertainers and candy-floss salesmen are good.

It is when these two ideas of goodness grow confused that I begin to lose my enthusiasm for the press. There are those, of course, who see its role as being more important than the chronicling of events as they seem to unfold, commenting on them and making jokes or indignant noises about them, as seems most appropriate. There are those who feel the press should have an active role in shaping events, influencing political decisions, exposing malfunctions of the administrative process and acting as a general coppers' nark. Nobody, so far as I know, has ever *asked* the press to do any of these things. It is a role which it has adopted on its own in a spirit of goody-goodyism, sometimes marred by self-importance and even spite.

The worst offender, apart from the *News of the World* and *Sunday People* which have traditionally worn a mantle of sexual purity to hide their shameful prurience, is undoubtedly the *Sunday Times*. We followed the holy campaign for the extravagant reimbursement of thalidomide victims patiently enough. Perhaps not many people agreed with my feelings that the cause was unworthy, the money an offensive intrusion into private grief. But even if they did agree, they cannot have supposed that great harm was done by the disbursement of these huge sums of money to a small number of people, however unworthy. It had the moral value, perhaps, of an up-market bingo game.

Similarly, I do not suppose that much serious harm will have been done if the *Sunday Times* succeeds in its long campaign to stop the sale of duty-free drink at airports. Some pipsqueak in the travel or aviation department decided this was a bad idea – no doubt he is a teetotaller – and the newspaper has been campaigning ever since, pointing out that bottles of drink in the passengers' cabin constitute a fire hazard, a health risk, a moral outrage. Never mind that aeroplanes must have now flown many billions of miles with never a single accident from this cause. But even if they persuade the British government to stop this harmless and amiable allowance – and mercifully there is little sign of it – they will only have succeeded in making a small nuisance of themselves.

29.1.83

*   *   *

Express Malice

Some time ago I had occasion to buy a copy of the *Daily Express*, something few people do nowadays, because a friend advised me that I was libelled in it. When asked to produce evidence for my theory that the English, as a race, are growing rapidly stupider, as well as less literate, I usually point to the *Sun*, whose intellectual level is so conspicuously lower than the *Mirror*'s of fifteen years ago, or to the *Sunday Times*, whose dismal books page and general intellectual banality may yet send the English back to church, if not to the one surviving literate weekly. Nobody thinks of the *Daily Express* as illustrating the point, partly because it was always nasty, philistine and half-witted, partly because since Mr Victor Matthews bought the newspaper, nobody who might discuss such matters appears to have seen it.

Perhaps it is time we caught up. Matthews has appointed as editor a fellow-Cockney called Derek Jameson whom I used to know slightly as the amiable, oafish pictures editor of the *Sunday Mirror* when I worked for that newspaper, writing captions for bathing beauties. In those days we never exposed a lady's breast, and I was interested to learn in a recent radio programme that Jameson has taken this scruple with him to the *Express*. The listening millions heard his solemn pledge: 'Us four oz Oim conncerned, ve *Dighly Express* will never carry nippoos'. (*As far as I am concerned, the* Daily Express *will never carry nipples.*)

Where on earth, one might ask in that case, *does* the *Express* think it is going? It is a crude and tasteless thing to mock a man for his accent unless it is upper-class, but to ignore Jameson's cockney would be more insulting, like ignoring the man who arrives at a party in a false nose. In appointing him, Matthews plainly intended to make a statement about something or other, whether about the future role of the *Express* or the new role of the Cockney in the modern world. Now it falls on us to unravel what the pair of them are trying to say.

On Monday 23 October 1978, the day of which we treat, the banner headline across the top of the *Daily Express* reads: TODAY: MY KINGDOM FOR LOVE. Edward and Mrs Simpson. ALL THIS WEEK THE STORY THAT ROCKED BRITAIN STARTING ON PAGE 28. The East End of London, of course, is famous for its devotion to the Royal Family, so I suppose a few senile Cockneys might be expected to read on; but if they turned to page 28, they would have found it entirely taken up with the day's TV programmes.

Eventually, on page 23, the *Express*'s aged readers may have found the Royal Romance retold yet again, this time in unmistakable pastiche of Sylvie Krin:

'When Lady Furness arrived at Fort Belvedere that Friday she found Mrs Simpson already having tea with the Prince ... Mrs Simpson, sitting with the teapot beside her in the position of "mother", was saying ... "And you, Sir? Another cup of your lovely English Tea? With milk, but I'll not give you any sugar, it's bad for you".'

Finally, on Lord Moyne's yacht, we reach the long-awaited leg-over situation:

'One night as they walked hand in hand along the deck and a song faded behind them under the sounds of the sea and the night breeze ... she shivered and let go his hand ... "I must go to my cabin" ...

' "Shall you be coming out again, later on?"

' "Not tonight, Sir." She kept her voice cool. She curtsied lightly, but slowly enough to leave some meaning in the action ...'

Is this ludicrous publication seriously to be called a newspaper? The question arose in its most poignant form when I saw the libel, glowing like stacks of £5 notes on a gaming table, from the William Hickey page: '*Auberon confesses*. He ignored a suicide warning sent to him by a woman who later died ...'[1]

No, we must be resolute. After some happy fantasies of spending the money – re-gilding my picture frames, restoring my Burges settle, draining and dredging my lake – I wrote Jameson a personal letter which, as he has not yet had the courtesy to acknowledge, I offer for wider scrutiny:

Derek Jameson, Esq.,
Editor,
The Daily Express,
Fleet Street,
London, EC4   24th October, 1978

WITHOUT PREJUDICE

Dear Sid,

I would not expect you to have much success in trying to follow a *Spectator* article, but it might have been prudent to employ a lawyer with greater powers of concentration before lifting a story from *Spectator* of 21st October, 1978, for your Hickey column of 23rd October, 1978: 'Auberon Confesses.'

This starts 'Writer and critic Auberon Waugh, son of novelist Evelyn, is

1. For the origin of this, see *Our Sacred Duty*, p. 219.

making the astonishing confession that he ignored a woman who wrote to him threatening to kill herself. Now the woman is dead.'

As anyone who read the *Spectator* article will know, there was no threat contained in the woman's card. She merely stated her intention of killing herself next day. As I did not open the parcel until nine days later, the moment was long since past and the only logical reason for pursuing an enquiry would have been to satisfy vulgar curiosity. After considerable thought I decided against this course of action and wrote the letter reproduced in full in *Spectator* but not, of course, in Hickey.

Your report omits to mention this vital fact, that I knew of her intention only when it was too late to do anything about it. Instead it creates the deliberate impression that I callously turned my back and ignored her 'threats' while the issue was still in doubt. Perhaps in your world it is perfectly acceptable to accuse someone of murder by neglect but the *Daily Express* lawyers, if you still employ any, may suggest that different standards apply elsewhere.

When your reporter, who said he was called 'John Roberts', telephoned I warned him of the danger of trying to compress a complicated and rather sensitive argument into a lurid gossip paragraph. He chirpily replied that he doubted whether this consideration would influence his superiors. In recklessly ignoring this warning, you also printed an account of my conversation with Roberts which is exactly opposite of what I said:

> 'Of course the mystery woman was not a "totally strange woman" to Waugh, as he says in his confession in the small circulation Spectator magazine.
> 'Yesterday he told me: "Frankly I know she has children. That is why I cannot reveal her name".'

If you ask Roberts to play you his tape of the conversation you will find I explain at great length how I know absolutely nothing about the woman beyond what is in the *Spectator*, but I was not prepared to reveal her name *in case* she had children.

Yet this false allegation – that I deliberately misled *Spectator* readers on a vital point – is Mr Roberts's only substantive addition to the story which he incompetently lifted from the *Spectator*. He also adds the usual gratuitous pieces of misinformation – that I will be forty next month, that I have written over fifty books – which are what pass for news nowadays, I suppose, on the *Express*. One day you might teach him how to use the standard reference books.

From my experience of the libel law (possibly not so extensive as your own), I should judge the gravity and recklessness of the main libel to be worth a minimum £5,000 in out of court settlement and any sum you care to name after litigation. The secondary libel – alleging deception of my readers – is of value only in establishing malice.

You may have read that I have a principled objection to suing for libel – even where such a rich and unworthy newspaper as yours is concerned. Alas, this is true although I am sorely tempted on this occasion. The injury is deliberate, damages are tax free. But I give you due warning, I propose to make various utterances on this matter in the course of the next few weeks and months which

116

may well include remarks on the subject of your personal habits and fitness for the job of Editor. If these remarks should seem in your judgment to exceed the proper limits of fair comment or good taste, please bear in mind that I am reserving my position over this malicious and unscrupulous attack on my character.

Yours ever,
Bron

Next week (hopefully): the story of Jacqueline – whatever happened to the first Mrs Jameson? The searing account of a marriage that failed; Partners with Pauline – the true-life romance of Sid and his second wife, from languishing looks to leg-over; A Mother Remembers: Mrs Elsie Jameson looks back on struggles with Sid – Part One, nappy rash. All in next week's star-studded *Spectator*. The voice of Britain.

4.11.78

*   *   *

Laughing Stock of the World

In the past fourteen years, when I have been following libel cases, I can only think of three which have come to court and ended with anything which might be described as a victory for the defendants: *Dering v Uris* (the concentration camp doctor case) of 1964, which ended with contemptuous damages of a halfpenny; *Brooke* (the Spanking Colonel) *v People*, which ended with nominal damages of £1, as I remember; and a strange case called *Gayre of Nigg v Sunday Times* which didn't cause much stir and where the defence, I imagine, was one of fair comment. No doubt there have been others but very, very few compared with the list of successful plaintiffs from Liberace to Telly Savalas or the even longer list of would-be plaintiffs who have been bought off with large settlements. One does not wish to touch any murky, demagogic chord of xenophobia, of course, but when English writers writing in England for an English readership can't even defame foreign politicians and deposed potentates like Dom Mintoff and Milton Obote (who live abroad) without risking huge compensation, then it is plain that England's press laws have become the laughing stock of the world.

In an unseemly exchange which took place on the correspondence page of the *New Review* a few years ago, the editor of the *Sunday Times* accused me of advocating a Licence for Liars, and in a sense, although I shrink from his lurid, alliterative English, he is perfectly right. What neither he nor any of the deferential press establishment seems able to grasp is that freedom to lie imposes its own restraints. A disreputable journalist writing in a disreputable newspaper will simply not be believed.

117

It would seem a perfectly reasonable defence – at any rate in mitigation – for the editor to plead that his newspaper is so disreputable and so rubbishy that nobody could possibly believe it; or, if someone was so stupid as to believe it, he would almost certainly have forgotten it within the hour. Unfortunately, this defence does not exist, and it is only within a system of imposed restraints, where all newspapers are supposed to be equally reliable, that liars cause damage.

In Italy and the United States, where laws of libel are much laxer, newspapers impose their own ethical standards or lack of them. But it is a characteristic of the caged budgerigar that it cannot understand the idea of freedom, and shrinks from it. The sadness is that these pretty captive preening birds should present themselves as our leaders.

18.11.78

*   *   *

The Real Censors

David English, the editor of the *Daily Mail*, has no matrimonial diffi-culties; he has never had a homosexual experience and has no lesbianism in the family. What a dull dog he must be. Never mind. A boyish forty-five, he still has time to catch up. It would be a sad day when every public post was filled by people with these negative qualifications. David English's recreations are listed as reading, skiing and boating. Ugh! His namesake Michael English, the paralytically dull Labour MP for Notting-ham (West), gives his recreations as 'reading history and the more usual pleasures of the majority of bachelors'.

Am I being particularly dirty-minded in seeing a sexual innuendo there? What *are* the more usual pleasures of the majority of bachelors? Not masturbation, I hope, or we must begin to entertain grave fears for Mr English's eyesight as he approaches the age of forty-six. This might impair his efficiency as an MP, and bring his recreations into the area of legitimate public interest, as opposed to the area of vulgar curiosity which he was presumably catering for when he listed them for *Who's Who* in the first place. Still, I suppose that for as long as he can still pursue his other solitary pleasure, of reading history, we must not worry. *Le vice anglais* surely consists in worrying too much about these legitimate areas of public interest.

Any discussion of rights of privacy is bound to be riddled with double-think or half-truth or both. I do not see that there is any respect-able medium between the two extreme positions – that everyone's private life should be protected from vulgar curiosity, on the one hand, and on the other the doctrine, that anyone who enters public life forfeits his or her privacy. Even Dempster's Law allows a certain amount of fudging on the point of who is engaged in public life. Politicians and show business folk, of course. Newspaper proprietors? Yes, certainly. Editors? I rather think so. But journalists – well, journalists are a little different, are they not? Quite apart from the possibility that it may be a sin against the Holy Ghost to reveal details of journalists' private lives, there is the important consideration that their work is of national importance, it is essential that they should be held in respect ...

But however much one may laugh at the more obvious contortions of a crooked conscience and however much one may try to avoid them oneself an element of hypocrisy undoubtedly survives. Two Sunday colour supplements have approached me in the last twelve months to ask if I would co-operate in a Profile of myself – the *Sunday Times* and the *Observer*. In both cases, after reflection, I declined, suggesting rather grandly that the country has enough to worry about without the unwholesome emotions of envy which might be excited by any inquiry into my personal circumstances. But the truth in both cases was that I felt the deep and, for me, unusual stirrings of a privacy-urge.

Almost anyone, I imagine, can be humiliated by one revelation or another. At a time when so many wives are either insane or obtrusive in some other way, they promise a rich harvest of humiliation for their menfolk. Some undoubtedly deserve it, like the terrible Pierre Trudeau, but the only two recent occasions when I have been shocked or embarrassed by an intrusion of privacy was on television where two women were seen talking about husbands who had by then been removed from danger of harm: Martha Mitchell, on the *Frost Programme*, and Mrs Ewart-Biggs, on BBC Television News. Both women, of course, were co-operating enthusiastically in whatever intrusion occurred. It must have made many husbands wonder if any of them is safe.

In the case which gave rise to recent debate, a female MP called Maureen Colquhoun, who is also a strident supporter of women's liberation movements, had left her husband, set up a lesbian ménage and was sending cards to advertise this new arrangement to her friends. The Press Council decided that the public interest was involved, and obviously the Press Council was right. A speech in favour of women's liberation has quite different validity if one knows it is delivered by a practising lesbian. But it would have been interesting even if the public interest had not been involved – if the lady had been the runaway wife of an unpleasant Tory MP, for instance. It is the crudest hypocrisy to pretend that one reads it only for those elements which are of legitimate public interest. Public interest is as capricious a way of deciding that a story is newsworthy as public curiosity, and so far as natural justice is concerned one might just as well decide that scandalous stories can be printed only if the victim has red hair, or was born under a particular sign of the zodiac.

119

The public surely has a right to be curious, even if it has no absolute right to have its curiosity satisfied. There is no conceivable obligation on anyone to assist in his own humiliation, but exposure is something we must all risk who have anything to hide. Arguments about the ill-effects of such exposure on innocent children are the crassest form of humbug, since such distress is caused by the message, not by the messenger. Whatever anyone says, and however many hairs are split in the definition of public interest, our attitude to a free press depends on whether we feel more threatened or more protected by it. Journalists, politicians and others in the public eye will always feel more threatened, but I don't think the public should allow them to get away with imposing their anxieties on everyone else.

*   *   *

The Morality of *Private Eye*

In the course of my professional duties I suppose I must have attended nearly a score of defended libel actions at one time or another, although only once as a defendant. On the other occasions I was simply an observer. Judged for their entertainment value they are usually a disappintment. The most depressingly predictable feature is that the jury, where there is a jury, invariably returns the wrong verdict, usually guided to it by the judge. But a more bizarre coincidence than this is that in every libel action I can remember the plaintiff's counsel, in winding up his case at the end, has suddenly remembered a few lines from *Othello* and produces them with an air of gravity, rather as if they came from the Sermon on the Mount:

> 'Who steals my purse steals trash . . .
> But he that filches from me my good name
> Robs me of that which not enriches him
> And makes me poor indeed.'

Counsel always pronounces the lines as if he had just discovered them, but I imagine they are to be found in some advocate's handbook of useful quotations. It is a pity that the same handbook does not reveal their source – from the mouth of Iago, the greatest villain in English literature.

Defence Counsel, for some reason, are usually less fluent with their quotations. I have never heard, for instance, any defence barrister quote the much more famous English proverb: sticks and stones may break my bones but words will never harm me. If that ancient piece of common sense were adopted, then the bottom would fall out of the lucrative libel

120

practice which allows lawyers to grow fat on the vanity, greed and vindictiveness of their fellow citizens. The central lie on which our oppressive libel law is based – that an honourable citizen is damaged by malicious and untrue gossip – is exposed every day in the normal intercourse of human society.

An exact measure of this justification for our libel laws – that a person's reputation suffers from defamatory references to him in the press – may be afforded by the case of Mr Jeremy Thorpe. When he faced the electors of North Devon in May 1979, he had not simply been the victim of a disparaging or insinuating article in the press, for which he could have collected tens of thousands of pounds of damage in the normal course of events. He had been formally accused by the Crown of some extremely unpleasant crimes. More than this, every newspaper in the country had given the greatest prominence to the details of these allegations, under privilege, for three full weeks. The actual effect of this onslaught upon his good reputation can be exactly measured: fewer than 5,000 of his Liberal supporters in North Devon switched their votes; 23,358 citizens continued to vote for him regardless. One can argue that in English law and in polite English custom a man is innocent until he has been found guilty in court, but if this is true of solemn indictments by the Crown it must be a hundred times truer of unsupported allegations by a journalist. In the case of many newspapers, it is only the existence of these draconian laws which lend any credibility at all to what they say.

When I am personally assailed – as on the occasion the then editor of the *News of the World*, Mr Bernard 'Slimy' Shrimsley, held me up before his eight million masturbating readers as Rat of the Year, or when his dear little red-faced brother Mr Tony 'Toady' Shrimsley, editor of *Now!* informed his own rapidly shrinking readership that I was a 'liar motivated by malice who does not deserve either to be employed as a journalist or to share the company of decent people' – I confess I rather enjoy it, as any practitioner of the vituperative arts is bound to do. But when I see a fellow-journalist with no apparent axe to grind (beyond, perhaps, his own future anxieties) striking high moral attitudes, criticising the *Eye*'s standards of 'accuracy' or questioning its beneficial influence on the whole fabric of our nation, I must admit I am slightly shocked. To me at any rate, it is rather like seeing Polish or Czech soldiers spitting on their countries' flags.

Obviously, they do not see it that way themselves. The emphasis of these attacks on *Private Eye* has shifted over the years. From original accusations of anti-semitism – if I were a Jew I think I would be intensely irritated by the practice of some fellow-Jews, when attacked, to accuse their detractors of anti-semitism – and insufficient respect for those with homosexual tendencies, the *Eye* is now most frequently accused of sadism and wanton cruelty, usually to small children. In a country which traditionally loathes its children, the suggestion that one cannot attack a man or woman in public life for fear of upsetting their kiddies strikes me as particularly rich.

Finally, there is the accusation of humbug – that anyone who reviles anyone else might necessarily be claiming greater holiness for himself. If this criticism were taken seriously, it would put an end to all invective, all vituperation, all scurrility and most of the fun of human society. Newspapers would emerge as some sort of cross between a charismatic love-in and a MRA public repentance forum.

21.2.81

*   *   *

Goldsmith's Injunction (1)

My reflections on the most suitable Englishman to lead his country out of its present decline were interrupted last week by a telephone call from a firm of solicitors: someone called Mr James Goldsmith (as he then was) proposed to seek a High Court injunction restraining me from any adverse comment about himself or his solicitor and friend, a gentleman called Mr Eric Levine, while they proceeded with a writ for criminal libel against *Private Eye*.

For some time I puzzled over why I should be singled out from the whole field of British journalists as the one most likely to inspire prejudice against Goldsmith and Levine. There are already perfectly adequate laws against such behaviour, and the laws of libel are more than adequate to deal with any defamatory falsehoods I might have had in mind. I am not and never have been an employee of *Private Eye* – it is just one of five newspapers and magazines to which I contribute regular signed articles, and it provides much less than a fifth of my earned income from writing. I do not think I have ever met Goldsmith or written about him, and I am reasonably certain I have never met or written about Levine. Neither suggests that I have ever libelled him.

Yet now I must hire lawyers and sit down to compose an affidavit, or possibly drag myself to London from West Somerset, losing two days' work in the process, to explain why I should be allowed to pass adverse comment on these two people if I choose. It is one of the scandals of our society that only the very rich or the penniless can afford to go to law, unless they are prepared to stake their entire fortune on what may prove no better chance than the toss of a coin.

But I bear Goldsmith no malice on that score. If I were as rich as he, I would probably be seeking injunctions all over the place, against people

I had never met and who had never heard of me, forbidding them from passing adverse comments or annoying me in any way. Although I have no intention of divorcing my poor wife – and it would be a scurvy trick to play on her after so many years of faithful service, etc – I often think it might be fun to institute proceedings from time to time, citing Sir 'Bill' Ryland, Mr Cyril Plant, the Right Honourable Lionel Murray or anybody else who happened to annoy me at the time. Then my wretched victim would have to go to all the trouble of composing affidavits to say that he had never had the pleasure of meeting the lady. But such diversions are restricted to the very rich, and I can't honestly suppose it would be more enjoyable than eating *pâté de foie gras* to the sound of trumpets.

There is a strong temptation not to defend the case at all and let the little fellow have his injunction, if that is what he wants. After all, I have spent the fifteen years as a journalist without once feeling the urge to make adverse comments on Goldsmith or his fat friend, and it should not be too difficult to restrain myself for a little longer. But in the few weeks remaining before the plea for an injunction is heard, I find a strange fretfulness come over me. Hold a cat by the tail, and however happy it may have been standing on that spot before, it will be prepared to pull its tail out by the roots in its anxiety to go somewhere else immediately. Obviously, I must use the weeks of freedom to pass as many adverse comments as I can think of, so long as they are (1) not libellous and (2) unlikely to influence a jury. It is not easy, because I have never met the fellow, as I say, and know practically nothing about him. But I have seen his photograph in the newspapers, and the first thing that needs to be said is that he has a disgustingly ugly face.

Looking at that dreadful face, I can't imagine, personally, what a nice, well-brought-up English girl like Annabel Birley sees there, but it is one of the tragedies of my life that the nicest, cleverest and most attractive women see qualities in other men which I can't see at all. You can't judge a girl by the men she chooses. Perhaps these men are exceptionally good in bed – not a quality to endear them to their own sex, whether it derives from greater agility, staying power, passion, tenderness or simply the possession of a larger organ.

There are those who say that the size doesn't count, and in any case I am not sure that it would be proper to speculate on the size of Goldsmith's organ at the present time. Under normal circumstances, it would be safe to assume he has one and even (on the principle that a cat may look at a king) to speculate about its size, but as soon as a man starts issuing writs for libel he immediately assumes many of the properties of an angel: his body is no longer the weak, farting, nose-picking thing we all recognise as a human body, but emerges in its glorified or resurrected state without spot or blemish.

123

Such speculations might even be held likely to influence a jury in criminal proceedings (the women jurors taking one point of view, perhaps, the men another) and that is something I understandably wish to avoid at all costs. So perhaps I had better confine my adverse comment to the proposition that Sir James Goldsmith has a repulsively ugly face. So, as it happens, has Mr Eric Levine, but these are only expressions of a personal opinion which a jury will be able to judge for themselves, if they think it relevant.

5.6.76

*   *   *

Goldsmith's Injunction (2)

The last time I wrote about Sir James Goldsmith at any length I was inhibited by the fact that he was plaintiff in about sixty-five libel actions. He was also seeking a High Court injunction to restrain me from making adverse comments about himself or his solicitor until the litigation was settled. So I confined myself to commenting that he had a repulsively ugly face, speculating idly about the size of his virile member and experiencing surprise that he should seek an injunction against me, who had neither met nor written about him before.

When the application came to court, Goldsmith employed the unbelievably brilliant Lewis Hawser QC to plead his case. Hawser did not dispute my comment about his client's face and had nothing to add to my tentative speculation about his other parts, but insisted that I had indeed written about him in *Private Eye* on 14 May 1976. He drew my attention to a sentence in which I discussed the famous libel action *Dering v. Uris* (1964 2QB 669): 'Obviously, Dering was ill-advised to bring such a libel action, even in England whose libel laws make it a haven for every sort of crook and pervert in public life.'

Although nobody was named, Mr Hawser felt that the description of 'pervert' must, in the circumstances, be taken to apply to a well-known politician, the description of 'crook' must be taken to apply to his client. I denied this, pointing out that there was no reason to suppose that Sir James was a criminal: that even if he had been one, he would by no means have been the *only* one around: there was also the Kray brothers, the Richardson gang, Mr Stonehouse, the Black Panther, Mr Poulson, the Cambridge Rapist, all of whom were protected at some time by the libel laws. In the course of his brilliant cross examination, Hawser persuaded me to admit that I might easily have been thinking of his client when I wrote the sentence, but I still maintained that I had no reason to suppose Goldsmith was a criminal and that thinking about him was not

124

the same thing as writing about him. Anyway, Hawser lost the case, and Goldsmith did not get his injunction.

31.3.79

*   *   *

9

RELIGION

The Folly of God

Montmaur, Aude

The martyrdom of St Lawrence is celebrated every year in the nearby village of Puginier, of whose parish church he is the patron saint, by dancing in the village square which lasts two days and two nights. On the first evening, a *grillade* is set up selling pieces of Toulouse sausage and other delicacies – possibly because the French seem to need an enormous amount of food to keep them in high spirits, possibly as a reminder of their patron saint, whose story is told them every year by the *curé* at the sung Mass which opens proceedings on the Sunday morning.

St Lawrence, or Lawrence as he then was, was sent to negotiate with some barbarians besieging Rome, as barbarians tended to do in the fourth century. They told him that if he would deliver the treasures of the Church, they would go away. Lawrence went back and collected all the blind, the maimed, the simple and the sick. He brought this collection of unfortunates – who were not, I suppose, fit for military service in any case – and delivered them to the barbarians, saying: 'Here are the chief treasures of my church.'

The barbarians were not all taken with this little joke and proceeded to roast him on a gridiron. When he was half done, he suggested that he should be turned and roasted on the other side. History does not relate what happened to the sickies, blindies and dafties of what might, I suppose, be called the Jolliffe Brigade. One rather dreads to think. But the Church took a favourable view of his initiative and canonised him in due course.

With their patron saint's little jokes in mind, said the *curé*, he wishes to preach a eulogy on the Folly of God. There were those who described these village fètes as foolish affairs, when normal standards of behaviour were allowed to slip. They were certainly somewhat gratuitous, he said.

125

But was not the most gratuitous act of all time God's creation of the world? God had created the world purely to amuse Himself. We were all part of a gigantic *divertissement* or entertainment. At other times and in other places, he said, it was normal to hold a *fête des fous* where simpletons were called in to act out, for a time, the roles of bishop, squire and policeman. But was this not, in a sense, the paradigm of all human society? God, in His wisdom, had even given us a contradictory set of rules by which to live, at one moment telling us that anyone who looks with lust on another woman is damned, at the next that he will almost certainly be forgiven for this understandable lapse. Should not the birth, life and death of Christ also be seen as gratuitous, he asked – sailing rather close to the wind, I thought, on this occasion.

But it did not trouble his congregation. The *curé* of Puginier is famous for miles around for the originality of his sermons and their high intellectual content, no less than for his personal sanctity. There must be worse ways to spend one's life than to amaze the gazing rustics ranged around. Clearly, his sermon was reaching some sort of climax.

'La sagesse des hommes c'est la folie de Dieu,' he proclaimed, and he hoped that they all had a most enjoyable fête.

> And still they gaz'd, and still the wonder grew
> That one small head could carry all he knew.

The reverend gentleman's sermon was directed, as he pointed out, towards the humorous aspect of God's nature. It is a part which tends to be disregarded nowadays, unless humour can be said to embrace the merely cute or twee. Undoubtedly the sculptors and painters of the Middle Ages were more aware of this underlying joke. Of the two great pagan schools of philosophy which have always struggled under the surface of Christian theology, the Stoics – ascetic, puritanical, self-righteous, ultimately elitist – seem to have finally triumphed over the Epicureans, among whose number I would certainly count Aquinas as well as myself and the *curé* of Puginier.

The reason for this may lie in the greater self-righteousness of the ascetics, or it may lie in the fact that this particular interpretation of life's purpose is painfully easy to refute within the conventional arguments of Christian theology. The most usual way to silence those who advance God as a joker is to point to the crucifixion and ask whether that, too, was intended as a joke. It is hard to argue the case for supposing that the crucifixion was, indeed, a gratuitous act of self-amusement without being accused by those of different persuasions of causing scandal or committing blasphemy, which is to play into their hands. If, indeed, the whole thing was intended as a joke, it seems almost certain that it was not a joke which He intended us to share. Far better to take refuge in cryptic utterances, whether before a slow-witted bucolic audience or in a foreign tongue: 'La sagesse des hommes c'est la folie de Dieu.'

At very least these speculations may provide an antidote to some of the ideas going around in ecclesiastical circles. The present disintegration of the Catholic Church does not seem to me so much a relapse into heresy – although one can spot a few heresies here and there – as a descent into feeble-mindedness. From St John's revelation that God is love it has been a very short step to identify 'love' with a state of vacuous euphoria involving an infantile dependence on group stimulation.

At the present time, the only antidote to the infantile 'clap-your-hands-for-Jesus' approach to religion is the sombre invitation contained in some writings by Graham Greene and others to contemplate what is called the darker side of God. The notion that God might have a darker side seems to me a revival of the Gnostic heresy, that mother and father of all heresies which, revived by the Cathars, caused such havoc in 13th century Languedoc. But Gnostics, historically, have tended to choose the left-hand path into Stoicism – ascetic, self-righteous and ultimately élitist – where now we have the *curé* of Puginier, in what I hope may come to be recognised as the key sermon of the decade, inviting his villagers to contemplate the lighter side of God in God the humorist. I may be wrong, but it seems to me that this must lead us back to the Epicurean dispensation of virtue as a means to an end, rather than as an end in itself. As monotheists we may recoil from the hidden dualism of this approach, but ultimately the two sides of God must be seen as one. And to the extent that faith is a product of choice, and choice the product of dialectic, there is little to be gained, really, by inviting people to stand up and clap their hands. That is to take the joke too far.

On the second night of the *fête* they cooked an enormous *cassoulet*, prompting further gloomy thoughts about the likely fate of St Lawrence's Jolliffe Brigade. Long after midnight, a peasant youth whom I know slightly – the nephew of a lady who stuffs geese and ducks for me – tapped my stomach and asked cheekily if I had eaten more than my share of the *cassoulet*, but that was the only social outrage of the evening. I do not think that the Lord of Disorder can have supposed it was a festival held in his honour.

23.8.80

*　　*　　*

Lust within Marriage

Ever since Pope John Paul II was elected – to the rapture of the Poles and the heartfelt relief of all who wish the Catholic Church well – I have been haunted by a terrible fear. One of the new Pope's most engaging tricks, I was told, is to seize a baby from its mother's arms, to fondle it, bless it and throw it 20 feet in the air before catching it and returning it to its mother. This trick always raises a cheer, they said, and I could well understand it. In my childhood I knew many Poles, after a large part of General Anders's army came and settled on an uncle's property in Somerset, and they could all do things like that; one could eat a lighted cigarette and make smoke come out of his ears; another could do unbelievably clever things with a piece of string; others, after Christmas lunch, would balance apples on each other's heads and shoot at them drunkenly with a bow and arrow. Luckily they always missed, but the arrows remained stuck firmly in my uncle's front door for many years as a reminder that there is a Providence which looks after fools, drunks, Poles, and drunken Polish fools most particularly.

My chief anxiety was that the Pope, being neither drunk nor foolish, was tempting Providence: that one day he would let a baby slip and smash itself to smithereens on the hard, cold Roman pavements. That would be the end of his popular image. However jocular the intention behind it, an act of accidental infanticide would simply not marry with the Church's strict teaching on abortion – not to mention contraception – and his Papacy would never be the same.

In the event, he has not dropped a baby. All he did was to make rather a puzzling remark at his general audience, held while an international synod of hishops was debating the whole question of sexual morality. What he said, so far as one can make out, was that the injunction in Matthew v 28 (from the Sermon on the Mount) 'that whosoever looketh on a woman to lust after her hath committed adultery with her already in his heart' should be extended to cover those who look lustfully at their wives.

What he meant is anyone's guess. I always thought that the original injunction was questionable, in that, given the Catholic attitude to sin – that one might as well be hanged for a sheep as for a goat – it amounted to an open invitation to commit adultery. A few weeks ago, there was a learned discussion in *The Times* about some sociological findings which seemed to suggest that although the Catholic population in the country as a whole was something less than a tenth, Catholics accounted for a quarter of the prison population and nearly a half of the registered drug addicts. It culminated in a spectacularly silly letter from a Redemptorial father in Lowestoft: 'Until very recently our church was almost obsessively concrned with theological orthodoxy and almost neurotically preoccupied with the observance of its laws ... It was regarded as a mortal sin to miss Mass, but in very few places was fellowship and community caring fostered. For Catholic religion was (and is?) conceived in too abstract and ideological terms. I am persuaded that a very large part of the answer, not only to delinquency but also to the whole sphere of growth and maturation, is to be found in meeting people's needs at the *human* level. The human need for community and friendship, for example, is just as necessary as theological truths. Fortunately, the Church has become aware of this . . .'

It is in terms of the flight from this new grinning, damp-eyed Christianity that one should study the Pope's suggestion, that a husband who lusts after his own wife is committing adultery in his heart. Pope John Paul has not actually dropped a baby, as I say, but many people seem to be pretending that he has. The suggestion that there is anything faintly disreputable about sexual desire in marriage does not so much run against the current of modern Church teaching as explicitly deny it. In fact the Pope would seem to be going further than St Paul (I Corinthians VII 8-9) and plainly did not intend to be taken literally. For all that, I find the many glosses which have been suggested even less satisfactory than the original statement.

First, the Vatican suggested that the Pope was condemning sadistic or otherwise intemperate sexual appetites in marriage. Lest this offend modern sexual theologians it was later refined to being a condemnation of married rape and wife-beating. But I see no suggestion in the Pope's words that he had married rape in mind, and this is surely not the moment in human history to condemn the ancient practice of wife-beating.

More fashionably – and even less honestly – it has been suggested that the Pope wished to discourage husbands from regarding their wives purely as sex objects. A deliriously enjoyable leader in *The Times* pointed out that sex should not, indeed, be seen as the main purpose of marriage. A prudent husband should also look to the wife's cooking, cleaning, mending, financial endowment, wit, breeding and general affability. All of which may well be true, but it is not what the Pope was saying.

A further explanation occurred to me – nobody else suggested it – that the Pope was condemning the *public* expression of sexual desire between married partners. Most of us have suffered at one time or another from the spectacle of married couples who feel bound to give demonstrations of public spooning, and most will have found it as embarrassing and as offensive to modesty as I do. But while this may be getting closer to the effect of the Pope's message, scrutiny of the text does not really support such as interpretation.

The true explanation, I am convinced, is more encouraging. We must remember that the Pope had just spent several weeks listening to bishops pontificating about the nature of sexual love, something which few, if any, of them know anything about. I am not suggesting that the Pope has any greater experience of it than they, but I suspect that he has seen a little more of the world and is wise enough to know that the current priestly attitude to sex is pernicious rubbish: that it is a joyous sacrament, undertaken as a token of personal commitment symbolising in its highest possible form the individual's commitment to the community in a spirit of fellowship and community caring.

Sex is nothing of the sort. It is an intensely personal thing between two people in which nobody else has a share. The instinct to privacy on these occasions is basic to human nature, and nothing could kill the sex urge more completely than the idea that Father O'Bubblegum, damp-eyed with sentiment, was blessing one's exertions through some misty spiritual windowpane. The invitation to sex, no less between a married couple than between illicit lovers, is an invitation to something intensely private and anti-social, naughty but nice. What St Paul understood and the present Pope understands, but the modern Catholic Church apparently can't accept, is that Father O'Bubblegum has no place in the bedroom. Take away the naughty element in sex, blanket it all with priestly approval, and you will have a generation of impotent delinquents.

18.10.80

*　　*　　*

Self-abasement

I have never read Freud or Jung and certainly don't propose to do so now, but clever dicks generally try to explain the power urge in terms of sexual supremacy, proof of virility, compensation for sexual inadequacy and all the rest of it. Obviously there is an element of sexual display in some forms of competition, or intelligent people would never have accepted this as an explanation for the power urge, but I am convinced it is not the only or even the major explanation for it. Above all, it does not explain the most fascinating phenomenon of all, which is that, as power seekers organise themselves to exert power, other and larger sections of the community are organising themselves to have it exerted over them. Teachers, sociologists, goodie-goodies generally and above all Catholic priests are now preaching that man must see himself first and foremost as a member of the community, as a cell in the social organism, rather than as an individual answerable directly to God.

An explanation which embraces the psychopathology of the power urge, its ascendancy, and the collapse of resistance to it must be found elsewhere.[1] The only two which occur to me must be expressed either in terms of good and evil as active forces in the world or in terms of the

1. See *The Power Urge*, page 90 and *Wetness of the Middle Classes*, page 47.

collapse of religion and its replacement, as one prefers. To accept my thesis – that in the hot, damp eyes of the Catholic priest facing his congregation and asking them to say after him *We believe*, one can see the first stepping stones by which Pol Pot's Khmer Rouge cross the Mekong River – one will need to start at the beginning.

God occupies that part of the human awareness which is emptied when finite reason instinctively recoils from contemplation of the infinite. At its simplest and barest, this occurs in thinking about death, when the intelligence contemplates its own extinction, or in grief over the death of a loved one. By extension, this area of awareness can be activated in any moment of perplexity, or by an operation of the will at any time, when it may be applied to matters which have nothing to do with death or eternity – the ordinary preoccupations of everyday life and human society. I do not propose to tackle the gigantic question of whether God has an external existence, intelligence or will, or whether He exists only in this perception of Him, because that is not relevant to my thesis. Faith may be a supernatural gift of God, but its first manifestation in human awareness is as an act of choice or the will in response to the urgings of Hope. We recoil in dismay from the infinite, from the prospect of eternity, and Hope leads us to Faith. Charity emerges, in this non-sacramental view of things, as the product of Faith and Hope. Charity may exist in somewhat perverse violation of the religious instinct, but it is of religion that I treat.

Man's relationship to God is therefore an intensely private affair, the most intimate and personal of all his relationships. The purpose of organised religion – church services, hymn singing, sacraments – is to help him develop that relationship. It is not – as primary, secondary or any other purpose – to give him a sense of belonging, to help him make friends, or to turn him into a useful member of the community. Its purpose, and the whole reason it was ever called into existence, is to reassure him, through his relationships with God, (even if God exists only in his mind) of his individual identity, his individual dignity.

In other words, the purpose of religion is exactly the opposite to that of political education aimed at teaching man to see himself as part of a bigger human society, of human history and social development. This notion is the one which can replace religious belief, or be forced into that area of human understanding which God has traditionally occupied. Religious humility is exactly the opposite of socialist humility, because it teaches that man is infinitely grander and more important, in the perspective of human history. Charity is a by-product of that awareness, but never its starting point.

But for socialism, or any other anti-religion, to triumph over religion it must first destroy that essential perception of individual dignity. It must emphasise man's role as a member of the community, make him obedient to the community's requirements, make him, in fact, amenable to the power urges of the few whose instincts are to lead and to exert power.

The essence of the Creed, and indeed of all religious observance, is contained in its first two words, 'I believe'. Never mind what you believe. Belief is an acutely personal affair, whether or not it is shared with those standing around. By shifting the whole basis of the liturgy from personal to communal activity, the Church is destroying the essential basis of religion. Worse than that, it is preparing the ground for the triumph of anti-religion. Beside the psychopathology of the power urge – or evil, to give it its old-fashioned name – we must examine the parallel psychopathology of self-abasement which a modern interpretation of the Christian religion certainly identifies with good. Look at them both how I will, I cannot escape the impression that they are working towards the same end.

27.10.79

*　　*　　*

Religion on Channel 4

There was something sweetly babyish in Channel 4's decision to use the evening of the Fifth Sunday in Lent, otherwise known as Passion Sunday, to broadcast the first of a series of three programmes questioning the historical authenticity of the New Testament. We are told that subsequent programmes, to be broadcast, no doubt, on Palm Sunday and Easter Day, will question whether Christ even existed.

Twenty years ago, when the white heat of technologial revolution was all the craze, such a suggestion might have been thought rather daring, even created a bit of a stir. In those days it was sincerely believed that modern 'experts' under the vague direction of the *Sunday Times* Insight Team would come up with something to prove not only that Christ never existed but that He was a homosexual drug-pusher of hallucinogenic mushrooms whose followers adopted the Cross as a quasi-phallic badge to proclaim their sexual orientation.

Since then, belief in technology has taken a few knocks. Christianity – or at any rate a form of it – is the new craze. With all its horses and all its men, technology has not even been able to prove the Turin Shroud a fake, but that is not the real reason for its failure as an alternative religion. Any day now some particularly fiendish geiger-counter or equivalent gadget may start authenticating the various Holy Foreskins and gallons of Virgins' Milk which sensitive, modern-minded parish priests have been tending to hide in their broom cupboards. Nevertheless it is irrelevant to my argument. Technology's failure as an alternative quasi-religious faith came about because it failed to satisfy religious hunger in three of its most important manifestations – the atavistic, the eschatological and the charismatic.

While the *Spectator*'s exciting new breed of younger reader looks up those words, I will observe that Channel 4 seems to have taken over from the old *Sunday Times* (which few, if any of them, will remember) in its relentless pushing of ideas which were considered novel or daring 20 years ago. The Channel's motives, on this occasion, are easy to understand; nor are they particularly to be despised. Nobody who, like me, is prepared to disregard the present fad for joyous or born-again religion can deny that the collapse of traditional Christianity has left behind it an appalling sense of confusion. Various of its more paradoxical tenets are still held to be philosophically respectable – even intellectually and morally axiomatic – long after their supporting structure of religious faith, hope and charity has been removed. Chief among these (to my mind, at any rate) is the Christian conclusion that worldliness is to be despised, poverty has moral value and personal wealth is wrong; on top of this came the earlier confusion which argued that since all men (yes, and women too) are equal in the sight of God, material equality among men (and women) on earth must be the universal goal. From this comes the glib identification of social equality with justice which inspires the entire canon of the *Summa Pilgerica*.

Since the removal of its Christian sub-structure, this piece of rubbish floats around in the post-Christian philosophical vacuum. The only answer to the question of *why* material equality is thought desirable must be that it is self-evidently so, an axiom. It is the piece of post-Christian débris which I happen to find most objectionable, but there are plenty of others. Perhaps the programme planners of Channel 4 were more concerned about the continued application of earlier doctrines on the sanctity of human life to the problem of unborn babies and 'the woman's right to choose'; perhaps they were even more concerned by the residual impact of Christian injunctions against sodomy as one of the four sins 'crying to Heaven for vengeance'. I do not know. But I can well understand the temptation to clear away all this debris by giving Christianity a final knock on the head.

I think they underestimate the scepticism of the audience they have chosen to address. Such wide-eyed gullibility as might, 20 years ago, have attached to the pronouncements of experts, unknown scientists and other technocrats has long since transferred itself back to one or other of the transcendental 'born again' religions. People are only too aware that many of the finest brains of the human race have been investigating the New Testament in all its aspects for the past 1800 years. There is a certain reluctance to believe that the new race of 'experts' is any more intelligent, or that it is going to turn up anything new after all this time. On top of this, I suspect that the new generation shares with Pontius Pilate a certain scepticism about the nature of historical truth. Perceptions vary, memory is fallible, gossip and persuasion intervene. Only the mind of God perceives and retains the whole truth; where our own imperfect perceptions are concerned – and especially in relation to events long lost from living memory – we must accept history as whatever tradition has accepted – history *is* tradition. It can be altered, but the label of truth attaches to it only by virtue of our choice, not by virtue of any property it possesses in its own right.

Channel 4's programme planners also misunderstand the nature of religious belief. Belief in God, or in Christ as a member of the Trinity, is a creative activity involving a conscious exercise of the imagination and the will. It is not a static condition, like being a negro. When I am occasionally asked by a lunatic in the train if I believe in Jesus, I answer 'sometimes'. This is not because I sometimes also disbelieve in Him but because at other times I am reading a book, brooding about Victoria Principal or whatever.

Nor is religion a mathematical proposition which can be proved or disproved within an accepted logical discipline. Religious belief, insofar as it is not inspired by divine agency, must exist as a conscious choice which involved rejecting its alternative, disbelief. People who say that they want to believe in God but cannot are deceiving themselves. Rejection of disbelief is as important a part of the process as acceptance of whatever one has chosen (or been conditioned) to believe. That is why I say it owes its existence to a hunger which may be broken down into three ingredients – the atavistic, the eschatological and the charismatic.

The charismatic – sacramental, or quasi-magical – element is the easiest to supply. You can do it with magic mushrooms, or incense, singing or dancing or just a heightened feeling of fellowship such as the army, the Boy Scout Movement, the new Catholic Church and the National Union of Mineworkers all manage to promote.

The eschatological element caters for anxieties about the disappointments of human life, its brevity and apparent pointlessness. It keeps adherents on the straight and narrow and provides a solace for them in their misfortunes.

The atavistic element is the most mysterious, but I observe that it has always existed in every religion which has lasted longer than a transitory craze. Even Christianity, it must be remembered, was grafted on Judaic roots. For some reason which I do not understand this sense of community with ancestors, of belonging to an ancient tradition, of treading where generations have trod, is an essential part of religion's survival.

The old Christianity died because it lost its charisma. The new Christianity has cultivated its charismatic appeal at some cost to its eschato-logical and to the virtual exclusion of its atavistic functions. Last week the Prayer Book Society revealed how theological colleges have been directed to drop the Book of Common Prayer in preference for the new liturgy, with its flat and banal language: 'We are the Body of Christ. In the one Spirit we were all baptised into one body. Let us then pursue all that makes for peace and builds up our common life.' 'Though we are many, we are one body, because we all share one bread.' I do not think they will share it much longer, after the present craze has subsided.

14.4.84

*   *   *

The Problem of Women

One of the great issues of our time which is seldom, if ever, debated in public is the question of the ordination of women. It might be helpful, I suppose, to voice a few of my doubts in case whoever eventually decides the point reads them and ponders. Can we be sure, for instance, that menstrual strain might not produce intemperate sermons? That the heavy sedation which so many women require permanently nowadays might not interfere with their sacred duties, if only the prescribed fasting? Many who still believe in the supernatural, quasi-magical properties of the sacraments have grave reason to doubt whether women would be effica-cious here. Their doubts derive from Scripture and from the earliest Christian traditions, but even agnostics who have watched women per-form at Wimbledon need not feel there is anything irrational in doubting whether women have that extra zing or whatever is required to turn bread and wine into the body and blood of Christ.

But of course these objections are only rationalisations of an intuitive feeling, what delicately nurtured left-wing thinkers call a gut reaction. The idea of women priests is something which is abhorrent to nature, like the idea of male hairdressers or female dogs in skirts and knickers or a man in a blue suit with brown shoes. I used to think that my reaction was a chivalrous one, prompted by the fear that such delicate and delight-ful creatures might make fools of themselves. Certainly, I never thought it was a misogynistic or even a sexist one in the sense of asserting male superiority, since I have never, even in my most religious moments, supposed that the supernatural powers of the priesthood conferred any superiority greater than a certain nuisance value on a man. Now, having read Marina Warner's fascinating study of the myth and the cult of the Virgin Mary, *Alone of all her Sex* I am not so sure.

It all depends, of course, on what you mean by misogyny. To Miss

135

Warner, I suspect, anything which tends to consign women to their traditional feminine role – child-bearers, comforters, upholders of kindness, gentleness, pity in human relations – is evidence of deep misogyny. This I hasten to add, is not because she finds such a role personally uncongenial, but because she feels it may be a subordinate one, and is certainly an unjustly imposed one.

The argument about sexual equality has always puzzled me, but since it is central to Miss Warner's thesis on the Virgin Mary and to my own feelings about the ordination of women, I suppose we had better let it all hang out on this occasion. I have never understood how equality can be said to apply, except in the most superficial sense, to any human relationship. By this I do not mean that we are all graded in some divinely-imposed pecking order, but that our essential differences make talk of equality meaningless. Study of the sexes is bound to identify the differing characteristics of each, and I cannot see how anything useful is achieved by asserting that chalk is equal to cheese, or should be equal to cheese and must be made equal.

Which brings us back to Miss Warner's rejection of the traditional, feminine role. She sees the myth of the Virgin Mary as an instrument of the Church to impose a particular social order, built around the domestication and subordination of women. She does not see the cult as a palliative, by which women found comfort in the less congenial role which nature had given them within the reproductive order, although she discusses this possibility – her manners throughout are beautiful, and the book is written with an intelligence and charm which are altogether captivating, even on the rare occasions when the blue stocking is allowed to slip and we are given a glimpse of something posing as angry young womanhood underneath. In fact, she makes a very good case for believing that the Church's obstinately held doctrine on contraception is a fierce rearguard attempt to impose this traditional misery at a moment in human development when it is no longer necessary. In any event, she is plainly right when she sees this attempt as doomed to failure.

Where she goes wrong, I think, is in her discussion of the cult's central contradiction – Virgin and Mother, absolute purity and abstinence from sexual relations on the one hand, the virtues of motherhood on the other. At one point she even goes so far as to complain that the twin ideal of virginity and motherhood 'cannot but be disturbing' on the mind of a Catholic girl. It is true that I have never been a Catholic girl, but I am not sure that she is entirely accurate (or even honest) in the account of her own spiritual Aeneid. She claims that the first terrible doubts assailed her with the carnal temptation of puberty: 'I sensed that the problem of human evil was more complex than concupiscence – at least in its narrow sexual definition'.

I doubt the truth of this observation. In fact the twin contradictory ideals enshrined in the cult of the Virgin Mary run very well in harness. At puberty, burgeoning sexuality is channelled into a powerful spiritual impetus.

'Bless me Father for I have sinned. It is one week since my last Confession, Father. Since then I have committed the sin of self-abuse.'

'How often, my son?'

'About fifteen times, Father.'

'Say three Hail Marys for your penance. Now make a good Act of Contrition . . .'

Ten years ago, I might have disapproved of all this as much as Miss Warner does. Now, in middle age, I tend to the view which Miss Warner attributes to her own father (a friend of the reviewer and a most blameless man) that it is a good religion for a girl.

Miss Warner is at her most beguiling when she delicately, almost lovingly, traces the history of the Church's teaching on Mary's perpetual virginity, exposes its lack of support in Scripture:

'The Gospel problems regarding her title to the very name Virgin Mary were and still are a straw before the belief in virgin birth. And my enumeration of the lack of scriptural evidence is not intended to pour an out dated, Protestant scorn on it, but only to show that from the earliest times, the New Testament was out of joint with the embattled desires and ideas of Christians . . .'

Where she is at her weakest is in her analysis of what has happened now. Briefly, at one point, she introduces the Chinese notion of *yin* and *yang*, where *yin* represents the (traditional) feminine qualities of gentleness, mercy, acceptance of suffering, while *yang* represents the (traditional) masculine qualities of strength, justice, self-defence, etc. The Virgin Mary, she argues, represents the *yin* face of the Christian religion, where sinners will be forgiven irrationally through her intercession, where love does not require its pound of flesh. Later, she drops this, and through concentrating on those twin ideals of virginity and motherhood, asserts that the cult of the Virgin Mary will soon be as dead as mutton in an age which consciously rejects both.

What she does not seem to realise, no doubt through neglect of her religious duties, is the extent to which the *yin* principle has now overtaken the entire Church. In other words, so far from stepping down, Mary has eclipsed the three Persons of the Trinity, remodelling them, to the extent that they survive, in her own image. Miss Warner is right to pour scorn on Paul VI's odious and pathetic attempt to re-project the Mother of

137

Christ as a Thoroughly Modern Miriam in 1974. She does not, however, appreciate the full depth of the fatuity involved.

9.10.76

*   *   *

A Thoroughly English Cardinal

'I don't mind your making a noise so long as you don't mind my stopping you', said Cardinal Hume when he was a housemaster at Ampleforth to some boys who were, presumably, making a noise. Twenty years later, he remembers this aphorism so vividly that he has to bring it up in the course of a television interview about his life as demonstrating his approach to discipline, his way with boys, his innate wisdom in earthly matters. If there had been a studio audience present at the interview, one may be sure it would have burst into rapturous applause. The Cardinal had that look on his face of a man who has just said something extraordinarily clever and is expecting applause.

I pondered this canny half-French Scotsman's *bon mot* for some time – he is, after all, the head of my Church in Britain, chosen for the job by Mr William Rees-Mogg on account of his Englishness, warmly supported by that powerful political thinker Mr Hugo Young – and decided that in its wisdom and profound spirituality it was probably beyond my reach. Why, if he did not mind the boys making a noise, should he wish to stop them doing so? What on earth did it *mean?* If the remark was intended to be funny, then it was the humour of the sadistic drill sergeant demonstrating the extent of his power over a squad of recruits, not the humour of a philosopher wrestling with the paradox of authority. Its closest echo is surely the prison warder in the early Peter Sellers film *Two Way Stretch* who says to a prisoner: 'SILENCE when your talking to *me*'.

But the prison warder (played, I think, by Maurice Denham in the 1960 production) was intended as a figure of absurdity, not a deeply spiritual philosopher. Of course I am not denying for a moment that Cardinal Hume is a deeply spiritual man. My point is that he is also a profoundly silly man, that his judgments on earthly affairs – from school discipline to industrial relations, the British Nationality Act to the Brandt Commission – are so silly as scarcely to be worth discussing.

I suspect that he is also a somewhat vain man, but that is beside the point. If he were not so clearly a *good* man he would not be such a public menace. But Mr Rees-Mogg was surely right in choosing him for the job in the sense that this sort of cocksure silliness has become a quintessentially English characteristic. Anything said or written in public which is intended to receive, or actually receives general assent is almost invariably

138

silly. We are led by silliness and silliness has become the consensus. Perhaps there is something deeply spiritual, even holy, in it all. As St Paul wrote (1 Cor I 21-24) 'It pleased God by his foolishness of preaching to save them that believed ... We preach Christ crucified, unto the Jews a stumbling block, and unto the Greeks foolishness ... Because the foolishness of God is wiser than men.' Again, in 11 Cor III 18-19: 'Let no man deceive himself. If any man among you seemeth to be wise in this world, let him become a fool, that he may be wise. For the wisdom of this world is foolishness with God.'

And so we have become a nation of damp-eyed, foolish, bearded, holy men, it may be thought. Certainly, one sees enough of them around. But before we settle into a happy, self-congratulatory reverie to reflect how pleasing we must be in the sight of God, it might be prudent to take a glance from time to time at those in our midst who are neither damp-eyed nor foolish nor bearded nor noticeably holy and see how they are prospering in this atmosphere of fatuous, all-embracing benevolence. I refer, in particular, to those like Mr Len Murray, Mr Moss Evans, Mr Clive Jenkins, Mr Alan Fisher, Mr A. Scargill and Mr L. Daly whose difficult task it is to harness this amiable undirected fatuousness into a concrete programme, and also to those like Mr Benn, Mr Hattersley, Mr Shore and Mr Silkin, not to mention Messrs Roy Jenkins, Rodgers, Owens and Williams, who hope to harness it to their own self-advancement.

A distressing aspect of the contemporary English silliness – at any rate for those of conservative inclinations – is the way it seems to lean left. Perhaps there is a logical reason for this, that socialism can now be seen by anyone who comes to look at it as an essentially silly creed, producing nothing but poverty and wretchedness, so all the abundant silliness in our society tends to lope and gambol towards socialism as the nearest refuge from the unwelcome truths or 'harsh realities' of the world as God made it. In other circumstances one would rejoice to hear that the Church of England has halted the decline in its membership and now seems set for a period of steady growth; that Cardinal Hume, according to an amanuensis of his on the programme has succeeded in 'making it fun to be a Catholic.' He should speak for himself. To many cradle-Catholics it has become a pain in the back-side.

7.3.81

*   *   *

Is Trifle Sufficient?

'Our heroic ages produce poets,' said a *Daily Telegraph* leader mourning the death of John Betjeman. 'Ours is an unheroic age, so we need poets

139

to match. We could have done so much worse than BETJEMAN, who loved the human race and the built forms in which it expressed its personality . . .

'No poet since KIPLING has done anything like so much to shape our thoughtways. He has gone, but something of him remains in us, as we view our surroundings with his eyes. Moreover, thanks to him, we now think of "Victorian" not as an epithet but as a heritage.'

Oh dear. It is rather a dirty trick, I suppose, to resurrect this surprisingly boorish and illiterate leader - no doubt intended well, quite possibly dashed off late at night under pressure of a deadline - to illustrate the inadequacy of our unheroic age to mark the passing of one of its very few heroes - certainly its only knight with the slightest claim to have worn shining armour. In France less important writers than Betjeman are given state funerals. Streets, squares, whole new towns are named after them, although this last honour might, perhaps, be inappropriate in Betjeman's case.

> Oh why do people waste their breath
> Inventing dainty names for death?
> We die; that's that; our flesh decays
> Or disappears in other ways.
> But since we're Christians we believe
> That we new bodies will receive.

Betjeman was always dissatisfied with his earthly body. It was never an appropriate vehicle for the exuberance of his emotional passions:

> Little alas to you I mean
> For I am old and bald and green.

Or again:

> My head is bald, my breath is bad
> Unshaven is my chin
> I have not now the joys I had
> When I was young in sin.

A happier age than our own would build a huge marble memorial in the baroque taste, showing his resurrected body, all flaxen curls and cherubic wings, ascending to heaven from the swamps of Lust, Doubt, Melancholy and Despair:

> O whip the dogs away my Lord
> They make me ill with lust.
> Bend bare knees down to pray, my Lord,
> Teach sulky lips to say, my Lord,
> That flaxen hair is dust.

140

Of all the odd sentiments to be found in the *Daily Telegraph* leader, the oddest is surely in the glib statement that Sir John Betjeman loved the human race. Of all the people I have ever known, I would say that he was the one who detested the human race most completely. He loved its humour, its fantasies, its occasional aspirations towards nobility, but I suspect it was his detestation of the human race in almost every other manifestation which drove him on his desperate quest towards religious certainty, towards the cosy, unquestioning acceptance of a benign God, revealed through stained glass windows, Early English arches and the ringing of church bells, which he supposed to be in the giving of the Church of England. If ever he could have convinced himself of its truth, he would have found that peace which passeth all understanding. But he couldn't, and he didn't.

Throughout his religious poems there runs the theme that none of it may be true. The debate within himself is endless and tortured; one can easily interpret his entire artistic career as the struggle to stifle these doubts and relapse into cosiness. Compare his poem on Christmas (from *A Few Late Chrysanthemums*, 1954) and his earlier poem, 'Before the Anaesthetic' or 'A Real Fright' (from *New Bats in Old Belfries*, 1945) with his hymn of praise for the Church of England, 'Septuagesima' (from *Church Poems*, 1981).

Here is Christmas, as seen in *A Few Late Chrysanthemums* (1954):

> And girls in slacks remember Dad
> And oafish louts remember Mum
> And sleepless children's hearts are glad
> And Christmas-morning bells say "Come!" ...
>
> And is it true? And is it true,
> This most tremendous tale of all,
> Seen in a stained glass window's hue,
> A Baby in an Ox's stall? ...

That, it must be remembered, was written almost a decade after 'A Real Fright'.

> I, breathing for a moment, see
> Death wing himself away from me
> And think, as on this bed I lie,
> Is it extinction when I die? ...
> St Giles's bells are asking now
> "And hast thou known the Lord, hast thou? ..."
> St Giles's bells they hear me call
> *I never knew the Lord at all.*
> Oh not in me your Saviour dwells

You ancient, rich St Giles's bells.
Illuminated missals – spires –
Wide screens and decorated quires –
All these I loved, and on my knees
I thanked myself for knowing these
And watched the morning sunlight pass
Through richly stained Victorian glass
And in the colour-shafted air
I, kneeling, thought the Lord was there.
Now, lying in the gathering mist
I know *that* Lord did not exist.

Compare this to the deliberate and almost avowed relapse into E. J. Thribb in his later poem, 'Septuagesima':

A somewhat unattractive time
Which hardly lends itself to rhyme,
But still it gives the chance to me
To praise our dear old C of E.
So other churches please forgive
Lines on the Church in which I live,
The Church of England of my birth
The kindest Church to me on earth.

There may be those who like things fully
Argued out and call you "woolly" ...
Well, let them be so, but for me
There's refuge in the C. of E.
And when it comes that I must die
I hope the Vicar's standing by ...
And at that time may I receive
The Grace most firmly to believe
For if the Christian's Faith's untrue
What is the point of me and you?

As we all know, he died in his sleep, at home, and not in any cottage hospital. It would be too much for those of us who loved him if we had to suppose that he died, as he had lived, tormented by the terror of death. On the face of it, he might seem to have recovered completely from his Real Fright, except that I doubt if he ever quite reached that cosy state. Just as his Christianity expressed itself in a fixed determination to be kind to the human race he detested for its meanness, its greed and its cruelty, to show a jolly face to the world when he was at his most melancholy, so I am almost certain he decided to affect a cosy certainty in religion which he was never within miles of feeling.

My purpose in this disquisition is not simply to argue that Betjeman was a good, kind and possibly saintly man, but also to suggest that his concerns were of more universal interest than anybody has yet suggested. Far from being a minor poet of local and temporary appeal, a genial light which has unfortunately gone out in the way so many genial lights are liable to do, like dear old Buffy Frobisher, I would suggest that his light may well go on burning with a fiercer brightness as the years go by. I would certainly imagine that his poetry will be being read with pleasure and profit long after the dimmest provincial university has finally cleared its shelves of Eliot, Pound and Auden.

He may have lacked Shakespeare's intellectual rigour and breadth of vision, he may have written nothing to compare with Keats's Odes and may never have attained the benign serenity of Wodehouse, but his place may yet prove to be among the truly greats – and we will be shown the greater fools for not having seen it.

26.5.84

*　　*　　*

PART FOUR

LIBERAL ISSUES

10

THE DARKER SIDE OF LIFE

Some Racist Jokes

'I know a lot of coloured people who don't mind being called niggers or wogs,' said Mr John Kingsley Read, of the Democratic National Party, at his first Old Bailey trial on a charge of inciting racial hatred. The words which he agrees he used at a political meeting in West Ham were these: 'Fellow racialists, fellow Britons, fellow whites, but I have been told that I cannot refer to coloured immigrants, so you will forgive me if I refer to niggers, wogs and coons.'

After explaining that his remarks were intended as a joke, Mr Read claimed that the crowd laughed. Another joke he was alleged to have made concerned the murder of an Asian youth who had been killed a week earlier in Southall: 'One down, one million to go.'

His acquaintance is obviously wider than mine. Try as I might, I can think of no coloured person of my acquaintance who wouldn't mind either of these jokes. Even if I thought they would enter into the spirit of good-natured persiflage, I should judge such pleasantries unwise as being likely to introduce an element of self-consciousness into the relationship by promoting colour-awareness to which so many of even the least sensitive coloured folk in our midst are understandably prone.

I suppose one learns these things by experience. There was a poet at Balliol in my day – nowadays, I believe, he is a Front Bench opposition spokesman in the House of Lords – to whom I frequently made such jokes in my ill-considered youth, but they never went down very well. That was before the Race Relations Act, of course, and undergraduates seemed to enjoy a certain immunity from prosecution for language likely to cause a breach of the peace. At any rate, the Old Bailey jury, which included one coloured person, was unable to agree on the first trial and acquitted him on the second.

In any case, whether Mr Read was trying to be funny or not, it was a rotten joke and I have long been in favour of savage penalties for those who make bad jokes in public. But there is a new development. Perhaps it is the result of the Race Relations Act or of some curious, collective decision produced by the climate of our times but there seems to be growing a sort of code whereby ethnic jokes can only be made by members of the ethnic minority to which they apply. The obvious exception to this rule is the Irish. Any of us can make hurtful, rude and provocative jokes about the Irish to our hearts' content – when the Irish make them they are called Kerryman jokes, referring to a type of Irishman who is even more Irish than those we know and love. Exactly the same jokes are told in New York about Americans of Polish origin, and probably in Australia about English immigrant trade unionists. It would be amusing to assemble a book of Irish, or Kerryman, or Polish, or Pommy jokes which would be sold in all four countries with appropriate alterations. But where Jews, West Indian Indians or coloured Englishmen are concerned, they have cornered the market themselves, as anyone who has read the novels of Philip Roth or Vidia Naipaul must realise.

A few years ago I told a Jewish joke in the *New Statesman* for which I was then working. By some oversight, they printed it. It is quite an old one and will be familiar to many *Spectator* readers – I used it to illustrate a complicated argument about the devaluation of our currency. Anyway, here it is again:

Q. Why are pound notes green?

A. Because the Jews always pick them before they are ripe.

I thought it quite funny but it didn't go down at all well in Hampstead. I don't know how many angry letters, threats and cancellations the poor Editor received at the time, but I still suffer repercussions. On my first day in the health farm where I have taken up residence after Christmas I was approached by a fellow inmate, a nice, intelligent, funny, well-read Jewish girl and asked if I was a member of the National Front. When I denied this, blushing, she asked me if I was sure. It transpired that she works for a Jewish organisation in London and they have a large file on me. Oh dear!

But my objection to Negroes, Jews and other ethnic groups monopolising jokes about themselves goes beyond the natural irritation of a professional joker who finds some of his best lines taken away. I feel there is a very real danger that, left to themselves, they will take the jokes too far. Perhaps I had better explain myself.

People who make jokes about other ethnic groups than their own are restrained in the first place by good manners, then by taste, finally by a judgement of what they can get away with. None of these restraints exist in self-mockery. None of us make jokes about Africans any more, so, left to themselves, they have produced the ultimate anti-African jokester in

146

General Amin. Few people, I fancy, will disagree with me when I say that as anti-Negro jokes go, General Amin goes much too far.

Last week, the Israeli Knesset passed a law making it an offence, punishable by five years in jail and heavy fines, for anyone to offer material benefits to induce another person to change his or her religion. The law was sponsored by Rabbi Y. M. Abramowitz, who in an explanatory note said the measure was designed to curb Christian missionaries, who had offered huge sums of money and other economic benefits 'to ensnare the souls' of the poor. The United Christian Council, which sent telegrams of protest to Mr Begin and other functionaries, has not even received the favour of an acknowledgment. Of course the law would equally forbid material inducements in the conversion of Christians to Judaism (according to *The Times*, 500 Christians are converted to Judaism in Israel every year, a tiny handful goes the other way) but Israel remains the only country of the civilised world which has seen fit to pass a law against its citizens being bribed to change their religion.

I hope I am not an anti-semite and don't think I am one, although it is true I often find myself brooding about the Jews, as many Europeans must after the terrible events of the last war. So I hope it will not be taken as a sign of latent (or even overt) anti-semitic tendencies if I admit, as a Christian of sorts, that the conversion of Judaism to Christianity and to the message of the New Testament strikes me as a worthy, beneficial and possibly salutary exercise. Not everybody will agree, of course, and I mention the matter merely to state my particular set of prejudices in forming the second conclusion, that Mr Begin is taking the Jewish joke too far, just as General Amin has taken the Negro joke in Uganda. Not to put too fine a point on it, the new measure strikes me as a dangerously unpleasant Jewish joke in the worst possible taste.

In fact, his latest move takes us right back to the roots of Christian anti-semitism (although not to the roots of anti-semitism itself, as a study of Exodus will show). The new Knesset law will not only catch modern missionaries who are so foolishly kind as to feed or clothe the poor, it would also, quite unmistakably, have caught Jesus at the feeding of the Five Thousand.

Possibly the only beneficial result of the Nazi experience has been to teach the terrible danger of holding groups of people in contempt or hatred. Nearly two thousand years of hostility between Christians and Jews were washed away in the blood of that horrible episode, and if it also prevents Gentiles from making Jewish jokes, that may seem a small price to pay. My only point is that this deprivation is not without its dangers. It is when such matters are removed from the world of humour and treated with total solemnity that we find ourselves stuck with these unspeakable characters: Hitler, the ultimate German joke; Amin, the ultimate Negro joke; now, perhaps, an ultimate Jewish joke in the nasty and dangerously stupid Mr Begin-it-all-over-again.

14.1.78

*　　*　　*

Towards a British Apartheid

The inspiration behind the Rampton Committee of Inquiry into what is euphemistically called the 'under-achievement' of West Indian pupils in British schools was at best silly, at worst mischievous, so we cannot really complain if the report published last week is outstandingly silly. It might have been worse. No useful purpose could be served by drawing attention to racial differences in academic achievement within a single community. The suggestion that racism is itself to blame for the phenomenon could scarcely in the sublime depths of its fatuousness, be better calculated to feed the racism which it claims to discourage.

However, there is all the difference in the world between saying that certain subjects are best left undiscussed in public – which I honestly believe to be the case here – and allowing other people to discuss them in public foolishly.

Nobody has yet disputed the Committee's central finding, which is that there is an enormous disparity in the level of academic achievement between different ethnic groups, of which the most extreme examples are those of West Indian descent, who come bottom of the list, and those of Asian descent, who come top. Others would appear to come closer to the Asian level, although they have not yet been broken down. What is certain is that the West Indians are stupendously behind the Asians, achieving satisfactory 'O' and 'A' level passes in a ratio of approximately one to six.

That is the central fact which has caused so much agony of mind in the race relations industry. To the question of what we are to make of it and what, if anything, should be done, *The Times* contributed a leader called 'Looking the Facts in the Face'. This is how we were invited to face them: 'Explanations exist to suit every prejudice. . . . The possibility that West Indian children are merely less clever than others is among the simplest and least useful. Intelligence is a cluster of aptitudes and putting a value on them cannot be a wholly objective process. . . .'

I think this means, in English, that intelligence tests are unreliable, but I am not sure. An idle reader might suppose it to mean that intelligence is not a factor in determining academic achievement. Let us proceed: 'Even if there are differences in aptitudes between races, they are so small compared to the variation within each race that they have no significance

148

for the treatment of individuals. The differences discussed here are far too great to be convincingly explained without reference to environmental factors.'

I do not quote this extraordinary string of non-sequiturs simply in order to berate *The Times* under its excitingly gritty new leadership. Presumably this piece was written by one of the newspaper's educational correspondents.

The writer seems to be inhibited by moral considerations from admitting the possibility that Britons of West Indian descent might be a great deal stupider than Britons of Asian descent. Nothing else can explain the bald statement that differences of environment within a group are less marked than differences of intelligence. We are dealing with a group, not with individuals inside it. The problem, if it is a problem, is a group one, not an individual one. Let us approach it from a slightly different angle, that there is nothing repugnant to reason or charity in the notion that one ethnic group might be significantly more intelligent than another. Where identical teaching is offered, and where there is no external handicap like a language barrier (which works against the Asians, in any case) or physical disability like deafness, there can be only two determinants of academic achievement. These are intelligence and application. 'Application' is used to replace the old-fashioned word 'industry', and has itself been replaced in America by the prettier-sounding 'motivation', but they all mean the same thing, and their opposite remains the same: inattention, laziness and bloody-mindedness.

The disparity in academic achievement between these two groups is given as being in the ratio 6:1. It must follow that if their intelligence is equal, the West Indians are six times lazier or less attentive or more bloody-minded than their Asian fellow pupils. I should have thought this proposition an absurdity, but even if it is not – and it has been seized upon by all the environmental determinists in our educational establishment as being the only true one – it is scarcely less humiliating for West Indians than to be told that through no fault of their own they would appear to be academically less intelligent. The course of sanity would be to tell them neither of these things and let them get along as best they can, but that option is no longer available thanks to the busybodies on the Rampton Committee of Inquiry.

So let us examine the suggestion that environmental factors are decisive. The Rampton Report agrees that the physical conditions of both groups, characterised by poverty and overcrowding, are very much the same, although the *Observer* sidestepped this on Sunday by blandly asserting, without a shred of evidence, that successful Asian candidates must come from prosperous East African Asian families. Somebody in the *Observer* really ought to do a little counting to test the likelihood of this assertion. If the physical conditions are roughly similar, as is otherwise generally agreed, then the environmental difference must lie in the spiritual or cultural background.

So perhaps it is true that West Indians are inadequate parents, alternatively neglectful and over-affectionate, over-permissive and violent, as has been suggested. No doubt it is also true that they have a higher proportion of single-parent families but I doubt a higher proportion of night-shift workers vis-à-vis the Asians. This seems to me to be the most insulting explanation of all, but that is not my point. The great question is what, if anything, should be done about it, and this is where the real mischief lies.

The *Observer* demands an 'action research project', whatever that might be, whereby the government would produce money 'to provide day-long care for nursery-age black children whose parents are at work, and employment for black youngsters.' The institution of these all-black nursery schools would kill two birds with one stone, the *Observer* points out. Sounds cosy.

The report itself recommends the recruitment of more West Indian teachers, school governors, government school inspectors and career officers, as well as praising the study of West Indian history and West Indian writers. Readers may notice that I have not yet mentioned English pupils on the grounds that they are irrelevant to our discussion of this very human problem, but I can't help worrying whether this course of West Indian studies, taught by West Indian school teachers, inspected by West Indian school inspectors, is really suitable for the much greater number of Asian pupils in our schools.

No, the whole tenor of recommendations to date has militated towards the idea of separate development, and whereas I can quite accept that many – if not most – West Indians in the bigger concentrations would welcome the idea of separate development on their own terms, I do not see why they should be allowed to get away with it. The crux of the matter, which nobody has mentioned, is whether the West Indian Britons in our midst should be treated the same as everyone else or whether they should be treated differently, on account of their special problems, whatever they are. A solution which is universally regarded as wicked and abhorrent to nature in South Africa suddenly emerges as the best and most progressive way ahead for Britain. On balance, I feel that the wisest course for government is to treat West Indians as being the same as everyone else, and, if they misbehave, hit them on their heads – just like everyone else, and certainly not a fraction harder.

27.6.81

*   *   *

150

A Quota System for Schools and Prisons

I remember hearing the late Richard Crossman, when he was Secretary of State for the Social Services, express the view that somewhere in the Central Statistical Office was to be found a cell of fascists, or at least right-wing militants, whose purpose was if not to falsify figures, at least to present them in such a way as to suggest unacceptably right-wing conclusions. Harold Wilson had similar suspicions, voiced in private, about the existence of a fascist cell in the Security Services, but his anxieties, I feel, come under another heading.

With the frantic collation of statistics on every conceivable subject, and their instant retrievability through what has been called the revolution in information technology, it is easy to see how a few dedicated information technologists can put a spanner in the works of any left-wing or even vaguely progressive philosophy. One begins to understand why home computers will never be acceptable in the Soviet Union, and why even those computers allowed in industry and administration must be kept under lock and key. All that information *must* be dangerous, unless it can be rigidly controlled and released only when it has been digested into the current political and philosophical orthodoxies.

Two undigested lumps of information have surfaced in the West. At first glance they would seem to be abhorrent to the anti-racialist philosophy - perhaps one should call it creed - which we all espouse nowadays. Let us see how we can reconcile them to the prevailing orthodoxies and make them acceptable to the Benign Computer in the Sky whom Dean 'Don' Cupitt has described as 'the Sum of our Highest Values', preparing a new Kingdom of Heaven which he describes as 'the Welling Up in Each Person of Disinterested Love of One's Neighbour'.

The first appeared in a research study undertaken by Mr Colin Guest, an assistant prison governor, into the pattern of youth custody sentencing in the South-East of England. He discovered that whereas young Asians outnumber young blacks in the area by a factor of three to one, young blacks outnumber young Asians in the youth custody centres by 22 to one.

Armed as we are by our faith in the non-existence of any racial or ethnic weighting in the incidence of criminal propensity, and knowing as we do that crime is the product of social deprivation and racial bias rather than of any natural inclination to be bad, or inability to be good, the only useful lesson we can learn from this otherwise completely *irrelevant* piece of information is surely that blacks are discriminated against more than Asians by a factor of 66-1. In fact it would appear that Asians are discriminated against even less than whites. In the population of the area they are outnumbered 20-1 by whites, but in these youth custody centres they are outnumbered 70-1. This would appear to give an anti-white discrimination factor of 3.5, but perhaps we should not dwell on that possibility as it might prove unhelpful to the great Welling Up, or, even worse, *irrelevant* to our inquiry.

The suggestion that young blacks might actually be more prone to crime than young Asians by virtue of the greater neglect or incompetence of their parents, or by virtue of any inherited characteristic is, of course, repugnant to all morality and right reason, not to mention the law and the prophets. But in the unlikely event of anyone being able to show that young blacks actually *commit* more crimes than young Asians (as opposed to being charged with them), it occurs to me that there might be a psycho-chemical explanation which would be acceptable to the theory of Britain as an anti-black conspiracy.

One hates to generalise, but I believe it is true that young Asians, by and large, have a lighter bone structure and smaller bones than blacks. This would mean that their bones store a smaller deposit of the deadly fluoride poison which local authorities have been adding to the water supply for over 20 years in the form of sodium fluoride. There is no proof that fluoride poisoning is a cause of academic failure, indiscipline or delinquency in the young, but these extremes of indiscipline are a recent phenomenon and seem to have affected blacks worst. If it is reasonable to suspect the existence of fascist cells in the Central Statistical Office and Security Services, I do not see why they should not also exist in the Department of Health and National Water Authorities. But perhaps the nation's blacks are already too bemused and stultified by all the poison pumped through them to take action against what begins to look like a diabolical plot against the black community, to make them fail their exams and keep vast numbers of them in prison.

The second undigested piece of information to emerge last week concerned the dismal performance by black officers of the New York Police Department in examinations for promotion to sergeant. Out of 11,583 officers who took the exam, which had been drawn up by a specialist consultancy firm under instruction to eliminate racial or sexual bias from the questions, only 23 of those who passed were black. Effectively, one in ten of the white candidates passed, one in 50 of the blacks, answering straightforward multiple choice questions about police procedures.

The New York Guardians Association immediately demanded that the results of the examination should be scrapped, and promotion to sergeant should be organised on a quota basis as is already applied in recruitment. This may be in line with SDP/Liberal Alliance thinking, as enunciated by Mrs Shirley Williams at the first Alliance education conference in February. There she said that the exam system was the biggest single barrier to achieving a classless society. What we needed was profiles, assessments etc, she said.

But there is no reason to suppose that blacks would do better under a system of profiles and assessments, given the almost universal racism of whites. In any case, this daft woman went on to argue that 'the line between academic and vocational education was at least as serious – and in some cases worse than – the old line between grammar and secondary modern schools.' I do not see that anything useful can be served by listening to her.

My objection to scrapping exam results and applying a quota system to everything – including, perhaps, admissions to prison – is that this solution tackles the symptoms without tackling the cause of apparent racial disparities. It is always possible that I am entirely wrong in my suggestion of fluoride poisoning as a possible cause, although it would surely be worthwhile to give the idea a try. In any case, I feel that applying quotas to everything must have the effect of drawing attention to the problem and therefore aggravating it. Such positive discrimination is unlikely to be conducive to the great Welling Up in Each Person of Disinterested Love of One's Neighbour. But there surely is a case to be made against the racial analysis of exam results, against inquiring into the racial composition of the prisons. This information is neither helpful nor relevant in an *intelligent* discussion of racial problems. Let it be expunged from all information technology immediately.

15.9.84

*   *   *

Che Guevara in the West Midlands

'We would restore real freedom of the press,' says Mr John Tyndall, chairman of the National Front in the course of an interview in this week's *Observer*. 'We wouldn't, of course, allow anything seditious or subversive or slanderous.'

Real freedom, in this context, presumably means a relaxing of the various inhibitions imposed by the Race Relations Act accompanied by a tightening-up of such freedoms as remain to insult, deride or criticise our political leaders. In all my years as a journalist, I have never once heard the phrase 'Freedom of the Press' used except to urge some further restriction on it. My settled conclusion is that practically nobody in Britain believes in it outside the tiny world of journalists, and precious few inside that world. Most people, I believe, prefer reading an un-shackled press – although some are even made uneasy by that – but as soon as this freedom threatens to disturb their own tranquillity in the smallest way they immediately adopt attitudes whose repressivensss is only matched by extreme moral high-mindedness.

153

I think the National Front have a right to feel discriminated against. Long before the passing of the Race Relations Act there were perfectly adequate laws against public conduct or language likely to cause a breach of the peace. They may well be a nasty, boring and humourless collection of fanatics, but I have never seen that there was anything more wicked about race hatred than there is about class hatred or religious hatred or the peculiarly intense and inexplicable hatred which my dear wife feels for Jimmy Connors, the tennis player. They are all part of the rich panorama of life. If I forbade my wife to express her true feelings for Jimmy Connors, I have no doubt they would fester inside her, creating little black eddies of resentment and paranoia which would eventually burst out in some hideous drama on the Centre Court at Wimbledon when Connors would expire, coughing blood, in front of the television cameras, with a lady's parasol sticking between his ribs; public subscriptions would create a Jimmy Connors Memorial Trust and we would be stuck with a hideous modern statue of the young man somewhere on those green and pleasant lawns. So, wisely, I let her have her say.

Another Sunday newspaper this week printed a long profile of Robert Relf, hero of racist advertising, which included an extract from one of his letters to an East African neighbour who received £109 a week in social security payments for himself, his wife and thirteen children. The newspaper – rather sniffily, I thought – dismissed his 'unsubtle line in venomous abuse' with the following comment:

'Normally the kind of language in Relf's letter would be considered unfit for publication in a newspaper but we reproduce it today because it is relevant in assessing Relf's motives and his public image.'

Ah yes, to be sure, it is most important that we should form the right assessment of Relf's motives and his public image. Many people's reactions, I know, will be quite different, but I must confess his letter had me rolling on the floor:

'So you bloated black Pig you feel that the State is not doing you any favours by paying you £109 per week to sit on your stinking great arse ... Well, you odious venereal black scum if I had my way ... by putting a rope around your fat slimy neck and stringing you up to the nearest lamp post ... Bloody good riddance you stinking fat Bastard.

signed R. Relf

PS. COME BACK HITLER ALL IS FORGIVEN.'

I can see many nice, easy-going, intelligent people pursing their lips at this point and saying no, it won't do, you can't pretend this sort of thing is *funny*. Think of the poor black man's feelings. This is all quite beyond the pale. One becomes positively indignant that anyone can be so rude, does one not? I can only say, as a student of the vituperative arts, that this letter scores fairly high marks in its own right and if one examines

154

it from the point of view that other people, who are neither its writer nor its recipient, are going to take it very seriously indeed, then it becomes an object of the most exquisite comedy. Add to this that Relf's recent hunger strike and victory over the Race Relations Board have made him a folk hero of the West Midlands, bringing him hundreds of letters of support and an inscribed volume from Ms Patience Strong, the poet and women's magazine writer – 'Salute to a brave and courageous English-man' – and the joke begins to assume cosmic proportions. Now Mr Relf is to be found at every function and fête organised by the National Front, to whom he has become the Che Guevara of the West Midlands.

Of course I can see as well as anybody that there is nothing funny about racial strife, nothing remotely funny about broken heads, spilt blood, terror and hatred in action. I keep a small file of letters I have received which are not so different in tone from the one which Mr Relf sent to his East African neighbour. Most of them, in fact, are from lady novelists and all are from authors. Once or twice in my career – certainly not more often than twice – I have even written such letters myself, always to novel reviewers. The error behind this form of abuse lies in supposing that it is possible to inflict any sort of wound by letter to a stranger. Only friends wound in that way. Just occasionally, perhaps, leafing through the file for a quiet chuckle, or to find a particular adjective which evades me, I experience a momentary twinge of unease over the depth and intensity of the hatred revealed. It is not so much what these people say as the evidence of their desire to say it which can occasionally give a man pause, if they catch him at a weak moment. But mostly, they are read for laughs.

I don't know why it is that race relations should attract so much foolishness and pomposity on both sides of the fence. I can quite under-stand people wishing there were fewer blacks around, and am not parti-cularly shocked to hear such sentiments expressed although I might say, 'Tut, tut'. I can quite understand people feeling it wrong that others should be discriminated against on account of their colour, and might even give a feeble clap or two if somebody put this case forcefully enough. But what I know in my bones to be wrong is this insistence that we should all be prepared to take Mr Relf seriously.

For myself, I see nothing to choose between the National Front and the Race Relations Board. Both are a collection of bores and busybodies and both are harmful to the extent they are taken seriously.

The chicken-and-egg argument of which came first out of Mr Robert Relf and the Race Relations Board may never be settled, but I feel certain that the only thing which gives the National Front glamour or popular appeal at the present time is the attempt by foolish, well-meaning people to suppress its views and treat its language as unfit for publication. The

Race Relations Board is now in a quandary over Mr Relf. He has beaten them all, and it is terribly hard for pompous people to admit they are beaten. The kindest and wisest thing to do is to laugh at them.

10.7.76

11

OUR FOUR-LEGGED FRIENDS

The Pleasures of Compassion

The RSPCA's decision to condemn fox-hunting did not go down well in West Somerset. Mr Jack Hosegood, joint master of the Exmoor Fox-hounds, issued a statement expressing concern at the terrible pain these animals will suffer if they are poisoned or snared; shooting is even worse, he says, because 'their bodies reject lead and soon develop gangrene'. Mr Ben Burton, joint master of the Dulverton East, opined that it was a 'retrograde step'.

They might have added that if foxes are not hunted, poisoned, trapped or shot they will probably die of something else – old age, perhaps, or hypothermia, which can be very painful – or measles, or Parkinson's disease, or over-eating, or they might choke on a chicken bone. Every time a fox dies in pain we are all diminished, are we not? Even as I write, I expect there is a fox in great pain within five miles of me. Well, if it comes to me I will offer it an aspirin.

I don't hunt nowadays although I frequently shoot at things, and even if I seldom hit them the intention is definitely there. But I can see what fun it must be for other people to try and stop me shooting. Quite apart from tender feelings for animals there is all the simple pleasure of stop-ping people from doing things they want to do and making them do something else they don't want to do. For myself, I am not tempted that way. I do not think it is a very healthy pleasure, and suspect there is just as great an element of sadism in it as there is in foxhunting. But even if one sees this busybodying as a degrading and anti-social form of enjoy-ment I don't see how one can try to stop people from indulging it without succumbing oneself.

So the wretched fox must cater for three human appetites – for those

156

who like chasing it, those who like to stop other people from chasing it, and those who feel affectionate and gooey at the sight of these dreadful beasts. I belong to none of these categories, but I am convinced there is no element of sadism in the pleasure of fox-hunting for the good reason that on the rare occasions I tried it I never once saw a fox, and I do not understand how anyone can be accused of rejoicing in the discomfiture of an animal he never sees. Perhaps it is a little undignified and absurd for parties of grown men and women to spend all day on horses chasing a small animal they never see, but then so are most human pleasures when one comes to think about them – eating oysters, taking a bath, scratching one's nose.

Fishing has always struck me as more sadistic, especially the idea of 'playing' a trout or a salmon, just as a cat plays with a mouse before eating it. The absence of opposition is probably because there are three million anglers in the United Kingdom, a fact which might suggest that degenerate, detribalised urban man has not quite lost his hunting instincts for all the goo he likes to read about foxes in the *Daily Mirror*.

Of all the cruel sports I have witnessed, the one I found most objectionable was bull-fighting. This was not so much because I found the sight of bulls being tortured and killed unpleasing, although I did, and it certainly wasn't because I witnessed scenes of bloodthirstiness or sadistic glee in the crowd, although I should probably have found them distressing if I had. In fact, I detected the opposite emotion in the crowd – a lively and vociferous compassion for the bull and this was something I found much more disgusting: the quick, clean kill was applauded precisely because it involved no pain to the bull; a bungled job was booed because of the unnecessary pain and distress it caused.

This seems to me the ultimate perversion: that an animal can be brought forward and tortured to death in public so that the crowd can indulge compassionate feelings towards it. There can be no doubt that such compassionate feelings are pleasurable – whole branches of the film, literary and journalistic worlds thrive on it and there was a school of criticism in the 1960s which judged novels exclusively by the amount of compassion they dished out to all and sundry. But of all the available candy-coloured tangerine-flake streamline consumer satisfactions available, the Kwick Kompassion Kick strikes me as the most distasteful.

Bullfights have never caught on in England as a means of exciting this enjoyable emotion of pity – partly, no doubt because they are not yet available in aerosol containers. Until recently, I thought our national equivalent has been established in the country's 400-odd thalidomide victims. They, too, were not yet available in aerosol containers, but Sunday colour supplements were plainly the next best thing.

Nobody with any human feelings can fail to experience a violent emotion on seeing these photographs. The first reaction, as at the Jew's funeral, was to try and measure the emotion in terms of money – other people's money, of course. Lady Hoare's Thalidomide Appeal was not spectacularly successful, and it soon became apparent that damages were being demanded on a scale which was not compensatory or even punitive so much as poetic. We soon became like Ismaili Muslims watching an obese Aga Khan weigh himself in gold who insists on another nine-course meal every time the scale begins to balance.

The real scandal of thalidomide, it seems to me, does not lie in the human error which brought it about, nor even in the Distillers' Company's initial reluctance to act as society's scapegoat. It may lie partly in the readiness of the Sunday colour supplements to dwell on these tragedies, week after week, year after year, ever since. But far more, it lies in the appetite of the British public for gawping at these unfortunates. Even the High Priest and the Levite had enough good taste to pass by on the other side of the road.

14.2.76

*   *   *

Death by Ferrets

Some time ago a six-month-old girl called Pamela Burgin was killed by ferrets in her parents' flat in Crystal Palace. The parents had gone out for a drink. Later, two policemen cornered the ferrets and beat them to death with their truncheons. If one had to produce a comment on the above sequence of events, it would surely be along the lines – 'Sad but interesting'. Sad, because any death of a child is always sad, interesting because it was such an unusual way to die. None of the newspapers reporting it could think of another incident when a child had been eaten, or mauled to death, by ferrets. The nearest they could get to it was in recalling the case of nine-year-old Linda Wright, attacked by a stray ferret at her home in Skegness last January. But Linda's assailant was, to all intents and purposes, wild and would scarcely be affected by legislation requiring owners of caged ferrets to be licensed.

The sad case of Pamela Burgin is interesting from other points of view, of course. It confirms a vicious streak in these animals which I have always suspected. No boy will ever forget the day he shot his first ferret. In my case, I had been asked by the keeper, with a twinkle in his eye, if I would like to pick the little creature up. Innocently putting my hand into the cape, I found my finger bitten to the bone. Everybody fell about laughing. Later, the ferret was put down a rabbit hole and we waited with shotguns at the ready for a rabbit to jump out. Thirty years later, I can't honestly remember whether I genuinely mistook the mean, trembling, pink-eyed creature for a rabbit . . .

But the *chief* reason, I insist, for finding the case of Pamela Burgin interesting as well as sad is its extreme rarity. No case has ever been recorded before, so far as I know, of pet ferrets behaving like this, and there is no reason to suppose that there ever will be again. Pamela Burgin, in her own small way, has made history.

So that, then, is the sum of my editorial comment on this unhappy event: *very* sad but *jolly* interesting. And there you might suppose we could leave the matter, turning to another page for other tales of adventure, passion, tragedy and good old British fun. But Mr Arthur Latham, Labour MP for Paddington, feels the matter should not be allowed to rest there: 'After this tragedy, there may well be a case for people to have licences enabling them to keep caged ferrets', he pronounced. Now we are given to understand he is urging the Home Secretary to review all laws on keeping animals. It is one of those rare occasions when one might almost be tempted to feel sorry for the Home Secretary, but of course such sympathy would be misplaced. Nothing would give him greater pleasure than to introduce a whole new range of laws on ferrets, forbidding them unequivocally from attacking small children, appointing neighbourhood ferret officers to enforce the law, requiring ferret owners to register with the police and submit to inspection by the local ferret authority, enabling ferret officers to enter any premises on which they have reason to believe ferrets are kept without a warrant, requiring anti-ferret devices to be installed on all doors and windows in hotels, lodging houses and public offices. The Health Education Council could then chip in with hours of television advertising on the dangers of ferrets and the import of live ferrets could be banned. Huge fines could be imposed on anyone possessing a ferret without the proper documentation.

Politicians live for these opportunities to introduce a number of fatuous, unnecessary and restrictive laws in response to what they see as popular demand. Next, a two-week-old baby in Neasden, almost certainly called Stephen, will die after swallowing a white mouse, and the whole thing will start again.

What is sad and rather frightening about Britain nowadays is that public opinion, to the extent that it exists, genuinely seems to support this response. Every bloody fool in the fish queue, all the old dears queuing up for their benefits in the Post Office, all the teachers, social workers and National Health supervisory staff who make up the rest of our population will agree, on learning of Pamela Burgin's horrible experience, that the government should do something about it. Never mind that both the ferrets and the baby are dead. Never mind that ferrets have never behaved in this way before, or that they would have behaved in just the same way if they had been licensed; never mind that there are already perfectly adequate laws against leaving your children unattended. Nobody uses the occasion of Pamela Burgin's death and the wholesome emotions it arouses to demand that the Home Secretary resign. This would be just as rational a response, since he has obviously let the ferret situation get out of control and the incident must raise doubts about his competence to deal with future developments on the white mouse front. Yet our invariable response to any new development, in the intellectual paralysis of the time, is that the government should somehow deal with it, extending its powers and restricting our own freedom – or more particularly the freedom of other people – whenever necessary.

*   *   *

The Case of the Suffering Goldfish

I turn to the Case of the Suffering Goldfish in some alarm, for the light it throws not only on the legal attitude to goldfish but also on our underlying social philosophy. This case is no longer *sub judice* so my comments on the prosecuting authority, the witnesses, the court's verdict and the magistrates who reached this monstrous verdict can be more or less unbridled.

The basis of the case is this. Mr Alan Garlinge, aged 23, bought a 1½ inch goldfish from Mr H. Sanders of Coldharbour Lane, Brixton, for 50p. Examining the fish afterwards, he noticed it had an abscess on one side and complained to the RSPCA. The RSPCA prosecuted, producing as witness Mr Alan Hanson, a veterinary surgeon, who told the court: 'The right course in a case like this would have been to dispatch the goldfish humanely. Unnecessary suffering has been caused by allowing the goldfish to continue living in that condition.' Magistrates, finding that he had caused the beast unnecessary suffering 'by omitting to provide necessary care and attention', conditionally discharged Mr Sanders for 12 months, ordering him to pay £60 costs.

This verdict seems open to criticism on grounds of law, of natural justice, of Christian morality and finally, perhaps most serious of all, on grounds of social philosophy. Let us first examine the legal aspects. In the famous case of R. V. Donaghy (Scotland) 1974, as I remember, it was found that Miss Eleanor Donaghy could not be guilty of cruelty to prawns by putting them on a hot plate and watching them jump around for the good reason that prawns were not animals and so did not qualify under the protection of Animals (Scotland) Act 1912. Miss Donaghy,

160

under cross-examination, rather felt that Scottish prawns were insects. So *mutatis mutandis* (or, as the lawyers say, *semble*) must English goldfish be. A clever lawyer could have made kedgeree of the prosecution's case but Mr Sanders, in a letter to the court, pointed out that defending the summons would have cost him £150, which was too expensive for a goldfish.

On the point of natural justice, I can only suggest that death is no less abhorrent to the animal creation than it is to human beings. The idea is repugnant to all natural observation that 'necessary care and attention' can involve killing. Any concept of justice which relies on such a proposition must be an abomination, at any rate from the point of view of the animals it is designed to protect.

So to the morality which regulates the conduct of Christians towards brutes. This is best contained in the *Summa Theologica* I, 1, 2, 3, 13, 75, 118 (fundamentalists can turn to Exod. xx 10, xxiii 12; *Deut.* xxv 4; xxii 6) and can be summed up thus; animals have no duties, being destitute of free will, *ergo* no rights. Brutes are made for man, who has the same rights over them as he has over plants and stones. He may put them to death for his food, and this without strict necessity; *ergo* he may put them to death or inflict pain on them for any good or reasonable end, such as the promotion of knowledge or health or even for the purposes of recreation, but with this limitation – that he must not take pleasure directly in the pain given to brutes, since by this he degrades and brutalises his own nature and might transfer the cruelty to his own kind.

Nobody claimed that Mr Sanders derived pleasure from the suffering of his goldfish, so we must conclude that his negligence was no offence against traditional Christian morality. Which brings me to the far more serious point of social philosophy. If these laws against animal negligence are not inspired by traditional morality, they must be inspired by simple human kindness towards animals, that is to say by an empathetic (or, as some would say, a sentimental) anthropomorphism. Animal suffering is repugnant to the extent that it reminds us of, or resembles, human suffering. Why, under these circumstances should animal death be more acceptable, unless we are prepared to put down humans in pain?

11.4.81

*   *   *

Handling a Bat without a Licence

No doubt it is whistling in the wind to expect any government to care much about the freedom of its subjects, least of all freedom from government. 'Freedom' is just another of those words which politicians bandy around, like 'patriotism' and 'compassion', to raise a cheer. As soon as anyone has involved himself in the political process, he has involved himself – however ineffectively – in the process of making decisions, shaping the community, bossing everyone else around. 'And a few men talked of freedom, while England talked of ale' (Chesterton).

Between those of us who vote Conservative for the simple reason that we wish to be left to live our own lives with a minimum of interference or help from the government, and those who collect our votes with the appropriate slogans, there is a far wider gulf than any which exists between Mrs Thatcher and Mr Benn, between Norman Tebbit and Alex Kitson. But even while the Conservative Conference organisers are busy pulling the wool over the eyes of the delegates and stage-managing the debates they ignore the extent to which they are pulling the wool over their own eyes at the same time. The urge to political power may exist, but to suppose that political power reposes anywhere in the democratic system – in Downing Street, or in Cabinet or Cabinet committee, or House of Commons, or party conference, or constituency association committees or in the electorate – is an illusion. Nobody exerts any overall control over anything. Things happen only because a handful of enthusiasts or busy-bodies in some particular field wants them to happen, or because there is not another handful of busybodies on the spot to prevent them happening.

A particularly flagrant example of this process emerged last week with the announcement of a new law that forbids anyone to disturb, annoy, harm, kill or interfere with any bats which choose to take up residence in his house. The penalty for disturbing a bat on its roost, or for handling one without a licence, is now £1,000 a bat.

There are some people who like bats. The late Mrs Ian Fleming was one. She would crawl for miles to glimpse them in caves or hanging from trees. Similarly, there are many people who do not like bats much but are not particularly troubled by them. The chance of a bat roosting in their attics or spare bedroom curtains may seem a remote one. They may feel that bat enthusiasts should be allowed their say in the running of this country, just like everyone else.

I do not happen to belong in either of these categories. Underneath my house, I have eight large cellars which for some reason bats have chosen to claim for themselves. For those who do not like bats, it is extremely disagreeable to have to fight a way through a colony of them every time they want a bottle of wine. Even more than that, there is a particular pleasure involved in the ownership of wine which has nothing to do with drinking it. There are some bottles in my cellar which, after serious thought, I have decided are too good to be served to anyone I know. There is nobody I like enough. But it is nice to go down and gloat over them occasionally. Bats entirely spoil this pleasure.

162

Until last week's law, the bat problem could be kept within manageable proportions by sending children down on a bat-hunt every three months, armed with old tennis rackets. They usually managed to kill a couple, and the result was to discourage the other bats from getting above themselves. Now they will probably take over the whole house.

Never mind about that. It is the principle of the thing. The general effect of this new law, which is an extension of the Wildlife and Countryside Act, is that nobody who finds his house invaded by bats can do anything about it. Who, one might ask, is the mastermind behind this new denial of human freedom? The *Daily Telegraph* came up with someone called Dr Robert Stebbings. He explains that bats are the gentlest, most misunderstood of creatures; people who find a stray bat in their house will probably not be prosecuted if they show it the door politely:

'This is one of the slight anomalies of the new law as it is written. But I'm sure that no one will mind if you pick it up and take it outside and hang it on a tree or the outside of the house.'

Even so, one will be liable for a £1,000 fine if one has not applied to the Nature Conservancy Council for a licence to handle bats. Quite possibly it will be just another of those laws to which nobody pays the slightest attention. But it is a melancholy fact that enthusiasts like Dr Stebbing have already passed a law forbidding people to pick wild flowers in the hedgerows; they are agitating for laws to prevent people picking fossils from the cliffs at Lyme Regis, as people have done for hundreds of years, and to prevent people treasure-hunting with metal detectors, an entirely new activity which answers one of the deepest yearnings in human nature.

None of these things was debated at any of the party conferences, none of them will appear in any election manifesto. They are wished upon us by a handful of specialist busybodies who are miles removed from any democratic process. Yet they cut deeply and intimately into our enjoyment of life. My house is full not only of bats but also of fossils collected by succeeding generations of Waughs, rediscovered by each new generation with wonder and delight. They cause more pleasure and give more instruction than they possibly could if they had been left among the thousands of tons of fossils at Lyme Regis, to be weighed by experts every ten years or so at taxpayers' expense.

Where will it all end? I notice there are many fewer wasps around than there used to be in my childhood, when every year I was stung four or five times. When a wasp came into the classroom, all lessons would stop while everybody threw books at it. Any day now we will learn of a new law making it a criminal offence to frighten a wasp.

Some may decide that no fundamental principle is involved in all this. When Franklin Roosevelt laid down the four essentials of freedom –

freedom of speech and worship, freedom from hunger and fear – it did not occur to him that it might be necessary to add freedom to turn unwanted bats out of the house, or freedom to kill wasps. We all tended to take those freedoms for granted. Now it is too late. Before worse happens, delegates at the Conservative Conference may care to ask themselves who is to protect us all from the bat-protectors.

9.10.82

12

OUR FOUR-WHEELED FRIENDS

Special Lavatories

A few days after the end of the 1967 war in the Middle East I remember waking up in the Tel Aviv Hilton without the faintest idea where I was. It was after rather a late night spent at Mandy's Discothèque, kept by the immortal Mandy Rice-Davies, in the company of the *Daily Mirror*'s Donald Wise, doyen of all foreign correspondents past and present, Mandy herself and a handful of other people whose names I have forgotten, if I ever knew them. My bedroom gave no clue and after I had studied my passport carefully, I decided that I could not think for the life of me what I was doing there. It was only half an hour later, after a hot bath and while I was struggling through the horrors of a kosher breakfast that it all came back to me, as they say.

But if Hilton Hotels are pretty well indistinguishable the world over, airports might be specially calculated to inspire dissociative amnesia. Most people at an airport look slightly mad, and one has no confidence that they would be able to reply accurately if one asked what country one was in, even if they knew themselves. After several hours spent at various airports last week, I noticed that they even have the same symbols to distinguish gentlemen's from ladies' lavatories. It has often seemed a shame to me that all the grandeur of the human male, the mystery and delight of the human female, can be reduced to such footling symbols, but I suppose that is what air travel does to us all. It would be a kind thought to supply a third set of lavatories, possibly distinguished by a question mark, to cater for amnesiacs who have temporarily forgotten which sex they belong to.

London Airport, however, is different. Arriving at No 2 Building, I spotted the difference immediately. The first sight to greet the traveller is a battery of notices, advertising sanitary arrangements not only for the usual sexes but also for a Third Sex, described as 'Invalids'. Their sign is a wheelchair, symbol of so much that is nicest and best about modern Britain. No visitor could hope for a plainer statement identifying the country he has landed in: You are entering a compassionate state, it says. Seat belts must be worn at all times lest you take more than your share of the delicious health services available free of charge; safety helmets and surgical trusses should be adjusted before leaving the lounge; all sharp objects which might be harmful to children if eaten must be left at Welfare Control. Visitors are warned not to feed the old age pensioners, as some of them bite.

I think it is very nice of the British to supply these amenities for the not-so-well and it is comforting for the able-bodied majority to reflect that if ever we are taken poorly at one of our airports, special facilities are there. As a matter of fact I am a disabled person myself, with disabilities permanently fixed at 100 per cent eighteen years after my army service in Cyprus, despite swindling attempts by various governments to reduce them. It occurs to me that I may have the right to demand entrance to these special, unisex arrangements. Certainly I have the right to sit among the *mutilés de guerre* and pregnant women on Paris buses, despite unpleasant attempts to deny foreign welfare to any Englishman who is self-employed. Those of us who are dedicated to the survival of privilege in any form should lose no opportunity to jump on every available bandwagon. I only wish I could represent myself as a battered single mother.

Which is why I have always felt especially tender towards Quentin Crewe, the wheel-chair good food warrior and champion of Invalid Power. As a matter of fact, Mr Crewe gave me my first job in journalism, and our paths have crossed several times. Once he helped me in a venture for the *Sunday Mirror* called the 'ABC of Beauty'. It involved writing captions for photographs of pretty women in bathing dress – by no means as easy as people might suppose – and one doesn't forget these acts of kindness from a fellow journalist. He once pluckily changed his name from Dodds to Crewe in commemoration of his maternal grandfather, the first and last Marquess of Crewe. How odd of Dodds to choose the Crewes, they cried, as the marquessate obstinately remained extinct. But I think I see his point. His struggle is my struggle and the struggle of most of us. What is our task? To make Britain a fit country for ourselves to live in.

Those who arrive at London Airport might receive the impression that our Quentin isn't doing too badly. Amnesiacs are less well catered for, as I say, and so, in fact, are the unattended blind, the mentally sub-normal and those unable to relieve themselves without a brass-band accompaniment (as soon as this disability is recognised by the Health Service, I intend to register), but our wheel charioteers, at least, have won recognition for themselves. So it was with real indignation, dismay, sorrow, pain and a keen sense of outrage that I read last Sunday how inadequate are the arrangements in the new National Theatre.

Quentin Crewe was sent on his tour of inspection by a Sunday newspaper which I have vowed not to mention for a year, so I shall identify it only by pointing out that its book and arts pages aren't much good. And it isn't the *Observer* either. He was accompanied on his tour by the National Theatre's Mr Lasdun, plainly a conciliatory sort of fellow but, as we shall see, not quite conciliatory enough.

It is true that a few token gestures have been made. There is an underground car park where a disabled person can drive straight in, park, and then wheel his chair to a lift which will take him to the foyers of the two main theatres, called Lyttelton and Olivier, where there are special seats and places available for the disabled, as well as special lavatories, or 'loos' as Mr Crewe calls them in his homely way. However, his eagle eye has spotted a flaw: anyone accompanying wheel-chair users into the theatre will have to sit in front of them, rather than behind. Disgraceful. Mr Lasdun promises to see if this can be re-arranged.

But wait for the next shock horror sensation. Although the two bars are readily accessible to people in wheelchairs, and it may be that food will be supplied in them, access to the restaurant and both buffets is by a *service lift*. My God! Just like second-class citizens. It makes you wonder what century we all think we are living in, does it not?

But far, far worse is in store when Quentin reaches the third theatre, called Cottesloe – an experimental, small theatre which is still unfinished. There are only four spaces available for wheelchairs; the special ramp is too steep for comfort. As if this isn't bad enough, and although the theatre was designed as late as 1972 – wait for it – *there are no special loos!* No wonder Quentin goes off the deep end:

'Oho. Was this not after the change of public opinion we all found so moving and proper? How did it happen that there was no loo? Why did they not plan for one when they planned the ordinary loos?

'They hoped ... It was a question of money. Now they had applied for money for a loo: £3,200. Yes, that is what they said. They showed me the space of it. "It will mean taking down a brick wall, there." Gosh.

'Suddenly, they lost my sympathy.'

Oh dear, oh dear, what can we *do*? Put knives on your wheels, Quentin, and run us down like Boadicea. Relieve yourself on us from a great height, using machinery which we will be only too happy to provide. But please, please, *please* never let us lose your sympathy.

Since finishing that excellent article, I have discovered plans for a new West End theatre specifically designed for the disabled. The Little Theatre Club of St Martin's Lane has formed a company known as the Living Theatre for the Disabled. I hope to God they don't forget anything this time.

10.4.76

*   *   *

The Country of the Disabled

I do not know what ceremony attends the investiture of a Disabled People's President – whether he is robed, anointed, crowned and exposed to the cheering multitude. Probably not. But there can be no mistaking the aura of veneration which attaches to the post. In a country which is torn by conflicting interests and class antagonisms, tender sentiments towards the disabled are just about the only thing we can all agree on. As I have said before, those ostentatious signs advertising toilet facilities for the disabled which greet travellers at Heathrow Airport are far more a symbol of the nation, and of its precarious unity, than the Royal coat of arms or the Union Jack. One day, perhaps, the wheelchair motif will be adopted as our national flag, and the mysterious third sex which has begun to appear at motorway comfort stations – Men, Women and semi-ambulant Duos – will be adopted as our official sexual identity.

All of which may sound a trifle bitter, but as it happens I am a disabled person myself and therefore, surely, entitled to be bitter. Since 1958 I have been officially designated as a hundred per cent disabled, although even at a hundred per cent I rank pretty low in the hierarchy of the disabled. I am not nearly so unfortunate, or so much to be pitied, as those who can claim mobility allowance, constant attendance allowance, invalidity pension or unemployability supplement.

But I am considerably more disabled than Lord Snowdon, the Disabled People's President, and while recognising a sort of logic in the proposition that in the country of the disabled the one-legged man should be king, I sometimes wonder what I and the other million-odd registered cripples in this country have done to deserve his concern for us. That his concern is prompted by nothing but the milk of human kindness can scarcely be doubted, since with an earldom in the bag he has nothing to gain. But as one of the miserable remnants of humanity to whom the prospects of an earldom is no longer available, I do not see why I should follow obediently under his flag, or acknowledge his leadership.

21.3.81

167

13

SMOKING AND DRINKING

The Temperance Fanatics

One of the least pleasing aspects of the British press is its extraordinarily sanctimonious attitude towards allegedly 'drunken' drivers. We all know that most, if not very nearly all, journalists have a weakness for the occasional tincture, or the cup that cheers, or whatever. We all know that most of them (in fact I should again say very nearly all, apart from those lucky enough to have an abstemious wife or girl friend) occasionally drive around in their motor cars with a blood-alcohol level over the permitted limit. We also know that the permitted blood-alcohol level is ludicrously low. It was possible to extrapolate from figures supplied last year for the proportion of those who, on a random check, were driving when technically 'drunk', when set against figures supplied for the proportion of those involved in fatal road accidents who were also technically 'drunk', that one has a better chance of avoiding fatal road accidents when 'drunk' than when sober. At the very least one was forced to conclude that figures supplied by the Ministry of Transport for road accidents involving one or more 'drunken' driver were seriously misleading, and that alcohol was not a significant factor in a large proportion of them.

As against this, one must obviously agree that it is a very foolish thing indeed to drive a car when seriously or hog-whimperingly drunk, and that criminal sanctions can reasonably be applied as a deterrent, especially against confirmed alcoholics. In partial mitigation, for all except persistent offenders, it might be observed that the decision to do this foolish thing is taken at a time when judgment is impaired. Among the logical and intelligent Japanese, I have been told, it was a defence against any charge of dangerous driving until well into the 1960s to prove that you were drunk at the time, and therefore not responsible for your actions.

Of all the offences which decent, law-abiding people can commit, 'drunk' driving is surely the one which in most circumstances (although admittedly not all) the British journalist should find it easiest to forgive. Yet when the Lord Chief Justice, Lord Lane, recently called for even stiffer penalties, almost the whole of the British press welcomed his words and at least two newspapers – the *Mirror* and the *Standard* – said his suggestions did not go far enough, calling for even stiffer sentencing than he proposed. For some reason the press has decided to give these unfortunate 'drunk' drivers the treatment usually reserved for sadistic child murderers, pederasts generally and certain kinds of drug-pusher. While it is easy to understand popular resentment against these other offenders as reflecting the anxieties so many parents feel for their children, I cannot see that the same applies to 'drunk' drivers. perhaps the resentment against them reflects a general hatred and terror which should more properly attach to the internal combustion engine. Masses of metal hurtling around under fallible human control inevitably cause appalling havoc when anything goes wrong.

Whenever I write about this subject I always get letters from people who have picked up slaughtered children and pregnant mothers in every conceivable posture of distress – their bones protruding piteously to the sky, or decapitated, their bowels strewn over hundreds of yards of motorway. Do I condone this, they ask. In fact, I have had one or two similar experiences, although I had no reason to suppose that the accident which caused the injuries was itself caused by drunkenness. Even by the MOT's unreliable figures, only a very small proportion of road accidents involve drivers with a blood-alcohol level above its derisory allowance. The truth is that these hideous injuries are caused by the nature of road transport, where every lethal machine is controlled by a different person in whatever state of sorrow or joy, health or sickness, alcoholic exaltation or teetotal depression he may find himself. Anybody who avails himself of the benefits of road transport must inevitably accept its risks.

Another explanation for this fury against 'drunk' drivers, especially in the 'popular' or lower-class newspapers, might be that editors imagine they are catering for the anxieties and resentments of those who do not own cars – the poor defenceless bicyclist or pedestrian, as he goes about his lawful business, drunk or sober, in the normal course of events. If so, these editors are out of touch. According to the latest General Household Survey, 59 per cent of households now own cars. Few of these households wish to see their breadwinner locked up for two years on a spurious, press-incited charge of 'drunken' driving. Editors are annoying more of their readers than they are pleasing by these silly campaigns, and I wish their proprietors would point it out to them.

But the most obvious explanation is that these editors have been deliberately misled and manipulated by the temperance brigade about the evils of alcohol. They feel guilty, like so many Britons, about their own self-indulgence and feel they can exorcise the guilt by expressing exaggerated outrage against the tiny proportion of 'drunken' drivers who are caught.

Time and again in these pages I have ponted out the extraordinarily high proportion of Scots Presbyterians and Calvinists (I am not saying they are all members of Moral Rearmament) in the Ministry of Health,

169

and the lying propaganda they feed to ministers and press about an 'epidemic of drunkenness'. A survey published last month, which was conducted independently of the Ministry of Health by the Central Statistical Office and involved the stupendous number of 21,000 interviews, reveals the true facts: abstainers from alcohol are more likely to develop chronic illness than drinkers, while even heavy drinkers have a much shorter rate of absence from work through sickness than abstainers. Just how many billions of pounds, I wonder, are these wretched abstainers costing the country in lost working days – and how many further billions are they costing the Exchequer (that means *your* hospital facilities, *your* kiddies' education and old people's welfare accommodation) in unpaid excise duty?

But the temperance fanatics are everywhere, and as drunken driving might seem to be the weakest point of the anti-temperance case they press their advantage remorselessly. To measure the extremes to which these anti-drink fanatics are prepared to go, one must look across at the other side of the herring pond where the New Jersey Supreme Court ruled by a six to one majority last month that a host who gave his guests liquor was liable (no less than a publican) for injury to other parties caused by the guests' subsequent drunk driving. As the one dissenting voice from this absurd ruling (Judge Marie Garibaldi, God bless her) pointed out, it means that hosts will in future have to monitor their guests' drinking.

Even more alarming, both houses of Congress passed a bill forcing States to prohibit sales of drink to those under 21 on pain of losingsome of their Federal Highway subsidies. The National Safety Council estimates this will save 700 lives out of 43,000 road fatalities in 1983, the lowest for 20 years. The law will discriminate against women, who scarcely feature at all in drunk-driving statistics for the age-goup of 19–21, and it will discriminate even more viciously against non-drivers – two out of three New Yorkers aged 19 and 20 do not drive.

Perhaps these absurdities and injustices pale into insignificance beside the decision of our own Mr Justice Woolf in the High Court who awarded £45,750 to a convicted rapist against the drunken driver from whom he had accepted a lift on the grounds that, having been a 'small-time crook' with a mistress before the accident, the man only started committing rape as a result of his injuries.

What, one wonders, has happened to the Providence which is supposed to look after fools, drunks and Americans?

14.7.84

*   *   *

170

Smaller Genitals

Not a day passes without some new and preposterous claim by the anti-drink campaigners – most of them as insulting to the intelligence as they are blatantly untrue – reported by press and television as uncritically as if they were cricket scores or pre-war train timetables. Most of them came from an international conference on alcoholism being held in Liverpool, but the height of absurdity was reached, as is so often the case, in the House of Commons when a new Conservative Member, called Dr Brian Mawhinney, demanded that people who became ill through excessive drinking or smoking should pay for their medical treatment.

In the asinine spirit of the times, and with the intellectual vacuity which I am sorry to say is fast becoming the chief characteristic of official utterance in Britain, the Under-Secretary of State replied that while Dr Mawhinney's suggestion 'has at first sight the advantage of equity and logic', the Government had no plans to introduce special charges for alcohol-related or smoking-related illnesses. He put the cost of smoking-related diseases to the National Health Service at £115 million, that of drink-related at £50 million to £69 million.

We all know perfectly well that these figures are chicken-feed, even if they are not grossly unreliable, since bronchitis, lung cancer, arterisclerosis and cirrhosis of the liver frequently have causes other than smoking or drinking. Excise duty on tobacco and drink pays for the entire Health Service several times over. If equity or logic had anything to do with it, there would be a strong case for charging non-drinkers and non-smokers for a proportion of their medical costs. Moreover if it is true, as is often claimed, that these brutes live longer than those who drink or smoke, then there is a very strong argument for charging them higher national insurance rates, too.

But then nobody has ever really pretended that the Welfare State had much to do with equity or logic. Its chief function may be to support a gigantic administrative structure, its chief characteristic may be its amiable inefficiency, but where the national pension scheme is concerned, the combination of inefficiency and coercion reaches such levels as can only be described as criminal extortion. Everybody concerned with it should be sent to prison.

One might be prepared to forgive Dr Mawhinney his attempts to add one further absurdity, one further injustice, to the whole tottering structure of indiscriminate state welfare if he were not attempting to discriminate, on this occasion, against a group which includes oneself as well as a large proportion of his constituents. His motives might indeed turn out to be religious, as so often proves the case on examination – he is a proselytising Ulster Protestant by origin who somehow got himself adopted for the marginal seat of Peterborough at the last election. I imagine the Soke will send him packing next time round.

Among the absurdities to come out of the Liverpool conference was one headline, 'Plight of the gymslip drunks', where 'a survey of alcoholic abuse among young people revealed that some schoolchildren take an early morning drink to steady their nerves ... other children claimed that their doctors advised them to have "a hair of the dog" to calm them down.' Several paragraphs down, the sociologist presenting these lurid 'facts' revealed that the survey showed 'that the great majority of young-sters appeared to drink very little'.

Most enjoyable of all was the evidence of Dr Anthony Morris, a 34-year-old gastroenterologist, who claimed that alcohol produced signs of effeminacy in men: 'Any man drinking more than five pints of beer a day (i.e. three glasses of whisky, as poured in a middle-class home) is running the risk of changing his shape and losing his sex drive ... Also male genitals tend to be smaller than those of men who drink moderately.' Among other risks we run, apparently, is that of increasing the amount of female hormones in our bodies, causing us to develop breasts and shapely curved hips.

This would be fascinating information indeed if we could be certain that Dr Morris's concern were entirely scientific, but before long his dismal, propagandist intention emerges: 'This certainly goes against the accepted idea that to drink excessively is masculine ... Perhaps if more people were aware of the effects that drinking had they would be less inclined to drink.'

Groan, boo. What is it to him if we choose to have small genitals, develop breasts and shapely curved hips? Why do these wretched people think they can treat us all like goody-goody lower-class 'kids' on a *Blue Peter* Outward Bound Course? How dare they tell us such preposterous lies for their own sanctimonious ends?

The only part of the Liverpool conference on which press and television chose to cast doubt was also the part which was unquestionably true – Lord Avebury's revelation that Churchill had been pissed as a newt through much of the war, and that Gaitskell had to be carried out of a reception in Russia. This last story not only appears in Philip Williams's official biography, published in 1979, but also in Denis Healey's memoirs (*Healey's Eye*, Cape £7.50) reviewed by me in *Book Choice* in January of this year. Healey, who was there, recalls that Gaitskell was too drunk to make any press statement on Macmillan's announcement of the 1959 election so Bevan, of all people, had to make one for him.

If Lady Gaitskell looks a bit odd announcing at this late stage that it is all 'an absolute, awful lie', she doesn't look half so odd as Young Winston doing his Lord Goodman act, blowing himself up like a bullfrog to talk of 'a vile and malicious allegation against a man who cannot answer back'. The whole country knew about Winston, and nobody thought the worse of him for it. Can't silly little Winston see that this information – that his grandfather was paralytically drunk on occasions during the war – is not a bad advertisement for his grandfather so much as a good advertisement for drunkenness? After all, old Winston did actually win the war. My own father occasionally had one over the eight during the late Twenties and early Thirties – a time when he was writing novels which were not only good but actually *memorable*. And what, precisely, has Lord Avebury achieved in his eight years of teetotalling which is remotely comparable?

The English are slightly mad about drink. Many of us are at least slightly drunk for quite a large proportion of the time, yet to suggest that anyone is even slightly squiffy is held to be a 'vile and malicious allegation'. Militant teetotallers are a tiny minority, yet somehow they make all the running. If only we could get rid of the ludicrous guilt attaching to a normal social practice, we might be a happier nation. This guilt led Bevan, Crossman and Morgan Phillips to commit perjury, Dora Gaitskell and Young Winston to make fools of themselves; but the *real* enemies I insist are Lord Avebury and his Liverpool Mafia. Let us concentrate on them.

18.4.81

*   *   *

ASH

The Duke of Gloucester waited ten years before making his maiden speech in the House of Lords. Perhaps it has taken him that amount of time to think of anything to say. Perhaps he felt the country needed ten years to recover from the shock of his father's death. It may well be that the younger generation of *Spectator* readers has quite forgotten the old boy, described in his *Times* obituary of 11 June 1974 as 'a true descendent of George III'. But it was in the same year of evil memory – the last weeks of Edward Heath, two general elections, two Labour victories – that the present Duke, then in his 30th year, became patron of an unpleasant and querulous organisation called ASH, Action on Smoking and Health.

Possibly the Duke felt he should wait until he was in his 40th year because we might not attach enough importance to the thoughts of a younger man. But as his remarks bear an uncanny resemblance to everything which has been pouring out of the ASH organisation all these years I fear we must ignore the noble lips and mature mind from which they

173

come. We might even forget about the Duke for a moment and concentrate on the matter and timing of his first unhappy foray into public life.

Nearly every word he spoke, as I say, came from the literature of ASH, the organisation of anti-smoking fanatics. The Duke has allowed himself to be led by the beard, possibly thinking of that earlier Gloster who remarked: 'Tis the times' plague when madmen lead the blind.' Our present Duke, unfortunately, seems to lack the same felicity of expression.

'I regret,' he said, 'that many schools regard examinations as more important than health education on how the body works and the effects of mistreating it.'

I wonder on what basis he makes that statement. My own impression, having educated four children, is that a large part of the education system is devoted to nothing else. It may not be true as I have read (or possibly written) that many education authorities have 'Reasons for Not Smoking' as a subject on the CSE curriculum, but it is certainly true that every school in the country of which I have any knowledge devotes a whole course of lessons to the subject. Diseased lungs in plastic containers are passed round as regularly as collection plates in church. And the final result of all this anti-smoking propaganda is a generation of children with extraordinarily bad examination results who smoke like chimneys. Perhaps my own observation is not typical, but it seems to me that those who are now aged 15–20 smoke about ten times as much as those in the age group 21–26.

'The Government receives 3.7 per cent of its revenue from smoking,' said the Duke, reading, I imagine, straight from his ASH brief, 'but the National Health Service spends £170 million on treating smoking-induced diseases.'

He went on to produce the familiar and grotesquely random figure of 50 million working days lost through smoking, comparing it with the much smaller figure lost through strikes. Never mind that strikes stop production while occasional illness of staff usually has no effect whatever. The most glaring *suggestio falsi* is contained in the apparently insignificant figure of 3.7 per cent of government revenue when set against the huge figure of £170 million spent by the Health Service. In fact government revenue from tobacco tax is nearer £4,500 million. The government makes a huge profit from the smoking habit, and any arguments against it based on fiscal convenience are a gross and deliberate perversion of the truth.

The fact that ASH is prepared to wheel out fiscal considerations in support of its case reveals better than anything else that it is an organisation of fanatics. When it talks of 'premature' deaths through smoking – maturity, presumably, being assessed on something like the average life expectancy in developed countries, which has increased from 65 to 73

174

since 1950 – it does not mention that there is no conceivable economic advantage, and considerable economic disadvantage, in prolonging life expectancy still further. Although there may be some loss to the economy in pre-retirement deaths among that proportion of the workforce which is productively employed, it is more than offset by the gain to the economy in 'premature' post-retirement deaths and pre-retirement deaths in the parasitic sectors – coalmining, steel, shipbuilding, social services etc.

So far as government health policy is concerned, we are left with a repudiation of the whole horrible and tragic phenomenon of death and a vague, Scargill-like feeling that the government should do something about it, even where people freely decide on a course of action which may shorten their lives. But there is a further argument for government action against smoking based on its anti-social aspects: that smokers cause a nuisance and create a health-hazard for non-smokers, too. It is for this reason that trains and buses have always set aside areas for non-smokers, and accommodation has generally (if not always) been made in places of common resort for non-smokers to avoid the society of smokers, if they so wish. I confess, for my own part, that I generally prefer the company of smokers, finding them more trustworthy and likeable, although I also prepared to put up with the company of non-smokers if they are not too boring and do not smell too bad.

All that has changed in recent years is that the anti-smoking fanatics have discovered how non-smokers are in the majority. Quite suddenly, the right to smoke has lost all moral justification. Every busybody in the country feels he (or she) has been given the green light to ban smokers from any and every public area, and anyone subjected to momentary irritation from someone else's tobacco smoke feels justified in demanding redress. My own answer to this is that almost any form of social intercourse involves annoyance. People offend me by their stupidity, by their ugliness, by their smell, by the noises they make, and increasingly by the things they eat. Wherever I go people blow their microbes over me in foul-smelling gusts of air with pieces of hamburger and vinegar-flavoured crisps, egg sandwich (one of the worst) and Kit-Kat bars. I just smirk and cringe and agree with whatever banal observations they have to make about the weather or John McEnroe. The only people whose susceptibilities are adequately catered for are those who object to tobacco.

Yet the anti-smoking fanatics now feel they can conquer the world. Nothing else explains how a newspaper like the *Standard* dared ride roughshod over the very substantial minority of its readers who still smoke in demanding a London Transport ban. Nothing else explains why the Duke of Gloucester should now decide to offer us his weasel face as a pious figurehead for all the oppressive frenzies of ASH. His words, as I say, were not his own. He is only a symbol. We will not be doing anything to stifle debate, merely responding to his own symbolic role, if we pelt him with eggs.

30.6.84

14

THE BRITISH WAY OF SEX

Inventing New Sexual Offences

I suppose it is only to be expected that as evidence of normal heterosexual activity in these islands becomes rarer, the press should be more and more excited by any it can find. Since the popular newspapers love a good headline about sex, we cannot really protest against the efforts of headline-seeking MPs to provide them with one. But I do feel there may be something wrong when MPs, aided and abetted by the press, respond to the present dramatic decrease in sexual offences – they have shrunk by 20 per cent in ten years, according to the Howard League report – by trying to create new ones. This would have been the effect of Miss Janet Fookes's Sexual Offences Bill, which failed to complete the report stage in the House of Commons on Friday and has now been consigned to the oblivion it deserves.

I do not think I have ever had the pleasure of meeting Miss Fookes, although she has been an MP now for 15 years. No doubt this former teacher has been too busy, what with her chairmanship of the Royal Society for the Prevention of Cruelty to Animals, secretaryship of the all-party committee on mental health, her co-chairmanship of the all-party equal opportunities group and her council membership of SSAFA and the National Canine Defence League (to name but a few of her activities) to go out in the world and meet ordinary chaps like me. But I warned her, several times and in the plainest terms, that she was backing a loser in her silly, giddy little attempt to invent new sexual offences and increase the maximum penalty for old ones.

Now the fair MP for Plymouth Drake says she is 'deeply disappointed, hurt and very, very angry' with two back-bench colleagues who spoke against her measure. Perhaps she will take a word of advice from someone outside the fray. There are plenty of good headlines to be won on stories about pet animals. Has she heard the one about the Indian restaurant

176

which had a pile of cats' heads on its kitchen table? A Bill making it illegal for Indian restaurants to sell cat-meat would certainly go down well in the *Sun*. Or, in case someone pointed out that this was already illegal, a Private Member's Bill to increase the penalties for cruelty to children would certainly catch the mood of the moment. It would take a very brave MP to filibuster that one. Perhaps a joint Bill, to Protect Children and Control the use of Cat-meat in Restaurants, with further clauses increasing the penalties for cruelty to cats and making it illegal to eat children or serve them in restaurants. Many children, in my experience, are quite genuinely terrified of being eaten, and if the House could send out a firm message that eating children was now against the law, it might do something to reassure them – as well as discouraging evilly disposed people from eating them.

People may accuse me of treating Miss Fookes's anxieties lightly, but her Bill would appear to have had no more serious purpose. It fell to Mrs Jo Richardson, Labour Member for Barking, to point out that there were already perfectly good laws to deal with offensive kerb-crawlers who harassed women. They were the main target of Miss Fookes's Bill. The problem was that the police tended not to give a very high priority to such complaints. Was there any reason to suppose they would give a higher priority to complaints under Miss Fookes's Bill?

One amendment, proposed by Her Majesty's loyal Opposition, would have made it necessary for the kerb-crawler to have acted in a manner causing nuisance or fear, but Miss Fookes was not having any of that. Such an amendment would emasculate the Bill, she said – a curious metaphor, I thought, to apply to a measure proposed by a woman for the protection of women. To suggest that nuisance or fear might be necessary for the committing of an offence was to misunderstand the whole nature of the problem, she said. It was the cumulative effect on residents of frequent kerb-crawling which caused the nuisance.

This was what worried Mr Matthew Parris, one of the two heroes of the hour. You could not prosecute someone who was not guilty of causing a nuisance himself, but who might unwittingly have contributed to a general nuisance. He would accept the Bill only if the Home Office minister concerned, Mr David 'Dave' Mellor, was willing to insert the word 'persistently' into the clause describing the offence.

This caused one of those enjoyable little scenes which occur whenever MPs feel they have morality on their side. Mr Mellors accused Mr Parris of blackmail, and said it was Mr Parris's ego which was on trial. At another point, Mr Mellor said to another MP who expressed doubts about Miss Fookes's wisdom – Mr Anthony Marlow (C. Northampton N): 'I am interested that the welfare of women is of so little moment to you.'

Mr Marlow described this remark from his own front bench as 'ill-advised, somewhat stupid and impudent', complaining that the minister had threatened to 'spread my face large and wide across the national press' if he dared oppose the measure. Mr Marlow's main objection was that innocent men would be dragged through the courts on the say-so of any madwoman. 'It would do us no good as MPs should we be picked up,' he pointed out.

All of which is probably true enough. When Nottingham's publicity-seeking Chief Constable, Mr Charles 'Campaign Charlie' McLachlan, started dressing his policewomen up as tarts, one of the first people he arrested was a high-ranking policeman from a neighbouring force. I believe the experiment has now been discontinued. But Mr Mellor made the point that his aim in promoting the Bill was not to encourage a large number of prosecutions, but merely 'that the House should send out the message that kerb-crawling is now against the law' – which it already was.

In other words, the whole thing was a PR exercise designed to make a few headlines and appease some female activists. I can think of many more mischievous ways for the House to spend its time. If it did nothing else, there would be fewer cries to have all its Members garotted and thrown into the Thames. But so long as it can only draw attention to itself by passing redundant and oppressive laws in compliance with some passing whim of the *Sun*, *Sunday People* and *News of the World*, the cries will continue.

Thanks to Mr Parris Mr Marlow and Mrs Richardson, the House on this occasion sent out an entirely different message. I wish I had space to spread Mr Marlow's face large and wide across my page, decorated by an appropriate halo and celestial choir of cherubim and seraphim. But it really is time that politicians and gutter press alike realised that the country is not behind them in supporting the demands of ageing spinsters, embittered housewives, feminists and militant lesbians that any woman should be able to send any man to prison whenever she feels like it.

18.5.85

*   *   *

Shameful State of British Prostitution

'This is one of the greatest revivals since Lazarus,' gloated Mr David 'Dave' Mellor, the Home Office junior minister, after he had successfully gerrymandered Miss Janet Fookes's Sexual Offences Bill through the Commons. Last week I rejoiced that two courageous men had arisen from the fawning, greasy ranks of Conservative backbenchers to filibuster this disgusting measure out of existence. The incident demonstrated, as I thought, that the Conservative Party could still show some heroes when the need arose, as it once produced Winston Churchill. On this occasion I thought the House of Commons (whose Members are now demanding a huge increase in secretarial and research allowances on top of the £12,437 they already receive, on top of their £16,000 salary, on top of their free travel, postage, telephones . . .) had spent a useful afternoon in seeing off the hell-cat Fookes.

In his new novel, *The Kingdom of the Wicked*, Anthony Burgess claims that Lazarus lived only a very short time after being raised from the dead. I am not sure what his authority is for this, as I can find no suggestion of it in St John's Gospel. The most interesting thing about the raising of Lazarus is that it marked the great turning point in Jesus's fortunes. Although it won Him a certain amount of instant popularity among the Jews, from that moment the High Priests really had it in for Him, and they did not let go until He had been crucified. This is rather how I feel about the New Conservative Dave Mellor, who in the course of Friday's debate, answered objections that the police would use policewomen posing as tarts to arrest punters:

> We deprecate and deplore the *agents provocateurs*. We aim to ensure in the discussions we have with police forces up and down the country that police . . . orders reflect the extent of public concern that would arise if such police tactics were to be employed.

So goofy and half-witted were the Members present despite all their gorgeous, pouting secretaries and slim, liberated female research assistants from North America, that they let the slimy oaf get away with this. Anybody who has read the newspapers at all in the last two years would know not only that there is already a law in use against kerb-crawlers but also that police have been successfully prosecuting under it and using policewomen disguised as tarts in a blaze of prurient publicity from the entire gutter press, which was too excited by any news about sex to express the slightest disapproval.

This particular raising of Lazarus is thought by the Government to enjoy wide support in the country. I think they are wrong. Either it will be completely disregarded by the police, or it will be a serious nuisance, proving a charter for blackmailers, madwomen and androphobes. Last week I was so exhilarated to have found two wise and courageous men among all the sycophantic, nose-picking vulgarians in the Parliamentary Conservative Party that I saw no need to explain the unpleasant consequences of Miss Fookes's half-witted measure, if it had been allowed to succeed. Now these two heroes – Mr Parris and Mr Marlow – have been revealed as whey-faced poltroons and toadies like everybody else in Mrs Thatcher's accursed *galère*, I had better spell them out.

179

First, what is a kerb-crawler? By Miss Fookes's act it is anyone who solicits a woman for the purpose of prostitution from a motor-car, or having just got out of a motor-car. Penalty: £400, or £2,000 if the woman complains he has done it in a frightening manner. This measure does not therefore cover what is the main nuisance for respectable women walking in respectable streets who find themselves followed very slowly by a menacing car whose occupant then makes a lewd suggestion to her. It covers only *bona fide* punters trying to pick up tarts in one or another of the half-dozen or so areas in the British Isles where tarts still defy the Street Offences Act by loitering in the streets. It protects respectable women walking alone in these particular areas, who, in nearly every case, can easily signify to the punter that he has made a mistake. No doubt there is a nuisance involved in having to point this out, but it is not an earth-shaking one. The punter then pushes off.

However, the measures now being taken to remove this very minor nuisance to a tiny minority of women will leave the field open for any madwoman, militant lesbian or man-hater – and, God knows, there are enough of them around – to complain to the police of any motorist anywhere in the country, who asks her the time of day, or whistles at her, claiming that she has been solicited for the purpose of prostitution. Perhaps the unfortunate man will get off, perhaps he won't, but in either case his name will be dragged through the courts.

Now let us look at the proposed law as it will affect the prostitute. She stands outside all day, a large part of her time being taken up with such badinage as this: 'How much?' 'Twenty quid, dear, short time, with a rubber.' 'For you? You have got to be joking.' 'Fuck off, then.' 'You're dead right, I will.'

British prostitutes, I should explain, have the reputation for being not only the ugliest and greediest but also the laziest in the world. Few even pretend to enjoy the job, they make no secret of despising their customers and being in it only for money. Many will tend to sympathise with them, but that is just part of the English disease. If a job is worth doing at all, it is worth doing well, and these women are a disgrace. The inevitable result of the Fookes Act will be that instead of saying 'fuck' these lazy women will say 'Fookes':

'How much?' 'It depends what for, dear.' 'You know.' 'You mean straight intercourse, dear?' 'Yes.' 'I have taken your car number and will report you to the police.' 'You have got to be joking.' 'Not unless you pay me £50.' 'For nothing?' 'For not reporting you.'

Soon half the unemployed female school-leavers in the land will be on the game, and totally innocent men (to the extent that any men are ever totally innocent) will find themselves facing blackmail demands. The Act could only work if every unsuccessful prosecution under it was followed by a prosecution of the complainant for wasting police time. But according to the Howard League Report, one in four allegations of rape investigated by the police is found to be malicious, dishonest or mad, and how many prosecutions do we see for that waste of police time?

Now this silly and hysterical measure goes to the Lords. Perhaps they will produce some heroes where the Commons so conspicuously failed. In retrospect one can see that the raising of Lazarus (whose sister, Mary – the foot-washer – is widely thought to have been a prostitute) was one of the worst mistakes Jesus ever made. The House of Lords should take note when they see the Bill, and listen to me when I say, 'Lords, by this time it stinketh.'

25.5.85

* * *

Changing Sexes

Some months ago, I was intrigued to read that a large firm of underwear manufacturers in this country was altering its designs to take account of the changing shape of English women: their breasts had grown smaller, their shoulders broader, and their waists thicker. At about the same time I read that there could be no question of a return to the Sixties' mini-skirt because English women's legs were now shorter and heavier than before. At the time I filed this information away as confirming my own observation of the matter; it offered only peripheral support to my main theory, that there is an epidemic of masculinity among young British womanhood, which can be compared, in the extent of its depredations, with the blight of the Dutch elm disease.

My main observation is that, as their bodies become less feminine and less alluring, their minds are invaded by many of the less pleasing characteristics of the criminal male psychopath: senseless aggression, perverse illogicality, power mania, and egomaniac disregard for others. Babies may be aborted, children neglected or deserted, parents consigned tooblivion, all in the pursuit of some fugitive notion of personal fulfilment.

Male reactions are the least reported aspect of the female revolution, apart from the reactions of those few quislings who are proud to be ridden, saddled and bridled through the women's pages of the *Guardian* or the *Sunday Times*, to announce that they have found a new fulfilment in changing nappies, emptying potties, and carrying a handbag. Others gloomily announce that they have been vasectomised, but for the most part we are the people of England that have never spoken yet.

Perhaps a study of male underwear may reveal some clues. In this week's murder trial at St Alban's Crown Court, a wife denied murdering

181

her husband, while apparently admitting at one point that she battered him to death after drugging him. She then helped throw his body over a bridge over the A1. Her reasons for this, she said, were that she objected to his wearing women's underwear, and also to the infrequency of sexual intercourse between them. Presumably, the defence is one of diminished responsibility. The husband, a former guardsman of 6'3" was called Fred Chapman. When the wife found him wearing a nightdress, he explained that 'it was just a little way of his'.

For all one knows, many guardsmen have these little ways. It was the violence of Mrs Chapman's reaction which first made me suspect that Mr Chapman's choice of underwear marked a new departure. But at that stage I attributed it all to the phenomenon of the changing female, rather than suspecting a masculine response to this new breed of womanhood, although the name Fred Chapman, so evocative of decent English masculinity, struck a poignant chord.

Then, on Thursday, my wife went to Taunton to buy some new underwear for her two sons, both of school age, and both acutely aware of sexual differentiation in all its forms. She reported that the men's departments were selling frilly women's knickers. I supposed that she had made a mistake and went to see myself. It was quite true. In the men's department of Marks and Spencer there are stacks and stacks of women's knickers, described as polyester hipsters, in a bewildering variety of shades: forget-me-not, fuchsia, mushroom, dark blue (possibly for nautical types) and white (no doubt for the darker skin). What puzzled me most was not so much their dainty form as their basic design. Not to put too fine a point on it, they were designed in such a way that no man wishing to relieve himself could safely do so without lowering his trousers first.

Plainly, something very odd is happening to English men. If their reason for wearing these inconvenient objects is to attract the new Englishwomen, they have the pitiful example of Fred Chapman to disabuse them. But I do not think that this is their intention. No, it seems to me that the sexes in England are in massive retreat from each other. The only possible reason for this absurd underwear is to repel the opposite sex. Yet the media have ignored this massive development, and so far as I know there is only one organisation in this country catering for it.

This, strangely enough, is organised by another person called Chapman. Gerald Chapman is a 29-year-old homosexual who, for several years now, has been running the Young People's Theatre Scheme at the Royal Court theatre. Until recently I ignoed it, assuming it to be just another of the left-wing indoctrination centres supported by the Arts Council, usually in the East End of London. But in the past few months Chapman, who feels that 'sexual liberation is crucially linked to the class struggle' has been engaged in a campaign to educate London schoolchildren in general – and black schoolchildren in particular – in the ways of homosexuality. The scheme's earlier courses of lectures generally mixed left-wing politics ('a discussion of racism in schools: in memory of Blair Peach') with sexual instruction' 'the Young Black and Sexual Roles ... Michael Hamilton, (16) will talk about his experiences as a young gay.'

But the most recent course has been entirely devoted to the theme of 'Youth and Sexuality'. At an earlier seminar, Mr Chapman was proud to announce that the 300 children attending included a party from the Roman Catholic convent in Brent. Throughout October and November, his Young People's Theatre Scheme was addressed by Anna Raeburn (on counselling); Angela Phillips (of the National Abortion Campaign); Maureen Colquhoun (described as an ex-Labour MP, feminist, lesbian); Rose Robertson (Parents' Enquiry for Gay Teenagers); Hazel Slavin (contraception); and Lucy Toothpaste (Rock against Sexism).

And the poor little things thought they were joining a theatre group! More conventional schemes, like the National Youth Theatre, have the greatest difficulty squeezing money out of the Arts Council, but Mr Chapman not only profits from the £305,000 subsidy given to the Royal Court but has also been appointed to a seat on the Drama Panel.

The best idea of what Mr Chapman is up to can be gleaned from the Royal Court Circular newspaper of his Young People's Theatre. The following is written by Rose Robertson of Parents' Enquiry, founded to counsel the parents of gay children, 'as well as to offer advice and support to the teenagers themselves': The heterosexual boy or girl from the age of seven or eight is enabled to indulge in horseplay which has an underlying sexuality in it. From the age of 12 or 13 they are able to go out with each other quite freely. The homosexual girl or boy is totally denied that opportunity ...

'What we do at Parents' Enquiry is to discuss sex with them. Because there's no book they can read where they can find out what happens between two gay people, it can be quite a frightening experience for a young person. They don't know what is going to happen to them. We teach them how to take care of themselves if they're propositioned; what to do, what to say. Imagine a young person in a gay pub or club for the first time – a mixture of feelings. They're flattered that they're noticed, they're frightened at what is going to happen to them. That's why we arrange for them to go in a group with an older person in charge.'

How touching to think that older persons can still make themselves useful in the new sexual revolution.

8.12.79

*   *   *

Naked Infants

After all the recent hysteria about the Child Protection Bill, when Mr
Ian Mikardo, the Labour MP, was practically accused of supporting the
vile trade in child pornography, we have at last been given a chance to
examine the Bill as it ambles its way through its second reading in the
House of Lords. To judge from press reaction, and from statements by
various opportunist MPs, one might have supposed that child pornography was a new and hideous development which somehow escaped
existing legislation on obscene publication and protection of minors, while
threatening to corrupt a whole generation of British schoolchildren for
the unscrupulous gain of these merchants in human misery . . .

At last, it seemed, the politicians, had found something to say which
would win them a little applause. What noble abhorrence they expressed
when Mr Mikardo threatened to delay this Bill, so vital to the moral
survival of our children! Anybody who could support such unspeakable
exploitation of children should be caned – not just caned, but thrashed
slowly, for hours at a time, on the bare bottom with a special, springy
lightweight twenty-eight-inch cutting cane such as only the British know
how to make. If volunteers were needed to deliver this correction, I have
no doubt we could rely on the sense of duty of a score of Tory MPs.
Why, child pornography is even worse than football hooliganism, school
vandalism, mugging and all the other crimes which give enthusiasts for
corporal punishment their occasional, tantalising moments of hope.

The English are undoubtedly an odd race, but not so odd as to produce
anyone with a good word to say for child pornography. The only problems for those who wish to say a great deal more about it, and pass new
laws against it, are (as the Home Office revealed during Friday's debate)
that in the first place it is almost non-existent in this country, in the
second place it is already against the law.

Lord Harris of Greenwich, Minister of State at the Home Office, was
able to inform their Lordships that since the second reading of the Bill
in the House of Commons the Home Office had made extensive inquiries
of the Director of Public Prosecutions, the police, Customs and other
authorities:

'The clear message the Home Office had received was that for practical
purposes the present law was capable of dealing with such cases as arose
of children being used for pornographic purposes. The usefulness of the
Bill was very much on the margins of the problem.'

It was simply not true, as vulgar rumour had it, that the use of children
in pornography was a 'widespread and growing practice'. Such material
as was to be found, he said, came 'almost exclusively from abroad'. It
was already seized by Customs and police whenever found. Where the

taking of such photographs involved the commission of more serious sexual offences against children it was already well covered by the criminal law, but even the simple act of taking an indecent photograph of a child was probably covered by the Indecency with Children Act, 1960. Both Customs and the Metropolitan Police advised that there had been no increase in the amount of such material in circulation.

But of course the Government would support this fatuous and otiose measure, he said – is it likely that any government would do anything else? – in recognition of its possible contribution in a problem that was 'more potential than actual'.

Of the various lords and bishops who spoke on the first day of the second reading, only Lord Houghton of Sowerby hinted that their Lordships were being led up the garden path. Wittily describing it as 'a Buffalo Bill, a stampede', he said that it was not legislation at all so much as a rush: 'It was a strange piece of legislation giving new rights to the police for intrusion on the lives of citizens. It had not been examined in detail for the evidence and justification for it.'

Lord Wigoder seemed to confirm this:

'The only practical distinction between the Bill and the Obscene Publications Act is that the Bill could catch a photographer who took pornographic photographs for his private purposes.'

But having studied the new Bill in conjunction with the Obscene Publications Acts of 1959 and 1964, the Indecency with Children Act (1960) the various post-war Sexual Offences Acts (1956, 1967, 1976) and the catch-all Act of 1885, it seems to me that the new Bill has one new application and one new application only. By its emphasis on the taking of indecent (as opposed to obscene) photographs for private purposes, it forbids parents to photograph their children or babies with no clothes on.

Now I agree that this is a very tiresome thing for parents to do. Such photographs humiliate their children when they are older, and can prove a grave embarrassment if they become bishops or Cabinet Ministers. But is the taking or possession of these photographs so vile and so despicable an offence as to merit a fine of £10,000 and/or three years' imprisonment, which is what the Bill proposes?

13.5.78

*   *   *

The Decline in Sexual Activity

The best news of July 1977 was the demise of Jack Ashley's Bill giving the Crown the right to appeal against whatever it regarded as a lenient sentence for rape or sexual assault. Not only was the principle of the Bill

185

repulsive – and this alone would have justified its humiliating defeat – but its application to the field of sexual offences was particularly incongruous. As Mr Nicholas Fairbairn, the flamboyant Member for Kinross, pointed out in opposing the Bill, rape and sexual offences are the only crimes which have been consistently falling for the last ten years, yet they are the only crimes which excite Labour MPs to ask for greater sentences.

This reduction in the number of sexual offences committed has continued despite the recently-imposed rule that a complainant shall have her identity protected while the victim of her complaint must see his name and photograph splashed all over the newspapers with any revolting details of his alleged offence – even when he is later found innocent.[1] Nor is a female's sexual or emotional history allowed to be taken into account when considering the plausibility of her story. Soon, I suspect, she will not even have to submit to a medical examination. At the time I demonstrated, in company with a few other wise men, how these measures created an open invitation not only for hysterical, jilted or otherwise unsatisfied women to use the courts for their own private vendettas, but also for unscrupulous women to blackmail any unfortunate men who fell into their clutches. And when the Criminal Compensation Board fixed the tariff for a proven rape at £1,000 to the injured party, one marvelled at the honesty of British prostitutes and escort agents, as they are now called, who continue to ply their trade at £20 a time (Arabs £30 extra).

But despite the official incitement to malicious or vexatious prosecution, the reported incidence of rape and sexual assault continues to fall. Perhaps the grotesque suggestion that wives should be able to prosecute their husbands for demanding intercourse when the wife does not wish it will do something to swell these sagging statistics, but I begin to doubt it. Whole ranges of new sexual offences may be created – inadequate attention to foreplay, insufficient post-coital discussion – but I can't help feeling that the number of prosecutions will continue to shrink, since they are part of the general phenomenon of declining sexual activity.

Whether this phenomenon is worldwide, or confined to the advanced industrial nations, or confined to the British Isles, is something which remains to be established. But evidence that it applies in this country is everywhere, and not only in the declining numbers of sexual offences. The Stationery Office's survey *Population Trends No. 8* shows that the birthrate fell so sharply again last year that the surplus of deaths over births doubled. Fewer and fewer people are bothering to get married – weddings dropped by 25,500, while divorces have shown the sort of rise one normally associates only with unemployment or the price of coffee.

1. This anomaly was later removed.

Fifteen years ago there was one divorce for every twelve marriages; last year there was one divorce for every 2.8 marriages. The most elementary graph will show that people who married last year are more likely than not to divorce, and that divorces will outnumber marriages very soon.

So the final projection must be for an ageing population of sexually inert single people, whether unmarried or divorced, whose few remaining acts of conception – something caught from the unisex public lavatory seats of the future, no doubt – are invariably terminated by abortion. Of course, one can see a few advantages to this – 'Children are such sticky things,' as Georgie Pillson remarks in *Queen Lucia*, 'specially after tea' – and it would obviously be unfair to blame it all on Mr Jack Ashley. Even Mr Nicholas Fairbairn – whom I do not think I have ever met, although he sounds a thoroughly good egg – shows sign of waning sexual activity. In *Who's Who* for 1974 he listed among his recreations 'making love'. The year after, they were merely described as 'creative' – a reference, I suppose, to his painting. This year they are given as 'bunking and de-bunking'. I am not surely exactly what is involved in the new recreation of 'bunking and debunking' but begin to fear that it may fall short of actual *penetratio ad vaginam*.

In fact, the extent to which such remaining sexual activity is nearly all in the imagination could scarcely be better illustrated than by the way in which the House of Commons is held up in the vulgar press as a hotbed of illicit sex. Anybody who has been there will know that they are all much too drunk for anything of that sort. There is a lot of dirty talk in the bars, smoking rooms and cafeterias, but nothing actually ever happens. To speak of marriages being broken there through pressure of work is, of course, even more absurd. Members of Parliament who divorce are merely conforming to the national pattern.

If I am right when I say that most sexual activity in this country now takes place in the imagination then it follows that most accused rapists must be innocent. Equally obviously, not all are innocent and I can imagine that it must be a highly disagreeable thing to be raped, one which might well have harmful long-term effects. It is perfectly reasonable that the law should seek to protect women from such an experience, as it has always done in every civilised community. But there are a number of equally unpleasant experiences against which the law provides no protection. A few years ago, I stubbed my big toe very nastily against some hard object or other. The pain was excruciating, lasted a long time, and might well have had deleterious long-term effects if I had been a more sensitive soul.

Obviously, the law can only provide a remedy where suffering (or long-term psychological trauma, or both) is caused by the malice or

187

negligence of another. It cannot heed the enormously greater part of humanity's suffering, as represented by my big toe, which is caused either by one's own error of judgment or by circumstances outside one's control. Of all the suffering around us in this vale of tears, I should not imagine that one thousandth part of one thousandth part is caused by rape. Of all crimes to which mankind is tempted, it is the one least likely to be influenced by the chances of acquittal or by the prospect of a heavier or lighter sentence or conviction unless, perhaps, we were to return to mutilation and the death penalty. So the question is bound to arise, as Mr Fairbairn raised it, *why are MPs so excited about rape?*

Let us thank heavens that these frustrated politicians, half-stunned by drink as they are, have returned to brooding wistfully over their perished members. Once they had set themselves on the course of revenge, there is no knowing where it would have ended.

30.7.77

*   *   *

Lord Wigg

'If you want anything, see my solicitor,' said Lord Wigg, as his final word on the magistrates' court hearing which acquitted him last week of having used insulting behaviour likely to cause a breach of the peace.

Wigg was charged with kerb-crawling in the West End of London and accosting women – six incidents were listed – in such a manner as to have endangered the peace. His defence was that he was merely seeking to buy a newspaper, to wit the *Daily Express*. The Wells Street magistrate, Mr Lawrence Tobin – a fearless, intelligent, honourable and experienced man, by all accounts – found that no threat to the peace had been proved, and Lord Wigg was duly acquitted.

Another great triumph for British justice. Even the police seem to come out of it well this time, which must be a source of great pleasure to such law-abiding people as Lord Wigg and myself. I found the Wigg incident absorbing for a number of reasons – not least of which was the identity of the character witnesses chosen. As a journalist and a Catholic myself, I was naturally gratified that a Member of the Queen's Most Honourable Privy Council, privy to many of Her Majesty's most intimate secrets, should, when his reliability was called into question, summon the assistance of a Catholic and two journalists.

Lord Mowbray, the Catholic in the case, gave evidence which, as reported, may seem to have been peripheral to the main point. He and his lady wife, who live opposite Lord Wigg's basement flat in Warwick

188

Square, were 'often struck by this rather weird figure out at night. He was walking forty yards or so, stopping, staring into space, and he gave one the impression he was officious or snooping.' Lord Wigg struck him 'as being a night bird.'

So much for the Catholic. Of the two journalists, Mr Chapman Pincher, who had known Lord Wigg for thirteen years, gave him the sort of reference one might give to a cook when there is plainly not much one can say about her cooking: 'I have never known him to tell me a lie in all the numerous altercations we have had. He sets enormous store by his integrity.'

The other journalist – Sir Harry Boyne, former lobby correspondent of the *Daily Telegraph* – was of particular interest to me, as I have been making a study of the relationship between politicians and parliamentary lobby journalists for many years. Sir Harry's testimony seems to mark a breakthrough in this delicate relationship:

'I would say he has two outstanding characteristics. One is truthfulness, another is his phenomenal memory.'

One or other of these outstanding characteristics must have been dormant on this occasion, if we are to believe the magistrate. Summing up, Mr Tobin said:

'I have the unenviable task of having to decide whether Lord Wigg, with a long and proud career of outstanding service to this country, is on this occasion lying as to these miserable events.'

With seemly reluctance, Mr Tobin came to the conclusion that Lord Wigg was, indeed, lying: 'Lord Wigg's account I cannot accept,' he said before commending the policeman, who had frequently been accused of lying by Wigg's counsel, for his straightforwardness and restraint. The only happy aspect of these miserable events is the vindication of Sergeant McNulty.

Mr Tobin was right, of course, to remind us of Lord Wigg's long and proud career of outstanding service: his period between the wars in the regular army; his gallant war spent in the Royal Army Education Service and ended with the rank of Colonel; his fearless hounding of Profumo out of public life and out of the Privy Council (for younger readers I should explain that Profumo had lied to the House of Commons about his sex life. Unlike Lord Wigg, Profumo was not on oath at the time, but it was the security aspect which worried our George, as he then was), for which he was rewarded with the nastiest job in Wilson's 1964 Government, allegedly that of spying on the Cabinet for possible security risks. Many would have shrunk from this snooping, spying and reporting on colleagues, especially on their sex lives, but the George of song and story did not shrink. Now, at the age of seventy-six, with only his various pensions, his parliamentary expenses as a Life Peer and his Presidency of

189

the Betting Office Licensees' Association to live on, he stands as a terrible rebuke to all Englishmen with a social conscience.

It was this aspect of the matter which first aroused my concern. I use the word 'concern' advisedly, since it might seem boastful to talk of the deep compassion I feel towards old men who may have sex problems. It may or may not be safe to assume at this stage that Lord Wigg *was* kerb-crawling and accosting strange women in the West End of London, as the magistrate decided and two policemen confidently testified. Again, he may or may not have felt so ashamed of his actions that he chose to lie repeatedly on oath, as the magistrate rather seems to believe. Let us thank Heaven, at least, that his behaviour, if such it was, presented no threat to the peace.

But should old men be allowed to kerb-crawl and accost at their will? If so, what about the unfortunate women so accosted? They can scarcely claim compensation from the Criminal Injuries Compensation Board, since no crime has been committed. If any more meaningful relationship develops from their encounters, of course, they can always claim to have been raped and collect that way. The going rate, according to the Board's report, is £1,000 for a rape which involves no physical injury and no exceptional psychological trauma. Now that rape victims are so well protected from impertinent questions about their past history, I am surprised that more ladies of the town do not adopt this policy.

Another suggestion for the humane and progressive treatment of these old men is that they should be put in homes where they can accost, ogle and even discreetly goose the nurses, many of whom will probably come from Jamaica or Pakistan, or even as far afield as Hong Kong. But this solution ignores important considerations of human liberty. What about those old folk who quite genuinely wish to buy the *Daily Express*, as they are legally entitled to do? Indeed it is the magistrate's opinion that this was Lord Wigg's intention when he set off on his ill-fated expedition to the West End. Quite possibly he only wanted to know what was in William Hickey – a comparatively innocent taste, and certainly not sufficient reason to confine him in an institution or sentence him to pinching black women's bottoms for the rest of his life.

Any discussion of this problem is bound to be clouded by an awareness that any of us might grow old and face a similar one. Those of us who missed the great teenage sexual revolution and can only watch it from afar, with whatever degree of vicarious longing, or jealous disapproval, or mature, principled appraisal – we, the lost generation, can be certain only that our problems are likely to get worse, not better. At the age of forty we will see the puzzled wariness in the eyes of twenty-year-olds we are trying to chat up give way to embarrassment and dislike. Far worse, at the age of fifty-five it will be replaced by embarrassment and pity. Then comes the kerb-crawl and that endless agonising search for a copy – any copy – of the *Daily Express*. God help us all and grant us a dignified old age, untroubled by such urges.

11.12.76

15

DRUGS

The American Example

Nearly four years ago I wrote an article in the *Sunday Telegraph* complaining about a mendacious campaign being waged against alcohol by elements in the DHSS. A toady on the *Sunday Times* had been briefed by a DHSS minister to say that Britain was suffering from an epidemic of alcoholism, swinging measures to combat it were being prepared by the government etc. After spending some time on the actual figures for alcoholism which showed there was no epidemic of any sort, nor any significant increase, I remarked that it was curious the DHSS should waste so much time on promoting a non-existent epidemic for alcoholism when anybody could see a genuine and growing epidemic of heroin addiction among the young.

That remark, which was based on my own observation, was made nearly four years ago, as I say. So far as I can see, the heroin epidemic continued to grow for about two years after that and then started to tail off, being replaced among the latest arrivals on the junkie scene by cocaine – equally toxic, equally lethal and capable of inflicting worse permanent brain damage, but slightly less addictive in that dependence is psychological rather than chemical. Another comforting aspect of the craze for cocaine is that much of the stuff sold to would-be ravers in the early stages of their involvement is, I believe, chalk powder, which probably does them little harm to sniff.

However, three years after I had noticed an increase in heroin taking among the young and about a year after it had started to tail off, the press took an interest, splashing endless stories about young junkies who had died. These stories usually featured a parent (who emerged from the story in heroic colours) on a trail of vengeance against drug dealers. Then, after a few desultory cries for the return of hanging, mandatory life sentences or the introduction of Chinese water torture for drug dealers

191

(especially those who sell their wares to the young) we ladies and gentlemen of the press turned our attention to the next thing, whether it was
'Star Wars' or skate boarding.

Now, a year later again, the House of Commons has decided to take
notice. Eleven backbenchers – three Labour and eight Conservatives, who
included this page's own Miss Janet Fookes – went on a ten-day junket
(oops, fact-finding tour) of a sort which is familiar enough to journalists.
We call them freebies. Presumably they saw a great deal of the US Drug
Enforcement Agency, an unpleasant body whose bread and butter
depends on playing up (if not deliberately exaggerating) the US drug
problem.

But surely no cub reporter on a first assignment for his school magazine
would have accepted without question – let alone printed as gospel – the
grotesquely pilgered figures produced by the DEA: that illegal drug traffic
in the US was worth between $90 billion and $100 billion a year; that
'each day there are 5,000 new (cocaine) addicts, mainly from the wealthy
and successful middle and upper classes, who spend up to $3,000 (about
£2,300) each a week to satisfy their craving.'

That 'up to' is a beautiful piece of pilgering. Just how many people can
possibly afford to spend $156,000 a year on cocaine? The British fact-
finders announce that 12 million people in the US now use cocaine. Even
the DEA claims only four million. Our fearless fact-finders continue:

> So much cocaine is being seized in the US that there is a shortage of
> storage space, and so many traffickers are being imprisoned that there
> is a shortage of prison space.

The idea that in the whole country there is nowhere to store three or
four tonnes of seized cocaine is not even laughable; we already have a
problem of prison crowding over here before Miss Janet Fookes starts
sending minor sexual criminals and drug dealers to prison for life. It is
the hallmark of deeply second-rate minds that they always think of punishing people first. Sir Edward Gardner, the group's leader, would have
preferred the death penalty for major drug traffickers, but gracefully gave
way to the idea of life sentences plus confiscation of property, with
confiscation of property for those who are merely suspected by the police
(or army, navy, airforce, MI5 – possibly the fire brigade, too, traffic
wardens and lollypop women). Their proposal is that the police should
be able to confiscate anybody's property at any time. To get it back, the
citizen should have to be able to prove that he had not acquired it
through dealing in drugs. Were the MPs really so stupid and ignorant as
to suppose this ludicrous suggestion would find favour?[1]

1. It did.

We should not be surprised that backbenchers are such deeply second-rate people when we examine what emerges on the Front Bench, presumably the *crème de la crème*. The only useful lesson to be learned from the United States is that whatever may be the best response to the drug problem, the Americans have not discovered it. Vast sums of money spent by the DEA have not succeeded in making any impact on the supply of drugs, nor have draconian penalties, nor the confiscation of property. Whatever the best policy may be, the Americans have consistently chosen the worst, and it is not intelligent to copy them at this late stage. If the Gardner-Fookes proposals have any effect at all, it will simply be to make drugs more expensive and increase the incidence of mugging and burglaries to pay for them.

To achieve such a doubtful advantage, these hysterical MPs will have given the police (not to mention MI5 etc) a hideous new battery of powers over the lives of us all. Obviously the problem is a difficult one, but these clowns do not even begin to have an answer. I should have thought that the best way to discourage new punters in the field would be to stiffen penalties for possession (since nothing will deter the dealers) sending the Takis[1] of this world down for a statutory 18 months plus fine, while flooding the market with chalk powder for cocaine and some inert soluble crystal for heroin. That seems to me the best way of discouraging the spread of the habit. But one does not need to visit the United States to work it out.

1.6.85

*　　*　　*

The Real Case against Heroin

Long before I started writing a regular column in the *Spectator* 17 years ago I was, if not beating the drum for drugs, at any rate making tentative little squeaks towards the idea that liberalisation might be a good idea. Geoffrey Wheatcroft[2] is quite wrong when he says that the subject carries a taboo in political and journalistic debate. It has been endlessly discussed. Eleven years ago I ended a piece in the *New Statesman*, after complaining bitterly about the noise and smells made by proletarian holidaymakers in the West Country, with a passionate plea for some narcotic which would stop them producing so many goods, earning so much money: 'History, having destroyed religion as the opium of the people,

1. Taki Theodorakopoulous, *Spectator* journalist imprisoned for six months for cocaine offences.
2. A *Spectator* journalist.

now requires that they should be given a taste of the real stuff,' I concluded rather grandly. Nobody complained.

Time and again I have urged in these pages that the same solution should be applied to the negro problem in the US and to our own unemployment problem here. Mr Wheatcroft is undoubtedly right when he argues that three-quarters of the present problems created by heroin are a product of its illegality – the muggings, the deaths from impure heroin and from overdoses of heroin of unexpected strength, even to some extent the deaths from blood poisoning and hepatitis due to infected needles and from malnutrition, which might be prevented if druggies lived less as outcasts from society. I am not sure of this last proposition, however. One of the chief characteristics of people who take heroin is that they become the most tremendous bores, unfit for the company of any but their own kind. I remain convinced, whatever I may say hereafter, that the main drive against heroin, which comes from the United States' gigantic Drug Enforcement Agency (almost a third great world power in many parts of the near, middle and far East, as well as an unwelcome addition to our own secret police and customs networks in this country) is a response to that country's terror of its own blacks. I do not argue that Americans are wrong to be terrified of their blacks, merely that it is a most unintelligent reaction to this terror. A more intelligent – if less high-minded – reaction would be to ensure that heroin and other comforts for the underprivileged are easier and cheaper rather than harder and more expensive to acquire.

Even these arguments from a basis of misanthropic *Realpolitik* are harder to sustain when one reflects that heroin was an important, if not decisive, factor in America's military defeat by the North Vietnamese. The fact remains that so long as the Russians are breathing down our necks we cannot put a large proportion of our productive workforce out to grass or to poppies, as the case may be. Until Russia collapses in on itself, we will simply have to put up with the stink and the noise.

In any case, there is all the difference in the world between urging a cheap opiate for the masses on social and environmental grounds, and arguing it on grounds of human liberty. It was Mr Wheatcroft's eloquent advocacy for the decriminalisation of heroin on libertarian grounds that finally convinced me there should be no change in the law. First, perhaps, one should look at his non-libertarian reasons for a change. To say that heroin is not a poison (unless taken in excess) or not addictive (because will-power is required to break the habit) is neither paradoxical nor clever but plain wrong. Heroin's toxicity is about 200 times that of ethyl alcohol, closer to cyanide than to strychnine or arsenic. It has a rapid effect on the respiratory function which can cause death in tiny doses. It induces not only a psychological dependence (which itself is a sufficient indicator

194

of addiction) but also a biochemical dependence whereby sudden withdrawal can bring about physical collapse. Heroin, which was removed from the British Pharmacopoeia in 1953, is now only used in terminal illness, and it unquestionably produces an addiction in patients. When Wheatcroft quotes his guru, Dr Thomas Szasz, we tend to defer, supposing that anybody with such a ridiculous name must indeed be wise. The truth is otherwise. What Szasz actually has to say is quite as silly as anything ever said by Steiner, de Bono, or the abominable Warlock–Jenkins–Runcie machine.

What the libertarian case boils down to is that man (yes groan, and woman, too) has the right to destroy himself/herself if it wishes, and heroin should be freely available for this purpose. The first question to ask is at what age man/woman inherits this right. Certainly not Wheatcroft, probably not even Szasz would argue that children of three or four have the right to knock themselves off in this way. So we must place it at whatever arbitrary age society has chosen as marking adulthood – 18 or 21.

Now we all know – Wheatcroft, I and probably Szasz – that all this talk of liberal individualism is so much whistling in the wind. There is not the slightest possibility that any sane democratic government will ever legalise heroin (morphia was separated only in 1803; the first Pharmacy Act was passed in 1868). We are just striking attitudes. It is only when one examines the *reasons* behind this impossibility that one sees the real weaknesses in the libertarian case.

The reason that no democratic government will decriminalise this fairly agreeable short cut to oblivion and death is nothing to do with agitation in the meejer. Two years ago, when the DHSS was conducting one of its periodic anti-drink scares, I pointed out in the *Sunday Telegraph* that we were in the middle of a genuine heroin epidemic. The idea has now caught on. I fancy I find the current campaign against drug-pushers in the gutter press, and appearance of a crusading rock star at the Conservative Party Conference, as irritating as Mr Wheatcroft does. At least drug-pushers provide a service, and if any section of our society would benefit from massive injections of heroin it is surely the rock music scene. The trouble is that when young persons reach the age of 18 or 21 they represent 18 or 21 years of care, effort, affection and even money invested by their parents. No parents will agree that Wheatcroft should allow their fledglings the opportunity to choose agreeable oblivion the second they are flown from the nest. So make the age of voluntary oblivion 40. By then, most people are married with children. Do spouses and children have no rights?

The truth is that Wheatcroft's concept of liberty is a chimera, applying only to orphan bachelors (and, groan, bachelor girls, too) or childless widows and widowers. The rest of us are held in bonds of affection and family duty, if not of responsibility towards employers or public. The degree of liberty which Wheatcroft seeks could be imposed only by a deeply unpopular dictatorship. That is the contradiction in his brand of 'liberal individualism'.

20.10.84

16

LAW AND ORDER

Nymph, in Thy Orifices

It seems unlikely that more than a thousand people in this country have read Mr Leon Brittan's Police and Criminal Evidence Bill, now going through its final Committee stages. I certainly do not claim to be among their number, having learned what little I know about it from various press reports, from rumour and gossip and from my faithful correspondent Mr George Stern, of the Highgate Archway Motorway Extension Act Group. Mr Stern, when last he addressed himself to the matter, seemed to be of the opinion that the Bill empowered any police constable in the country to stop any private citizens he chose, with or without grounds for suspecting them of a crime, and not only search them but make them submit to an *intimate body search*.

In fact, closer scrutiny suggests that this power of intimate body search will be restricted to cases where people are taken into custody, and that before a police officer is permitted to undertake any search, rather than a doctor of the appropriate sex, it will have to be authorised by a police superintendent. For those who are puzzled by ranks in the police force, I think it is accurate to say that a superintendent is about the equivalent of an army major.

The most significant aspect of Thursday's debate in committee was the appearance of a group of Conservative MPs who opposed restrictions on the police right to conduct intimate body searches when and where they might choose. But before exploring these wilder shores of modern authoritarian Conservatism, as represented by the unbelievable Mr Eldon Griffiths, perhaps we had better glance at what the Bill *will* allow in this sensitive area.

On Thursday, an Opposition amendment to insist that such searches should always be carried out by a properly qualified doctor was defeated in committee. Not to put too fine a point on it, this means that on the nod from a station superintendent, any one of us taken into custody is liable to find his arse being groped by a policeman; any woman is liable to be searched in her anus and vagina by a police officer of the same sex. We may not have been charged with anything, and we may never be charged, but we must submit to these searches on pain of having whatever force is necessary used against us, and on pain of being charged with obstructing or assaulting the police if we resist.

The justification for this is that we may be carrying weapons in our bottoms. Apparently some people do. In fact, this is the only thing the police are allowed to search for. If, in the course of their explorations, they find the Ruritanian crown jewels, an illegally imported and obviously rabid chihuahua or a forged London Transport old age pensioner's bus pass, they will be in honour bound to ignore it. Obviously, in fact, they won't.

But very few of us carry any of these things in what Mr Eldon Griffiths insists on describing as our orifices. What is horrifying to most of us – and I really wish that more people would take an interest in the matter – is not the fear of being found out, or of having our most secret objects exposed. It is quite simply the humiliation of being searched in this way. There is a blinding inconsistency in the attitude of law-and-order enthusiasts who wax eloquent about the humiliation suffered by respectable women when they are whistled at, ogled or otherwise propositioned by strangers in motorcars, but are yet prepared to force respectable women to submit to an internal body search at the whim of a police officer. The effect of this sort of violation on a sensitive person of either sex is unlikely to be much less severe than that of anal or vaginal rape, when one makes allowances for the atmosphere of threat, suspicion and hostility in which it is bound to be conducted.

Mr Warren Hawksley, Conservative MP for the Wrekin, tried to re-inforce the Bill by extending police powers to conduct intimate body searches where they are looking for drugs. Mr Hawksley, I should explain, is 40 years old, a former bank clerk, Shropshire county councillor and member of the West Mercia Police Authority. He told the committee he had heard that 200 grams of heroin with a street value of £20,000 could be concealed in the vagina. If the Bill was passed as it stood it would be a charter for drug pedlars, he said.

No doubt Mr Hawksley means well. His face, as revealed in *The Times Guide*, does not inspire confidence. But even a man of very small intelligence should be able to understand that a policeman, given the power to search anyone's anus or vagina for weapons, can perfectly well search them for anything else, while claiming to be looking for weapons. Where drugs are concerned, Mr Douglas Hurd (the Home Office minister) suggested that dangerous drugs might count as offensive weapons, in any case. Why on earth did this unappealing man open his mouth (another orifice which is liable to be explored under the new regulations) in the first place to give us his grisly opinion about how much heroin can be carried in the vagina?

What Mr Hawksley seems quite incapable of understanding is that his own orifices are in danger. As soon as a police authority decides to have a drive against drugs - as 'Campaign Charlie' McLachlan's Nottingham force decided to have a drive against 'drunk' drivers over the Christmas and New Year season - every former bank clerk in the place will be bending over with his trousers down.

Perhaps Mr Hawksley is the sort of patriot who is prepared to have his orifices examined *pro bono publico*. Perhaps he would even welcome the fulfilment of a public duty. Mr McLachlan's score over the festive season, as I never tire of pointing out, was 2,671 sober and respectable citizens stopped, made to get out of their cars and submit to humiliating tests in exchange for exactly 46 arrests. I imagine that even fewer of us are in the habit of carrying weapons or dangerous drugs in our anuses than might be tempted to have a drink at Christmas time. If Mr Hawksley imagines that 2,671 citizens (other than himself and his fellow enthusiasts on the Tory benches) are going to show his commendable dedication and allow Mr McLachlan's men to poke around in their bottoms without complaint, then it is not his orifices but his head which needs examining.

No. I am sorry. If Mr Hawksley wishes to have his bottom examined he must arrange to have it done privately. Perhaps the National Health might be persuaded to extend its service to accommodate these predilections, but not the police force.

Mr Eldon Griffiths (whom I suspect, perhaps wrongly, of being the *fons et origo* of the great orifice movement) had even more alarming evidence to give the committee. He quoted from a random sample of the provincial police forces in 1982 and 1983 which revealed that among more than 100 objects recovered from body orifices were drugs, £200 in notes, explosives and a detonator. A radio transmitter concealed in a person's anus relayed an interview conducted by Thames Valley police to an accomplice, he claimed.

Perhaps this is true, although I have my doubts. If people think about anuses long enough, it is wonderful what they can come up with. But my point is that the evil involved in the occasional eccentric who chooses to carry a radio transmitter in his anus is much less then the evil involved in allowing policemen unbridled freedom to search for them in all our anuses. Perhaps there is a case for allowing intimate body searches on

convicted criminals, under certain circumstances. There is no case whatever, and can never be, for allowing them to be inflicted on free citizens
in a free country. The orifice enthusiasts will simply have to allow us to
walk around with radio transmitters in our bottom, if that is what we
want to do. Leon Brittan is mad if he thinks he can get away with it.
The first innocent citizen who is searched in this way will bring the
Government down – and that, I suspect, is giving rather more power to
the individual policeman than even Mr Eldon Griffiths would want.

3.3.84

*　　　*　　　*

The Low Taste for Hanging

Nobody I knew has ever been hanged, and very few have been murdered.
Off-hand, I can only think of poor James Pope-Hennessy. I was sorry to
see him go, of course, but suspect that the risk of violence or sudden
death may be part of the thrill for those with his particular tastes. Nor
could I see how it would make the situation any better if the wretched
man who murdered him was sent to be hanged. Those who are loudest
in their demands for the restoration of capital punishment must either
have peculiar tastes of their own or must be suffering from some failure
of the imagination which prevents them from seeing that judicial execu-
tion can never cancel or remove the atrocity it seeks to punish; it can only
add a second atrocity to the original one.

The trouble with a referendum on the abstract point is that it protects
voters from the consequence of their action. If hangings were shown on
television voters would at least know what they had voted for. A jollier
idea might be to have a separate referendum for each hanging or, on the
principle of the Athenian ostracisms, citizens might be invited to nomi-
nate candidates for hanging. Public executions are popular events in
various parts of Africa, but I doubt whether they would be very popular
here, just as I doubt whether, if we were asked to cast our votes against
named individuals, many would do it.

Of course, I may be wrong. It is possible that public executions would
prove immensely popular, that referenda in every case would keep the
hangman busier than he has been since the Bloody Assizes. One could
argue that since capital punishment for murder can only be of inconvenience to a tiny minority, and since the idea of it – if not the practice –
gives such enormous comfort – if not actual pleasure – to a huge number,
then it should be allowed on the principle of the greatest happiness for
the greatest number.

It goes without saying that a few innocent men and women will always

199

suffer, but I do not think that has ever been a very serious objection to the principle of capital punishment. Innocent men and women are just as likely to fall down a manhole which has been left uncovered. There is almost no end to the list of unpleasant things which can happen to an innocent man or woman. Someone in a Graham Greene short story, as I remember, was killed by a cow or pig falling from a balcony on his head. All these incidents provide an opportunity to ponder the fragility of human happiness, but blame must attach to the negligent man-hole coverer, balcony builder, to the stupid or cruel judge rather than to the man-hole principle, the balcony system, the idea of the death penalty.

Nobody who has studied our courts closely can doubt that several innocent men have been hanged. It is a sobering thought, is it not? that Lord Goddard was not only in a position to send men to the gallows but frequently did so, usually (by all accounts) with a horrible smile playing about his lips.

The main objection to killing people as a punishment is not, as I say, that innocent people will be killed. It is that killing people is wrong. Two wrongs don't make a right. One could get away with it in a religious age, when one could at least pretend to believe that, shriven and prepared for death such people had a better chance of eternal salvation than they might normally have had. But in an irreligious age, when there is no further hope, it can't be done. So long as one sees killing as wrong there is no need to waste time with the deterrent argument, since it would be nonsense to try to prevent a theoretical evil in the future by perpetrating an actual one in the present.

Others may see the end of capital punishment as part of the general collapse of discipline in our society, illustrated as it is by the daily difficulty of finding someone else to clean one's shoes. I agree that the shoe problem is serious, but I do not think that hanging is necessarily the answer. And it is here, in the strange barren ground between the frustration of cleaning one's own shoes and a muddled, self-righteous belief in retributive justice, that one should look most closely. If Paris was worth a Mass to Henri IV, surely Westminster must be worth the odd topping of some malevolent lout to Mrs Thatcher? An end to the punitive taxation which is tearing our poor country apart? The reintroduction of secondary education, suppression of the Equal Opportunities Commission, Arts Council, Open University? The prospect is too delightful to contemplate without risk of sin and the price – of stretching a few criminals against our better judgment – seems absurdly low. Put like that, the temptation is formidable.

But I am afraid that Mrs Thatcher has made a grave electoral miscalculation. She misjudges the quality of support for capital punishment and the quality of opposition to it. No life-long Labour voter, however working-class, is going to vote Tory to bring back the rope, but many Liberal voters who might have voted Tory will refuse to do so. A majority of workers may, on balance, be in favour of capital punishment but it is a luxury opinion of very little relevance to their daily lives, and the great suburban Liberal vote is made up almost entirely of people who feel very strong indeed about capital punishment and have already allowed it to determine their votes. Far from making her election more certain, she is putting it at risk.

Judicial killing has been found necessary as an instrument for promoting social change; time and again it has proved necessary to maintain the great social advances of the revolutionary working class – I do not think there is a single socialist country in the world which does not have the death penalty, often for trivial economic offences. But Conservatives and Liberals should acknowledge that the defence of private property is neither so urgent as to require this nor so noble as to sanctify it. Let dogs delight to bark and bite for God hath made them so. The working classes may enjoy hanging each other because it is the sort of thing they understand but we should really not encourage them in case they hang one of us by mistake. Lord Goddard is waiting for us, a wintry smile playing around his thin, red lips . . .

But there is one serious question I would like to plant like a grain of sand in the oyster of readers' minds – gentle, intelligent, kindly, educated readers of the *Spectator*. Here it is: *if the majority cannot be allowed to decide about capital punishment, why should it be allowed to decide about anything?* If readers can ponder this and reach the conclusion that majority preferences are, by and large, things to be avoided and where possible frustrated, they will have taken a giant stride towards that tranquillity of mind which, in an irreligious age, must fill the place of our being's end and aim. On capital punishment, at least, let us agree that the People must not decide.

17.6.78

PART FIVE

DECLINE AND FALL

17

THE SAD STATE OF BRITAIN

Surly, Incompetent, Dishonest

Returning to Britain a few years ago I complained bitterly in the *Spectator* about the prominently advertised Disabled Persons' Toilets at London Airport. These are still the first thing to meet the eyes of the bemused traveller, but the image which they once projected – of Britain as a compassionate, fussy old woman just waiting for the last of our fingers to drop off so she can help us down with our trousers – have been overtaken. One does not have to travel far into Heathrow – surely the vilest major international airport in the world – before suspecting that the country has left its heart in its public toilets. Those vaunted facilities for the disabled might look good on the travel posters – I am not sure whether the British Travel Authority has used them yet or not – but a more appropriate notice, to be placed beside the rabies advertisements at every authorised point of entry would read like this:

NOTICE TO VISITORS

Visitors to the United Kingdom are warned that their luggage is liable to be ransacked and anything valuable removed from it before it reaches the Customs shed. In this event they will have no redress, since the state of industrial relations in Britain does not allow prosecution of ground staff personnel for theft.

They are also warned that if they proceed through the 'Goods to Declare' channel, they will be kept waiting between one and a half and two hours, while three Customs officers process approximately two thousand travellers.

In London, they will find that few taxis will stop and even fewer will accept them as passengers unless they happen to be travelling in the same direction as the driver. Their hotels will almost certainly be unpleasant and overpriced, shopkeepers are liable to be surly, incompetent, and dishonest.

Use of toilet facilities for the disabled is, however, free, and we hope you will avail yourselves of them where appropriate. Welcome to Britain.

3.11.79

*   *   *

The Laziest People on Earth

'If the Fourth Commandment is rejected by the State, what hope is there for the rest?' demanded Mr William Benyon, Conservative MP for Buckingham, debating the Shops Bill on Friday night. As most people will be aware, the Private Member's Bill to remove restrictions on Sunday trading was defeated on a free vote by 205 votes to 106.[1]

In fact very few of the Ten Commandments are accepted by the State. Strange gods and graven images are tolerated, neither swearing nor adultery is forbidden, nobody is required to honour his father or mother. So far from its being a crime to covet one's neighbour's wife, it is generally thought good manners to put up a pretence of coveting her, while the sin of coveting a neighbour's goods has been elevated by much modern Christian theology, let alone by the law of the land, into a major civic virtue; rechristened 'standing up for your rights', or less selfishly 'concern for social justice', it is now one of the few dynamics of the modern democratic State.

What on earth did Mr William Benyon *think* he was talking about? Of all the Ten Commandments, and apart from the strange anomaly of Sunday shopping, only three are enshrined in our laws – the injunctions against murder, theft and perjury. Was Mr Benyon seriously arguing that if Sunday shopping restrictions are lifted, the State will also be tempted to lift its prohibitions on murder, theft and perjury? If so, by what perversion of the rules of ordinary human politeness was the House prepared to sit and listen to him? Why do the newspapers repeat it as if he had made a valid debating point?

To some extent, I suppose, the phenomenon can be explained by the Englishman's traditional respect for other people's sincerely held opinions. It has always been a bit of a Bloody Fools' Charter, that one, as the nation's bloody fools know only too well. They have only to take their pipes out of their disgusting, nicotine-stained teeth, wave the dribbling stem around a little, and say: 'Yes, but I happen to be of the sincere opinion that ...' Then a respectful hush falls upon the company while

---

1. It has since been reintroduced in modified form.

the bloody fool ceremoniously lifts his tail like a cow in the milking parlour: any amount of nauseating drivel pours out to make cowpats all around, and we walk in these cowpats at our peril.

The first thing to learn about Sincere Opinions is that they are not opinions at all. They are not the product of any identifiable reasoning process. When anybody is asked to explain one, it is immediately apparent that the steps by which he has reached it are even more asinine than the Sincere Opinion itself. One may suspect that the reasons given for these passionately held beliefs (or fatuous opinions) are seldom the real ones, but in Britain it is considered libellous to speculate about a person's real (as opposed to avowed) reasons for anything. Nor can I think of any reason, even a libellous one, for Mr Benyon's religious objections to voluntary shop-opening on Sunday except that, through no fault of his own, he is a prize ass. It is true that the Bible suggests observance of the Sabbath should be extended to man-servants, maid-servants, cattle and strangers within the gates, but it also forbids the eating of pigs, rabbits, prawns, lobsters, owls, cuckoos and tortoises, while encouraging people to eat locusts, beetles and grasshoppers (Leviticus xi). Perhaps, if he has good luck in the ballot for Private Members' Bill next time round, he will see fit to enact all this.

Bloody fools have as many rights as anyone else, even if I would dispute that one of them is the unqualified right to a respectful hearing: there is little to be gained by inviting those incapable of rational discussion to take part in it. But nobody can seriously argue that bloody fools should be encouraged to impose their ghastly opinions on the rest of us through the democratic process. Obviously he has a perfect constitutional right to vote for his own sincerely held opinions. I just wonder what Conservatives in Buckinghamshire feel like when they have to vote for this clown.

Conservatives in Hove have another problem. Their constituency association has chosen to present them with a grocer for candidate in Mr Timothy Sainsbury. Mr Sainsbury's objections, like those of the other grocers and grocers' friends who voted against the Bill, were founded on the extreme inconvenience of opening his shops on Sundays. In an ideal world, of course, all grocers would refuse to do so, but a few would inevitably break ranks and then he would have to open, too, for fear of losing custom.

'The way of the slothful man is as an hedge of thorns' (Proverbs xv, 19). 'The desire of the slothful killeth him; for his hands refuse to labour' (ibid xxi, 25).

Are the British, I wonder, now the laziest people on earth? Opinion polls show that a huge majority of the population – some 73 per cent – would welcome Sunday shopping. The House of Commons, being more than anything else a vehicle for special interest groups, rejected the measure by 205 votes to 106. But however much one may berate the stupidity of the unions for encouraging the more vociferously lazy among their members to shape their policy – an idle man, as we all know, is an unhappy man, and I attribute almost all the misery behind the Women's Movement to the fact that so many women have nothing to do – and however much we berate grocers and MPs and grocer-MPs for the same reason, the fact remains that they are not the worst offenders. Why do the rest of us put up with Mr William Benyon as our representative?

The nation's lazy people are more energetic in defence of their own laziness than the rest of us are on the opposite side. While we complain bitterly about being governed by idle grocers, greedy shop-assistants and roaming, demented bloody fools we are none of us – least of all me – prepared to do anything about it. 'By much slothfulness the building decayeth; and through idleness of the hands the house droppeth through' (Ecclesiastes x, 18).

12.2.83

*   *   *

Roll on the Wealth Tax!

Genuine moral indignation is a rare and beautiful sight. How else can one describe the reaction of the Press to the 'news' that a re-elected Labour government will introduce a wealth tax in its first parliamentary session? Listen to the *Daily Express:*

'Wealth, whatever the socialists say, does not exist in nature. It has to be created by the human mind. Even if it was inherited, it still has to be created by somebody. A wealth tax, then, will be a tax on what mind and effort can create.

'Can that be right morally?'

Well, I don't know. If it isn't morally acceptable, it seems to rule out nearly all forms of taxation – income tax, VAT, capital gains and transfer taxes, company taxes and every other means of raising revenue, except possibly dog licences. Is it reasonable to expect the nation's doggies to bear the whole burden? I will have to ask Father O'Bubblegum about that one:

'If you attack the rich ... you destroy the incentive to invest and thereby do the ordinary man out of a job.

'A wealth tax, then, will not only be thoroughly immoral in principle, it will, in practice, injure the poor ...'

Is it terror of doing the ordinary man (especially if he's poor) out of a job which explains this fine moral rage against the wealth tax? In the quiet hours of the night, as I lie contemplating the nation's problems, I feel that it must indeed be a pretty hellish thing to be an ordinary man; to be done out of a job on top would plainly be the last straw. It might make any of us feel strongly against his so-called wealth tax. A better name for it would surely be the Ordinary Man (Job Deprivation) Immoral Measure.

The Shadow Chancellor attacked the tax as 'gravely damaging in its effects on family businesses, on investments, on employment, on savings and on the national heritage'. The Association of British Chambers of Commerce is worried that the tax will inhibit the creation of new jobs, while my beloved *Daily Mail* is worried about its effect on small firms. 'Major sufferers will be the small firms,' it says.

Oh dear. I'm not a small firm myself, but I can see it wouldn't be much fun, especially if one is to be a major sufferer. So it seems that the proposed measure is thoroughly immoral and undesirable from the following points of view:

The ordinary man	The poor
The national heritage	Small firms
The wealth creators	New jobs

Miraculously, the list doesn't seem to include me. I don't like to think of myself as an ordinary man, I'm certainly not poor nor can I honestly describe myself as a wealth creator; I am not a small firm, not looking for a new job and I think it would be asking for ribald comments if I tried passing myself off as part of the national heritage, like Westminster Abbey or the Beaufort Hunt. In fact, if I wriggle a bit, divorce my dear wife and burn a few pictures, I might escape the tax altogether. It almost makes one begin to wonder whether there might not be something to be said for the tax, after all.

I think there is, and the first point in its favour is the moral indignation it generates. From the point of view of destroying the capitalist system, events have already made it unnecessary. The conditions for capitalism no longer exist in Britain. Rates of inflation, equity growth, personal income tax on investment income, capital gains and transfer taxes ensure that it is no longer possible to derive any benefit from saving money.

Since the capitalist system entirely depends on people's readiness to save rather than spend their savings it must only be a matter of time before the system collapses. We are now enjoying the time-lag between a historical development and general awareness of it. The process is stretched while the nation, individually and collectively, spends its savings, and prolonged still further by a few fools who continue to invest, by corporate investors – insurance companies and pension funds – who have no choice, and by government intervention, but it is nevertheless inexorable. Britain no longer provides a sound base for capital investment, so there can be no question of the capitalist system surviving without some violent change in our political and social institutions.

And that, of course, is what I am writing about. The socialists are too stupid, too impatient and too mean to wait for everything to fall into their laps. They have to force the pace. In point of fact, as the latest volume of the Central Statistical Office's *Social Trends* shows, nearly everything has fallen into their laps. By far the largest part of the wealth of the country is in housing (43 per cent) followed by life policies (15 per cent) and building society deposits (7.5 per cent). Ordinary shares come a very poor fourth at 5.4 per cent. Total income from rent, dividends and net interest has so fallen in the last ten years (while social security benefits have so risen) that social security benefits have now overtaken it as a proportion of total income, the figures being 9.5 per cent and 9 per cent respectively. So much for the capitalist system.

But by aiming a last, vicious kick at that disappearing nine per cent of total personal income which still derives from rent, dividends and net interest, the socialists achieve two things. They create a small area of highly articulate, highly motivated resentment, and they spread a general awareness of what is happening in the country. The greatest danger, it has always seemed to me, is that nobody notices what is happening as we slowly, imperceptibly slide into moral, material and intellectual mediocrity:

My own realisation came during the Christmas festivities. We saw the Shadow Chancellor trying to sing what he thought was an amusing parody of 'Twelve Days of Christmas' on Television News. He sang badly and the jokes were feeble. Next we saw the real Chancellor of the Exchequer appearing on a BBC Nationwide pantomime called 'The Wizard of Oz'. Here, the jokes were not so much feeble as non-existent, the production was shoddier than any village pantomime of my youth, and for the first time I really began to feel sad about my country.

But once our eyes are opened, the evidence is everywhere. Sir David Hunt has emerged as the BBC's Mastermind of Britain. He is the ugly, dim FCO functionary who, as High Commissioner in Lagos, advised the Wilson government of 1966–1970 on its policy for the Nigerian civil war which implicated our country in the genocide of two million Ibo civilians, mostly children. Now he goes on to a 'Supermind' contest, meeting winners of the 'Forces' Chance' and 'Top of the Form' radio series. This is what has been left behind in the general exodus.

A photograph in the *Daily Express* last week drew attention to the legs of an actress appearing in a rubbishy film about fishes. 'There's nothing fishy about lovely Lea Brodie's legs', drooled the caption writer - how I sympathise with him, having myself once been a caption-writer for pin-up photographs in the *Sunday Mirror*. 'Should make a splash!' he concludes. *But Lea Brodie's legs are no better than my own.* All the best British legs, one must conclude, have gone to Las Vegas or Qatar or the British Embassy in Washington. Roll on the wealth tax, roll on the Glorious Counter-Revolution!

31.12.77

*   *   *

Nothing to be Done

The greatest impertinence of Americans and others writing about the sad state of Britain is in the assumption that we can't see these things for ourselves. It is part of the same assumption, I fancy, which led the United States to its debacle in Vietnam, an assumption that the rest of the world wants to be prosperous, efficient, glutted with consumer goods and as much like the United States as possible.

Some people in Britain undoubtedly suffer from this distressing condition, but very few - according to a survey conducted by Opinion Research Centre and published in the magazine *New Society*, fewer than a third. Of a thousand people interviewed, five hundred and ninety said they wanted to work as hard as was necessary to live a pleasant life, seventy didn't know, while three hundred and twenty were prepared to work harder for more money.

New Society became very excited about this, talking about the revolution of falling standards, and suggesting that the British are remarkably unambitious, but I have been printing this out for years and years. It is something which the ambitious minority seem quite unable to get into its head - that most of us are lazy, unambitious and content to eat any lotuses available. The proper function of government is certainly not to cater exclusively for this laziness and self-indulgence; but a democratic government will certainly have to cater for it to some extent, and nobody is going to vote for higher incentives if he doesn't want higher incentives.

How then are *we* - the rich, the clever, the greedy - going to survive? Certainly not by making petulant noises every time something is taken away from us. Nobody apart from ourselves cares a hoot whether our wine coasters are of gilded silver or of Sheffield plate. Nobody even cares whether our port is of the finest vintage or whether it is Grocer's Ruby. We are on our own, and the sooner we realise it the better. We may feel strongly that other people should have an *incentive* to be as rich as we are, should be allowed *freedom of choice* between good and bad port, but it is a waste of time saying so. Others do not agree, and any appeal to the Englishman's traditional sense of fair play is an appeal against ourselves in the defective moral climate of the times.

After considerable thought, I have decided that no hope of survival resides in Mrs Thatcher or the Conservative Party under the present political system. Others will disagree with me violently, but I can only repeat that I think they are wrong. Like all politicians, Mrs Thatcher wants above all else to be elected to office and stay there. It is *office* which is the lure in British political life; not power, but the trappings of power – the telephones, the civil servants in attendance, the official residences and motor cars, the social cachet and illusion of being in the centre of things. It is the political system which has created the present economic climate and the economic climate which threatens me with grocer's port, but the political system has neither the power to reform the economy nor the will to reform itself, so I must look elsewhere for my treats.

As I say, we all know what is wrong, and we don't need foreigners to tell us. This is Mr T. D. Allman, an American pundit, writing in *Harper's*:

'While failing either to generate capital or to discipline labour, Britain took it upon itself to provide all its citizens with the combined amenities of consumer capitalism and the socialist millennium'. So we did, to be sure, and it worked rather well. The workers aren't yet eating their babies and I still have some fine old port. If things change we'll ask Mr Allman for more advice:

'The British government is bankrupt of economic solutions but ... it has successfully generated political acceptance of the fact that there may be no economic solutions for Britain.'

On the contrary, I know perfectly well what is required to solve my own economic problems: instead of the present graduated income tax, there should be a higher flat rate (after allowances) of forty pence in the pound; the Exchequer would gain from this, everybody would have incentive to work harder and I could order some more port. Tra-la-la. If one was feeling altruistic about the national economy, of course, one would also have to suspend the trade unions for three years, introduce legally enforceable labour contracts and break rather a lot of heads in the process. One would also disband the Parliamentary Press Lobby and repeal all the libel laws which protect crooks and incompetents in public office. I confess that when I think of all the things which need doing I find a certain lethargy overcomes me, a feeling that these things are better left to the people who enjoy throwing their weight around.

And there can be little reason to suppose they have any intention of taking the necessary steps. As our American pundit puts it:

'If the threat of a totalitarian Britain is negligible, so alas are the possibilities of any "historic compromise". The essence of the British condition is not one of political menace but the absence, on both sides, of any kind of force at all.'

Any solution to my own or the country's economic problems must be a political one, and the great impediment to any political solution remains our existing system, with its appalling certainty of producing one or other of two unacceptable choices. It is not at all surprising that our politicians should regard any change in these arrangements as the worst possible catastrophe – far worse than economic collapse or an outbreak of baby-eating in the North, bad port in the South – but it is surely more surprising that they have managed to persuade large sections of the articulate minority that this is the case. As Mr T. D. Allmann puts it (and if a foreigner says so, it must be true):

'Britain's political stability and economic instability are manifestations of the same condition. They are opposite sides of the same devalued coin of exhausted national purpose and apparently inexhaustible British complacency.'

In other words, there can be no question of a cure to our economic ills until we have rid ourselves of this dead weight of political stability. The enemy is now clear to see.

I am not suggesting, of course, that we should actually *do* anything to create conditions of political instability. That would be troublesome, undignified and possibly dangerous. Others may be tempted to put bombs under the Prime Minister's car, blow up local tax offices, visit Inland Revenue officers in their homes, ravish their wives and strangle their domestic pets, but when the issue at stake is simply the quality of luncheon port, this seems a bad bet.

I do not even think there is much to be gained by joining the National Front, the Socialist Workers' Party, the Young Liberals or any of the other quasi-revolutionary parties which spring up and multiply like mushrooms in horse manure. That, too, would be too much effort, out of keeping with our lethargic and complacent beliefs.

Political instability can only be brought about by economic catastrophe, and for that we must let events take their course. My reason for describing what is happening in Britain now is not to urge a particular course of action, simply to indicate the sanest attitude to it, and the one most conducive to peace of mind. Thus we should welcome the fact that Britain lost more than a million days through strikes last month; we should rejoice when North Sea oil wells blow up, when Concorde is grounded, when the pound sinks. Fair is foul and foul is fair, hover through the fog and filthy air.

When the hurly-burly's done, when the battle's lost and won I might put in an order for the 1977 Fonseca which, they say, may prove quite an interesting vintage for those who can afford it.

7.5.77

* * *

Morocco as the Model

One tends to see the whole of Morocco as a Signpost for Britain in the Eighties. Of course, the parallel can never be exact, since Morocco has a firmly established national religion to comfort and sustain its people in their adversities. On top of this, the population is extraordinarily young – not so young as in Thailand, where the average age is fifteen, but with over half the population under twenty it is grotesquely different from our own.

On the other hand, the Moroccan young – Arab and Berber alike – do not show many of the characteristics normally associated with youth; they are not thrusting, or dynamic or politically active, and take to unemployment like the proverbial ducks to water. But they appear to have alert, inquiring minds and are probably more to be compared with our beloved old age pensioners than with our own listless, incurious young people, stupefied by the variety of sweets and reading matter on offer: *Beano, Dandy, The Sun, Topper, Whizzer and Chips* etc. etc. Moroccan youths have no such embarrassment of choice. But illiteracy among the fifteen to nineteen-year-olds in Morocco is 75 per cent, and in this matter they are still a long way ahead of us.

The growth of illiteracy in Britain, especially among teachers, is a separate study, and this is not the moment to speculate on the final stages of what was once one of the world's better education systems. Let it suffice that education has always been something at which the middle classes have excelled, so that in the new, stupid, union-dominated society of the future, education must be reduced to a minimum. Such weighty affairs of state are not for the likes of us, but I was amazed that nobody has yet taken up my suggestion which, I feel sure, contains the only long-term hope for the newspaper industry. This is for a new national comic to challenge *Beano* as the main reading matter of the up-and-coming generation. *Beano* is still read by the university élites, but there are whole groups of school-leavers, students in technical colleges and teacher training establishments who fail to identify with its old-fashioned attitudes, and need something more down-to-earth.

One reason for this may be the prudishness of the publishers. A down-market *Beano* for the new generation of non-élitist, comprehensively-educated adults would eschew all advice on how to clean

212

their teeth and wash behind the ears. Instead it would have brightly coloured 'adult' comic strips specialising in lavatory jokes and mild forms of sexual innuendo. Its naked ladies would be fat, middle-aged and copiously endowed with pubic hair. Other photographs would show small, furry animals. Occasionally, the two might be photographed together, but the main message would be carried by cartoons and comic strips pointing out, through jokes about false teeth and going to the lavatory, what an essentially humorous, easy-going race the English are.

The formula can't fail, and if it is tied to some simple daily competition with large cash prizes so that every copy sold acts as a lottery ticket, it would cater for every identifiable English taste. The element of topicality would be supplied by a daily interview and photograph of yesterday's winner, and a page would be devoted to readers' complaints about their various illnesses. It is with such bright ideas as this that we should face the future instead of brooding glumly over Larry Lamb's horrible face as he boasts of the phenomenal success of *The Sun*.

But as with Morocco, all the brighter, keener people have left. In Morocco there are now only 1,500 doctors to cater for a population of fifteen million, and this is plainly the way we are heading in England. Those who remain in Morocco are perversely content to sit by a small pile of quartz or fossils on some unfrequented tract in the ante-Sahara on the off-chance that a tourist will pass by to barter for his findings. After we in Britain have sold all our Warwick vases and Canalettos we can start trying to interest the German tourists in our lace doyleys and Edwardian chamber pots. We are for the most part too old to try any of the other tricks that the Arab boys get up to.

Even in Morocco, it is not possible to find anyone to clean the lavatories on camp-sites or clear litter from the beaches. Unemployment is impossible to estimate in a country where two thirds of the population are peasants, and the ten per cent in industry produce half the gross national product. The Arab attitude to work would appear to be much the same as the English – five are usually required to do the work of one – but without the element of moral righteousness which makes the English feel it is humiliating and wrong for them to work, something which only their supine good nature allows them to contemplate, occasionally, as a treat for their employers.

Instead, the Arabs seems surprisingly happy to beg. This is something the English will never do, of course. 'Ah doon't give money to beggars,' one of our group explained, as if he were enunciating an unalterable moral principle. The English are used to demanding their *baksheesh* as of right. I wonder how they will fare when, after the collapse of education and the national health, our beautiful system of unemployment benefit, supplementary grants and allowances begins to totter.

213

Wandering around the villages of southern Morocco, where small children of five always seem to be carrying a baby on their backs, its eyes covered with flies, where village idiots howl and gibber at the gates and obviously mad dogs rush around biting everyone in sight, and seeing it all in this rather strange light as a vision of Britain's future, I found myself asking rather an awkward question: just how conservative is one, or are we, or we ought to be?

Britain resoundingly rejected the vision of a high wage economy, high productivity, fat men in their fibre-glass ocean cruisers, thin men competing manfully in the sheets – and we all breathed a sigh of relief at the time. It is perhaps merciful that the alternative, more austere vision of a conservative future – massive unemployment, collapse of public services, poverty, illiteracy and slow decay – should be ushered in as a product of Mr Callaghan's political know-how, Mr Benn's progressive idealism and Mr Moss Evans's noble stupidity. I am not sure that I regard our Moroccan future with quite the right degree of dismay or consternation, but I am very glad it is the Labour socialist and proletarian leadership which is giving us the chance to try it out. Mrs Thatcher should stay out of sight for a little longer yet. Morocco is not too bad once you get used to the dirt.

14.10.78

*   *   *

A Possible Cure for Paralysis

Attempts to analyse the British sickness cluster around our class system – the public schools, a tradition of non-communication between the classes, simple, old-fashioned snobbery and the resentment it generates – on the one hand, and our primitive tax-structure, powerful unions and indulgent welfare system leading to a collapse of discipline in family, schools and factories on the other. For convenience, one might label these the left-wing and right-wing explanations. For my own part, as regular readers of this paper may be aware, I attribute all these problems to the cruel and beastly system of primogeniture which has concentrated wealth and alienated the intelligentsia from the capitalist system, but that is all a matter of past history. It is too late to do anything about it now, when the government leaves too little personal wealth to share.

All these explanations for the English disease seem to me equally true. The only one which misses the mark puts the blame on uneven distribution of wealth (the richest five per cent own ninety-five per cent of the wealth or whatever) since anyone can see that what little personal income survives is more evenly distributed in Britain than anywhere else among our trade competitors.

When all has been said, I do not think that the disease can usefully be contained any longer by tackling its causes: abolition of the public schools would cause me infinite pleasure; so would removal of the punitive element in taxation, introduction of Continental laws on inheritance, smashing of union power and restructuring of welfare and penal arrangements to restore parental responsibility, school and industrial discipline. But the reason that none of the necessary reforms can be introduced is the same as the reason that they are needed. What has overtaken the country is a paralysing wetness, and as soon as one can identify this characteristic as the root of our problem the distinction between causes and symptoms blur into unimportance. Perhaps this wetness is a product of political ineptitude and opportunism, perhaps it is the cause of it, or perhaps it is a bit of both, but the most important thing for anybody who wants to change it is surely to recognise and work with, rather than against, the dominant national characteristic of our times.

In France the problem is exactly the opposite. Where we are absurdly deferential for the most part (I do not refer to the criminal classes) to incompetent government and unjust laws, they are unreasonably hostile to sensible government and necessary laws; where we abdicate all individual responsibility in philosophies of social collectivism and moral determinism, they abdicate all social responsibility in philosophies of anarchic individualism and penological vindictiveness.

We are both sick, perhaps, but the immediate thing is to find a cure for the English disease. Obviously, it cannot be cured within the present system, since the essence of the disease is that it cannot and will not cure itself. Westminster, Whitehall, the army, the police force, law courts, industrial management, schools, parents and children are all hopelessly infected. The great popular demand to bring back capital punishment does not, I am convinced, reflect a sadistic delight in cruel or unnatural punishment, or even a reasoned conviction that crimes of violence would be more effectively deterred. It reflects no more than an awareness of the encroaching wetness, and represents a reaction to it. Yet to reintroduce capital punishment at this late stage would achieve nothing beyond allowing a few gruesome and irrelevant horror shows on the periphery of national awareness. The fact that the enormous demand for capital punishment has not, in a democratic system, been able to achieve its end, reveals how essentially wet and ineffective the demand is.

The Socialist Workers Party, for all its faults, is not wet. Nor, for all its faults, is the National Front. If I could point to others on the political scene who are not wet I would happily do so, but I can't. The Front may have greater popular support, but such support should not be measured in terms of quantity so much as effectiveness, and the left is certainly better organised with more militants in the field. Both, however, are tiny beside the great wet mass of Conservative, Labour and Liberal voters. If I am right that the country needs some sort of electric convulsive therapy, then these would appear to be the only two dry points between which the current can pass. Under the circumstances, I feel we should give them both the maximum encouragement and wish them both the best of British luck.

27.9.77

*   *   *

The French Solution

For a beleaguered Englishman, wrestling with the fact that the pound is only worth 8.3 francs and a glass of orangeade in a bar therefore costs 42p or eight and sixpence, there is certain comfort to be derived from the discovery that large parts of French society, too, are going mad. I first began to suspect this at the seaside when I noticed that most Frenchwomen now bathe topless. For five weeks now I have been brooding and puzzling over this. A few women look quite charming in this state, although once it is common property even the most perfectly formed breast becomes no more erotic than a well-turned ankle or finely chiselled nostril. But most of the women were old enough to know better and looked extremely silly.

Whatever considerations drove them to this behaviour they cannot have included the traditional nudist argument that it is somehow healthier and more natural to expose one's private parts. Without exception they kept their lower parts covered. Yet by demystifying her breasts, the human female renounces one of the most formidable weapons in her sexual armoury. Curiosity is the trigger mechanism to the whole chain of male sexual response – a chain both in the sense of progression and in the sense of shackle or confinement. Curiosity is not heightened by this premature exposure, but diminished. Perhaps it was their intention to discourage or repel bathers of the opposite sex, but I am almost sure this was not the case. The simplest and most obvious explanation for this loss of modesty is surely the true one – they have gone mad.

Confirmation is available from other sources that this same crisis of modernism which, in the space of twenty years, has destroyed the Roman Catholic Church and left Europe virtually defenceless to Russia is now afflicting many parts of French society with madness. The chief of these is French television, and the most extreme example on French television is a programme called *Les Grandes Personnes*. It shows children talking to adults. In effect, this means that a single long-haired youth, prepubescent and epicene, is interviewed by any of a number of middle aged, vasectomised pederasts with horrible, wrinkled, understanding faces

216

and smug, left-wing views. The interview seems interminable, but probably doesn't take more than thirty minutes. Under the indulgent eye of the pederast the 'boy' trots out a little library of left-wing views about his school and the modern world – how he is disenchanted with capitalism, how religion means nothing to him and is only for his parents, how they are not taught enough at school about things which really interest them, like racism and neo-imperialism in the third world. The pederast beams at him and draws a little closer. 'Yes, yes', he says understandingly, 'religion was, shall we say, a romantic invention for the times,' and the plump, androgynous mannikin smirks gratefully back.

These are the new goody-goodies, the children who at my school would have been teachers' pets, sitting at the front of the class with the right answer to every question. It would be easy to be alarmed by the fact that the entire younger generation in France – or at any rate, all those under twenty-five who might, in happier times, have been capable of mastering the Christian catechism, have now been brainwashed – or 'educated' – into a rejection of the capitalist system. Whatever silly things the French may say to each other in their schools and on television, however dramatic their apparent rejection of the system under which they live, the fact remains that capitalism is in an amazingly healthy state in France. Even the French Communist Party is a long way to the right of our own beloved Conservatives on such vital matters as wealth, inheritance and personal taxation.

Yet in England where education has scarcely been politicised at all, capitalism is in ruins. Our educational policy, designed to accommodate the backward or inept pupil has produced a generation of politically apathetic sluggards. The French education system, which is the fiercest and most competitive in the world, has produced an élite dedicated to the destruction of capitalism, which continues to thrive. The English education system, surely the wettest and sloppiest outside America, has produced a generation of ignorant woolly-minded idlers who have all but destroyed capitalism at home.

Our problem is not insanity so much as feeble-mindedness, a refusal to think things out at all. We watch Bruce Forsyth instead. Last week's news that he had been signed up to make twelve new programmes for £180,000 – to stand in front of the cameras for 1800 minutes at £100 a minute – filled me with unutterable gloom. Of course, there is no reason to be jealous. The same vacant-minded audience who will gasp with delight every time he says 'Nice to see you, to see you nice' will also demand £83 per minute in income tax from his earnings.[1] I do not envy

1. The maximum rate of income tax was reduced by Mrs Thatcher's government to 60 per cent.

him his horrible house or the bogus Tudor bar inside it, or his pasty-faced new wife or his new plasticine baby or his nasty new moustache or even the genuine affection and respect in which he is plainly held by the British public. Apart from an intense personal loathing for the man I have no particular interest to declare. But last week's confirmation of the fact that in order to capture the attention of the British public, one must show them Bruce Forsyth does rather illustrate my point that the English are being encouraged to relapse into imbecility. It is not the sex or violence of British television which is worrying, still less its Marxist bias – just its vulgarity and stupidity. Where the French are going mad from the excitement of their intellectual processes, we are consciously and deliberately opting for the Stupid Society, where working class tastes will determine our culture and working class ineptitude will determine the level of our prosperity.

If we are to decide where we would stand in the great late-night debates of our time, we must do so in the privacy of our own libraries, studies or bathrooms because nobody is going to hold them with us. So sit a little closer, dear reader, and let's begin.

The trouble with capitalism, especially efficient capitalism, is that it not only makes the working class rich and free to exercise their loathsome consumer choices to the detriment of civilisation as we know it, it also make the working class powerful. When, in the exercise of this power, various inalienable characteristics of a working class are brought to bear – its brutal stupidity as well as its natural greed, is vindictive bloody-mindedness as well as its natural idleness (what the French call *la sale mentalité ouvrière*) one sees how capitalism must carry within itself the seeds of its own destruction.

The trouble with socialism is that in the process of keeping the workers poor, oppressed and docile it must depart so far from its own sustaining rhetoric of liberty, equality, fraternity, prosperity and workers' control as to create a psychotic society requiring mass imprisonment.

So we are left with a shaky, unthought-out belief in inefficient or mixed capitalism as our only protection against the drift into proletarian ineptitude and brutality. The French solution, of adopting the rhetoric of socialism while practising tooth-and-claw capitalism, carries with it the risk that our womenfolk will stand barking like dogs and exposing their breasts. That may be all right for the French, but it isn't really what we want to see at Bognor Regis.

2.9.78

*　　*　　*

218

Our Sacred Duty

Three years ago I received a letter out of the blue from a lady living at the other end of the country. She claimed to detect a resemblance between me and a portrait of the first Lord Herbert of Cherbury or Chirbury (1583-1648), the English adventurer and braggart, in a 1770 edition of Lord Herbert's *Life* which she possessed, and wrote to ask whether I had any idea how much the work was worth.

I replied on a postcard that I already possessed the 1886 edition, edited by Sidney Lee; that the portrait in this edition bore no resemblance, although it was true that Lord Herbert (brother of George Herbert) was a first cousin of mine, many times removed; that I had no idea how much her copy was worth, but would offer her a fiver for it.

There the matter rested. I do not think she answered my postcard. Then, soon after my return from France in September this year, I found a parcel among the pile of correspondence which took a week to clear. In it was the copy of Lord Herbert's *Life*, and two cards. The first was my own postcard of three years earlier. The second was from her:

'This present in appreciation of your articles in *Spectator* and *PE*. I much enjoyed today's 'The French Solution'.

Why is P.E. so anti poor J. Thorpe? ... I'm killing myself tomorrow so I won't know. So no need for you to write to thank. No reason really, just inclination and general tact. I'm sixty one anyhow and my throat bleeds - and of course there's Bruce Forsyth pending - etc. Also I'm petty-minded which is depressing. Widow, no window cleaner, gardener, sweep - all v. boring. Lots on dole. Washing machine on blink.

I really do enjoy you, and many thanks. All best wishes,

Yours,

...

When I read this it was already eight days after she had written. A reasonably responsible citizen would probably have discovered her telephone number and found out whether she had carried out her intention, or at least telephoned the local police or Samaritan organisation. Psychiatrists and others will declare that this was a classic cry for help, addressed to a stranger from whom she expected sympathy. I can only say that having thought about the matter, I decided it wasn't. There was a sporting chance she was a lonely, loopy, self-pitying woman who had no intention of doing anything but draw attention to herself, but I decided she was a sane, intelligent and likeable woman who, if she had changed her mind, would be gravely embarrassed to receive telephone calls from Somerset, or from her local Samaritans, or visits from the local

219

police and welfare *apparat*. I am not yet a disciple of the mysterious Thomas Szasz, who seems to be emerging as patron saint of the *Spectator*'s back pages, and whose practice, as I understand it, is to advise those patients who wish to commit suicide to go ahead and give it a whirl. But it seemed to me then, as it does now, that I had no business to intrude on the personal arrangements of a totally strange lady. So, instead I sat down and wrote her a letter:

Dear Mrs ...,

Thank you very much for your magnificent book *The Life of Lord Herbert*. It has caused enormous pleasure and I look forward to reading it from cover to cover.

Your parcel was awaiting my return from France and I can only hope that you did not carry out your declared intention. It seems to me a great mistake, however much one is depressed by Bruce Forsyth or sympathetic towards Jeremy Thorpe. There are always pleasures to be found in life, and none with any certainty thereafter. Of course, if you carried out your intention I am wasting my time and speaking to myself. But I hope not, and that you will come to accept that if you can enjoy my articles in the *Spectator* and *Private Eye* there are many enjoyments left to you.

In any case, please accept my sympathy in your depression and my sincere thanks for your present, which has caused me so much happiness.

Best Wishes,
Yours sincerely,
Auberon Waugh

In retrospect, of course, I am appalled by the inadequacy of this letter, dictated on 12 September 1978 while I was desperately trying to tidy up my affairs before going to Morocco. To have quoted my own scribblings in the *Spectator* and *Private Eye* as a possible reason for staying alive is quite exceptionally odious, and it is an aspect of the narrative which might easily have been suppressed if it had not been crucial to my reasons for telling the story here.

How much more eloquently I might have argued the case! I might have quoted my cousin George Herbert from his poem *The Flower*:

> 'And now in age I bud again,
> After so many deaths I live and write;
> I cannot more smell the dew and rain,
> And relish versing: O, my only Light,
> It cannot be
> That I am he,
> On whom thy tempests fell all night'

Or, in more pedestrian vein, the whole of To Be or Not To Be:

> 'But that the dread of something after death
> The undiscovered country from whose bourn
> No traveller returns, puzzles the will,
> And makes us rather bear those ills we have
> Than fly to others that we know not of?'

In the event, it would not have made any difference, as I was speaking to myself. On my return from Morocco, I found a buff envelope from the Post Office waiting in a pile of correspondence which took several days to clear. It had 'Returned Postal Packet' printed on the outside, and inside was my letter. Two lines were drawn through the address and the word 'deceased' scrawled beside, apparently by the local post office.

So I must assume that an unknown woman at the other end of the country had taken her own life after sending me a card. It is an odd and moving tale, and I am aware in telling it that some readers may be moved to anger by my own part – or lack of part – in the unfolding narrative. But it is not that aspect which makes me most uneasy.

Among the things which depressed my correspondent was the thought of Bruce Forsyth's return to television, and I fear I may be responsible for this, as I drew attention to the impending threat in the *Spectator* a few weeks earlier. In fact, this page nearly always seems to be drawing attention to disagreeable matters. I think I am right to castigate these horrible developments, but we must never allow ourselves to become depressed by them.

Let us examine the case of Bruce Forsyth. Since my warning, I gather he has, indeed, returned to television. I would not dream of looking at him nor, I imagine, would many *Spectator* readers. We can scarcely claim that he has impoverished the quality of our lives. He is just one of the numerous disgusting things happening on television. For my own part, I watch practically no television except the ten o'clock news and even then am nearly sick by the advertisements in the middle – why do the daddies always wear woollen cardigans and pudding-basin hair styles? No Englishman I know wears either; they might be creatures from outer space, these typical English daddies. There are countless horrible things happening all over the country, and horrible people prospering but we must never allow them to disturb our equanimity or deflect us from our sacred duty to sabotage and annoy them whenever possible.

21.10.78

THE END